LUCKY DEVILS

LUCKY DEVILS

HOW THREE TECH-MAD GAMBLERS BEAT THE ODDS AND MADE MILLIONS

KIT CHELLEL

monoray

First published in Great Britain in 2026 by Monoray, an imprint of
Octopus Publishing Group Ltd
Carmelite House
50 Victoria Embankment
London EC4Y 0DZ
www.octopusbooks.co.uk

An Hachette UK Company
www.hachette.co.uk

The authorized representative in the EEA is Hachette Ireland,
8 Castlecourt Centre, Dublin 15, D15 XTP3, Ireland
(email: info@hbgi.ie)

Hardback ISBN: 978-1-80096-325-2
Trade Paperback ISBN: 978-1-80096-326-9
eISBN: 978-1-80096-328-3

A CIP catalogue record for this book is available from the British Library.

Printed and bound in Great Britain.

1 3 5 7 9 10 8 6 4 2

This FSC® label means that materials used for the product have been responsibly sourced.

FSC www.fsc.org MIX Paper | Supporting responsible forestry FSC® C104740

For Callum, Isla, Lachlan, and Bob-John

CONTENTS

PROLOGUE

MAY 11, 1977

The ground floor of Harveys Resort Hotel & Casino in Lake Tahoe pulsed with noise and light. Ranks of slot machines clamored for attention from elderly ladies clutching pots of quarters. High rollers with porn star mustaches and shirts unbuttoned to the navel tossed their chips at dealers. Everywhere was decadence, and decay.

The United States was reeling from defeat in Vietnam, its economy in turmoil. Even in Nevada, insulated by wads of tourist dollars, there were signs. Elvis Presley had come to Lake Tahoe a few months earlier to perform at the Sahara. The King had sweated his way through the show, stomach bulging out of a white jumpsuit, forgetting the lyrics to songs he'd been performing for decades.

Inside Harveys, though, it was easy to forget that the outside world existed. A blue haze of cigarette smoke hung over the blackjack tables in the liveliest section of the casino floor. Here gambling was a spectator sport. Bettors sat on one side of each table, groaning if they busted out, whooping if they didn't. On the other side were uniformed dealers, impassively flipping cards. A crowd had gathered around a young woman who was steadily building an impressive stack of chips. That fact alone made her unusual.

Blackjack might seem like a fair game. Both dealer and players take cards from a shuffled deck, aiming for a total of 21 and no higher. But it isn't. The dealer has an advantage. Because he or she gets to play last, there's a good chance that the players will go bust first, surpassing 21 and thus losing.

The young woman, dressed professionally in a pantsuit and leather shoes, was enjoying a run of luck that had lasted for an hour and counting. A gangly kid in his twenties hovered nearby, staring intently at the table with one hand lodged in his pocket. At six foot seven, his height was enough to make him stand out. But there was something else, something about his unblinking concentration.

There were many eyes inside Harveys that night looking for anomalies such as the tall kid with the fixed stare. They were watching from behind one-way mirrors or hidden corners of the gaming floor. Men with thick necks and dark suits. Casino security.

One of them appeared at the kid's side. "Can I talk to you for a minute?" he said. The kid nodded and followed him to the edge of the casino floor, where he found himself facing a door leading into a stairwell. "I'm not going up there," he said, but by the time he turned around there were three security guards standing behind him. One of them shoved him through the door and jostled him up the stairs into a small office, barely big enough for a single desk.

Now there were at least five security operatives jammed into the room, including an older guy who had the bluster of a small-town sheriff. They all looked furious. "Strip him," the boss ordered. The kid could hear the young woman from the blackjack table being dragged up the stairs into a separate office. She was pleading with the casino staff, "Please don't hurt me. Please don't hurt me."

The kid's wallet identified him as Keith Marty Taft, from Sunnyvale, California. He went by Marty, not Keith, which was his dad's name, but he didn't feel like correcting them. The security men started pulling at his pants. They seemed to know exactly what they were looking for and quickly found it. Attached to Taft's waist was a metal case about the size of a matchbox with wires threading out. "That's the central processing unit," the casino boss said. The wires were connected to a keypad strapped to Taft's leg with four metal buttons. He'd been tapping them through a hole in his pocket.

"How about we plug you into the grid, see what happens?" one of the guards snarled.

"What about your friend?" the security boss asked. "Where is her computer?"

Taft smiled nervously. "It's just me. I play alone," he replied.

The atmosphere in the room grew heavier. The men in suits crowded around their captive, telling him he was in serious trouble and needed to cooperate. He was going to jail, they told him. They talked about driving him out to the desert, about putting his female companion into an X-ray machine. Taft tried to act like a harmless kid. He chatted away and told them nothing.

Eventually, after what seemed like hours, the casino called the cops. When Taft saw the uniform from the South Lake Tahoe Police Department, he was so relieved he could have kissed the officer wearing it. A one-way trip to the desert no longer seemed likely. In the presence of the law, the casino staff's attitude changed abruptly. The gruff threats were gone, replaced by ingratiating smiles. "We didn't do anything to him," they explained. "He's a cheat."

The cop, a young man himself, seemed more sympathetic to Taft. He agreed to handcuff him in front of his body for a more comfortable ride to the station, then draped Taft's jacket over his hands to hide his arrest from other casino patrons. "There's a lot of stuff going on in these places," he said. "It's not all straight up and down." He led Taft downstairs and across the casino floor, past the blackjack dealers who smirked as he went by, past the roulette wheels gliding smoothly around brass axles, past the old ladies sitting transfixed in front of slot machines.

Some of the gamblers stopped to rubberneck at the procession, but only for a moment. Soon they lost interest and turned their attention back to the real action: giving away their money one chip at a time. The casino accepted it, rewarding them with free drinks and the promise that their luck might change if only they played a little longer.

INTRODUCTION

For me, at least, this story began a decade ago, on a rainy afternoon in 2017. My friend and I were hiding from the weather, drinking beer and talking about my father-in-law Jim's passion for betting on the horses. Every few days Jim would share a hot tip for the next race. Horse X can't fail, he'd say. Get everything you can on it.

Of course, Horse X did fail, as often as not. It became a running joke. Even when his picks did cross the finish line first, it wasn't enough to make up for the money sunk on losers. Jim was coy about his methods, but it appeared to us that he always favored certain jockeys or trainers.

There must be a better way, I said to my friend Greg. Something more scientific.

Greg thought there was. He'd been working with tech investors and heard rumors about a couple of guys in Hong Kong who had created an algorithm that could predict the result of horse races. Fed by powerful computers and decades of data, the pair had apparently made a billion dollars. "You should write about that," Greg said.

At the time, I'd been working as a journalist for half my life and was tired of the repetitive stories filling the news. Another low-rent political scandal; interest rates up or down. This was something different, even if the number Greg floated seemed far-fetched. No one could make a billion dollars on horses unless they were *taking* bets, I thought.

Still, even if those mysterious gamblers from Hong Kong had tried and come up short, I wanted to know about it. There seemed to be a kind of noble futility in attempting to rationally predict something as chaotic as sprinting horses. That urge—to seek order in the complicated mess of existence—has been behind some of humanity's greatest achievements and most endearing failures.

I made up my mind to find them. Without having names or identifying details, it wouldn't be easy. Months of fruitless searching passed. I'd almost given up when I spoke to a Wall Street trader who told me about what he called "computer syndicates" operating in Hong Kong. "Those guys are insanely profitable," he said. He compared them to the high-frequency traders in financial markets, betting incredible volumes, millions at a time, powered by algorithms, not human judgment. There was one problem: The only gamblers who will talk openly are the ones who don't make money. The successful ones keep their mouths shut.

He did have a name, though: "The godfather of computer betting is Bill Benter."

Armed with this information, I found someone in Hong Kong who'd worked for Benter. He tried to warn me off, urging me to write about something else. "People in this business don't want to attract attention." But the idea of high-tech gambling hedge funds was too compelling to drop. Technology conferred an advantage that was almost magical, like a window into the future.

Eventually, I tracked down Benter. I was relentlessly persistent, and he was too much of a gentleman to refuse. When I showed up in Pittsburgh, his hometown, he agreed to meet. In the wood-paneled luxury of his private club, he told me about his career as a computer gambler. Benter and his partner, Alan Woods, were the ones who'd created the billion-dollar horse-betting operation my friend Greg had heard about.

My story about it was published in *Businessweek* in 2018. Before meeting Benter, I had found it difficult to imagine that such a thing could exist without word getting out to the general public, regular gamblers such as my father-in-law. Afterward, though, I met some of Benter's friends. They introduced me to others. I soon realized that they were part of a secretive subculture. They'd come up with what they claimed were mathematical solutions for any activity you can bet on and a good few you can't. Hardly anyone seemed to be aware of their existence.

Marty Taft, the tall gambler arrested in Harveys in 1977, was an early member of the club. His family had built one of the first wearable computers to process blackjack odds thirty years before the arrival of the iPhone. Others crafted devices that could track the movement of the ball and wheel on a roulette table, predicting the winning number with freakish accuracy. One individual used a computer from his top secret job designing nuclear reactors to crunch numbers for bets on college sports. That was back in the 1970s, when computer programming involved punching holes in numbered pieces of card and most people had never seen one.

Benter and his peers don't consider what they do to be gambling. Gambling is for suckers. Instead, they call themselves "advantage players." That means they play only when they have established with scientific precision that they have the advantage, when they are more likely to win than lose. A generation of advantage players came of age in the Las Vegas card-counting scene of the late 1970s and early 1980s. They had emerged from a singular place and moment in time, I discovered, when science had collided with professional gambling in the city of sin.

None of them are widely known outside their own tribe. They've never appeared on the front cover of *Forbes* magazine. But the more I learned, the more I saw how advantage players had influenced society in subtle ways. I started to see them everywhere.

The "father of information theory," Claude Shannon, was an advantage gambler who wrote software to play chess and tinkered with roulette computers. Shannon, who laid the foundations for electronic communication in the 1940s, is the reason computers transmit ones and zeroes. John von Neumann, a keen card player, invented game theory using poker to distill human decision-making into mathematical form. His theories underpinned the American doctrine of nuclear deterrence and shaped the course of the Cold War. The mathematician Jess Marcum advanced radar technology and worked on the neutron bomb. He also developed card-counting systems to beat blackjack and eventually gave up his research career to work as a professional bettor and casino consultant. These are the original heroes of advantage play—scientists with chalkboards, not the flamboyant risk-takers of gambling lore.

The modern-day acolytes of advantage are no less extraordinary.

A decent portion of Wall Street's billionaires paid their way through college by using their superior ability to navigate the risks of poker. Many of the scientists currently developing artificial intelligence at Google and Meta learned their craft while teaching machines to outwit professional poker players. The owners of two Premier League soccer teams in England—Brentford FC and Brighton & Hove Albion FC—made their fortunes with computer-generated sports bets. The list goes on.

It took me a while to identify what I found so intriguing about Benter and the others. It certainly wasn't their ability to make money by gambling. Whatever part of the brain rewards risk taking with dopamine, mine is undersized. I can't spend more than an hour in a casino without getting a headache from the constant clanging of slot machines. Eventually I realized that it was the way advantage players *think* that kept pulling me back.

Von Neumann was once asked why he preferred poker to chess. It's the uncertainty, he replied. With chess, all the information you could ever need is right there on the board. In poker, you can't see your opponents' cards, so you have to guess. You must lie and bluff. Sometimes you can make the right choices and still lose. That's what life is like, von Neumann said.

Advantage players spend their careers searching for ways to make better decisions. They don't always succeed, but they give themselves a better chance than the rest of us.

Not so long ago, gambling was illegal in the United States outside of Nevada and a few other safe havens. Today it's a $500 billion industry that has exploded into mainstream culture. Aggressive lobbying by casino companies and bookmakers has persuaded politicians around the globe that if people are going to bet anyway, they might as well do it legally and contribute to the public purse. The rise of online gaming means that anyone can wager on anything, anytime, just by reaching into their pocket and pulling out a smartphone. Even kids can bet legally using digital tokens in online computer games.

The zero-sum nature of gambling hasn't changed, though. Every dollar won is a dollar lost by someone else. To judge by the profits made by bookmaking companies, the decision-making ability of the average gambler hasn't improved much, either. Those with the knowledge to do it differently have kept it to themselves. The Wall Street trader who told me Benter's name was right: Real winners keep their mouths shut.

This book is, in part, an attempt to redress that imbalance. It will tell the story of advantage gambling through the eyes of three men. Each achieved remarkable feats in their chosen games. One of them is Bill Benter. The others are his friends Rob Reitzen, who worked on poker, and Bill Nelson, who mastered roulette and wagered on sports.

This isn't just a guide to successful betting, though; it's a story about obsession and what it costs to win. Because in real life, beating the house isn't like the movies. Only rarely do advantage players get to take home the prize after one big score. Mostly, it involves hard work, night after night toiling in front of a screen. Finding an edge can take years of research. Making sure it pays out takes thousands of attempts. There are moments of pure, adrenalized terror when the players try out their system in a Darwinian arena patrolled by guardians who might beat them senseless or worse. All the while, they must hide what they are doing and who they really are.

Benter, Reitzen, and Nelson would eventually find their advantages, but it took decades of struggle against casino bosses, bookmakers, police, gangsters, jealous rivals, and bad luck, the ever-present bogeyman stalking even the most mathematically gifted player. Along the way, there would be brushes with bankruptcy, courtroom dramas, and nights spent behind bars. Fortunes would be made and lost. Betrayals, real and imagined, followed moments of such improbable, unprecedented success that the biggest problem was what to do with all the cash.

One of the three would end up a millionaire many times over, a respected philanthropist, his every dream realized. Another would retire from the game in disgust, happy never to see a casino again. The third would walk away hardly better off than when he'd started but with enough stories to fill several lifetimes. Advantage gambling is a devil's bargain. Winning comes with a price. Still, I'm not sure that any of them would change a thing. Their glories and failures were their own. In a business dominated by greed and corporate spin, they learned something about how the world really works, something true.

When I first heard about Benter's billion-dollar betting syndicate, I assumed it was another gambling myth. I was wrong. Like everything else in this book, it really happened.

A NOTE ON SOURCES

What follows is based largely on extensive interviews with Bill Benter, Rob Reitzen, and Bill Nelson over the course of several years. Wherever possible, I tried to verify what they told me with official documents, such as police reports or legal files. Where it wasn't, I sought out multiple witnesses or found contemporaneous media reports to corroborate their accounts. All conversations are based on the best recollections of participants, albeit sometimes many years later.

PART 1

THE DAY OF THE LAMB

When a lamb goes to the slaughter,
the lamb *might* kill the butcher.
But we always bet on the butcher.
—Unnamed casino owner,
quoted in Edward O. Thorp,
Beat the Dealer

The day of the lamb had come.
—Edward O. Thorp, *Beat the Dealer*

PART

THE WAY OF THE LAND

BILL NELSON

The Goldman Sachs recruiter sat opposite Bill Nelson, fiddling with his silk tie and running his hand through immaculately coiffed hair. He was holding forth about the proud history of his employer, the proper functioning of capital markets, or some other subject Nelson couldn't care less about. Nelson, his attention slipping, was imagining how the conversation would go if the recruiter said aloud what he was actually thinking: "How would you like to come and eat shit on Wall Street for a few years? A handsome young man like you would be great at persuading rich old folks to shuffle their money over to Goldman Sachs."

No thanks, Nelson thought. It was 1975. Many of his brightest friends at the University of California, Los Angeles, were planning to use their MBAs to secure jobs in finance when they graduated the next year. Nelson had thought about it himself. It was why he was at the UCLA careers fair pretending to listen to the man from Goldman Sachs. He'd even flown to Chicago for a couple of interviews. Bear Stearns had a cool name, at least.

Nelson knew he had the brains to make it as a banker. In his junior year in high school, he'd taken a practice version of the SAT and gotten a mediocre score. He hadn't cared much about his academic performance until then but had decided to take that one test seriously. It can't be that hard, he told himself. He bought study books on how to ace the SAT and drilled with hundreds of tests. When he did the real thing, he rated in the 99th percentile, with a perfect score in math. He went on to attend the University of Florida before moving to California for his MBA.

Nelson's looks wouldn't have held him back in banking, either. Now twenty-five and six feet tall, his brown hair was brushed gold by the California sun. And his blue eyes—Paul Newman eyes, a friend had once said—were the kind that made both men and women want to know what he was thinking. He suspected he'd qualified for a grant to study business at UCLA only because the guy behind the counter at the placement office had taken a liking to him.

As the Goldman Sachs recruiter droned on, all Nelson could think about was what he was going to do on the weekend: He was going to drive up to Lake Tahoe to play blackjack. Again.

A few days later, he climbed into his convertible Volkswagen Beetle, baby blue, and hit the freeway. Soon he cleared the LA sprawl and was skimming across the lengthening shadows of hills with the top down and warm wind in his hair. The drive to Tahoe was at least eight hours, and the used Beetle wasn't built for speed. He had plenty of time to think about his life.

Nelson didn't consider himself to be a gambler. He'd made his first bet at the age of twenty-one while on holiday in the Bahamas. Encountering a roulette wheel in the local casino, he'd bet $20 on black and won. He'd taken his $40 and vowed never to do anything so stupid again. Why anyone would waste their time on an activity with a better-than-average chance of losing was beyond him.

After a chaotic childhood, Nelson didn't care to risk what little he had on a *game*. His father had run a cemetery in a small town outside Philadelphia. A medic in the Second World War, Nelson Sr. had been so traumatized by the experience that he'd wake up screaming at night. He'd had little time for his son, who had been left to his own devices. One of Nelson's earliest memories was literally dancing on his own grave. The family had bought a stone and a plot in advance, leaving a blank space for their names.

After Nelson's parents had split up, his father had sold the cemetery and moved to Florida, where he had sunk into drugs and despair. He would retreat for days at a time into his office with his guns and coin collection. All that had left Nelson with a mistrust of authority and the indelible sense that he would have to look after himself. He'd gotten his first motorbike at the age of fourteen, a Honda 50cc that he'd ridden around with no helmet. Too prickly and idiosyncratic for the cool kids at high school, he'd hung out with the chess nerds. He'd graduated high school as salutatorian, second in his class, and gotten his picture in the local paper.

Whatever his destiny, Nelson needed to be in command of it. Life had become simpler after he had moved in with his mother, who was dating a wealthy businessman. With their support, he had gone to college, then to business school. His mother's new partner wanted to see Nelson follow him up the corporate ladder. One day he sent his stepson an article from *The Wall Street Journal* that ensured he never would. It was about a mathematician named Edward O. Thorp, and it would shape the course of Nelson's future.

Thorp's book *Beat the Dealer: A Winning Strategy for the Game of Twenty-one*, first published in 1962, was a sensation, although hardly a page-turner, filled with dense numerical tables and charts. What it did, for the very first time, was show that a casino could be defeated with mathematics. "In the modern casino game of blackjack, the player can gain a consistent advantage over the house by using the strategy presented in this book," Thorp wrote.

That was nothing short of a revelation. What makes blackjack special, Thorp said, is that it's a game with a memory. Every card dealt impacts the chances of future success. The high cards—aces, kings, 10s, and so on—are advantageous to the player because they increase the chance of hitting blackjack or getting close to it. The more high cards left in the shoe (the plastic case holding undealt cards), the better for the player. If, for example, the first cards to be dealt are all lower than 7, the proportion of high cards in the remaining stack must have increased. Therefore, in the next round, the player's odds are better.

Thorp wasn't the first blackjack enthusiast to notice that. His real innovation was using an IBM computer to crunch the numbers and work out *precisely* how the odds changed. The IBM 704 was a clunking behemoth powered by vacuum tubes, a magnetic drum, and punch cards, taking up as much physical space as the average Buick.

At the time it was state of the art, with the ability to execute forty thousand instructions per second.

Using the IBM's electronic brain, Thorp calculated that in certain situations the player's advantage over the house was around 10 percent and might sometimes go as high as 100 percent. That kind of edge meant a gambler could double their money in the space of a few hours. Thorp devised a simple system to keep track of the dealt cards by giving each one a score: lower cards were plus 1, high cards were minus 1. The higher the count, the more a bettor should bet. Thus card counting was born.

Beat the Dealer changed the world in two main ways. First, it inspired a generation of young men (and they were almost exclusively young men) to try their luck as professional gamblers. Those card counters were a different breed from the swaggering risk-takers who'd taken on casinos in earlier decades. They were shy and awkward. They didn't drink or curse or holler at the blackjack table. They sat quietly, watching and thinking. In short, they were nerds.

Second, it led to an explosion in the popularity of blackjack. Previously a somewhat unloved casino game, it became America's favorite. The idea that it could be beaten with enough skill was irresistible to gamblers of all stripes, especially in a country that prizes opportunistic individualism. In reality, most gamblers couldn't make it pay, even when counting cards. The system required discipline, patience, a good head for numbers, and careful management of bet size. Even Thorp himself didn't profit much from the trick. After publishing his book, he returned to academia, then sought his fortune in a more dependable field: financial markets.

That was why Bill Nelson could walk into a casino in 1975 and count cards. American casino operators were still making around half a billion dollars annually from a game that was known to have an Achilles' heel. Some observers argued that *Beat the Dealer* was the best thing that had ever happened to the industry. "The one thing about system players is that they lose systematically"; so the saying went among casino bosses.

Armed with Thorp's book, however, Nelson found the opposite: It was almost too easy to win, like waving a toy gun in a bank and walking out with a bag of hundred-dollar bills. He'd return from a weekend gambling trip and spread out the cash on his bed. "Look, Paul, I won again," he'd say to his roommate. "Can you believe it?" He could scarcely believe it himself.

Maybe it was his nerve or his roving intellect. At college, he jumped from courses in math and physics to psychology, getting a solid grounding in different sciences. However he did it, he made nearly $15,000 in a few months from a standing start of $200.

The sun had begun to set by the time Nelson and his blue Beetle finally neared their destination. When he saw the bright lights of South Lake Tahoe twinkling through the pines, he felt the familiar tightness in his stomach. Card counting wasn't illegal or even against the rules of blackjack, and casinos knew it. But that didn't mean they liked it.

Nelson's adversaries had four main defenses: They could throw players out or wait for them to go broke from a run of bad luck; they could shuffle the deck repeatedly, slowing down the game and scrambling the count; or they could simply cheat. An experienced dealer could cut the cards any number of ways to make certain that a player would lose. Nelson saw it all. It made him more determined to win.

He parked the car and strolled into Harveys, the nearest casino. Once known as the Wagon Wheel, it had lost the name but not the tacky Wild West decor. There were slot machines inside prairie schooners. The casino's logo, mounted ten floors up in neon blue, depicted a wheel and a hollow-eyed steer skull, a reminder of the risks to an unwary traveler in this corner of the American frontier.

The blackjack tables had pride of place on the Harveys gambling floor; they were laid out in ovals at the center and crewed largely by middle-aged women powered, Nelson assumed, by hair spray and scorn. He sensed that they got a kind of sour enjoyment out of taking people's money, and he hated them for it.

He bought a stack of chips and sat down. If he was honest with himself, his encounter with the Goldman Sachs recruiter a few days earlier had only confirmed what was already a near certainty. He knew exactly what he wanted to do when he graduated. He'd known it since he'd first tested Thorp's method inside a casino and walked out with more cash in his pocket than when he'd walked in. He'd known it the day he'd called his college professor from a pay phone near the blackjack tables to delay his final accounting exam because he was on a winning run that was too good to quit.

It was a simple certainty, as hard and pure as a diamond: Card counting made sense. The math was good.

BILL BENTER

WE RESERVE THE RIGHT TO EXCLUDE PROFESSIONAL CARD COUNTERS FROM PLAY AT OUR BLACKJACK TABLES.

Bill Benter paused for a moment to take in the sign at the entrance of the Resorts International Casino in Atlantic City. *My God*, he thought. *It must work.*

He stepped nervously inside and saw bedlam. It was summer 1978. Resorts had opened its doors just weeks earlier, becoming the first legal American casino outside Nevada. The people of the Jersey shore had responded appropriately, with complete and total abandon. On the opening day, a queue of avid gamblers had snaked along the boardwalk and continued for a mile. Their appetite had not waned since. There were reports of customers wetting their pants rather than give up a place at the blackjack tables.

This was Nevada-style gambling but with a different flavor. Benter gawped at the glamorous women dressed in furs. The place was packed wall to wall with what looked like extras from a Martin Scorsese movie, the kind of men who chewed fat cigars and greeted each other with a kiss on both cheeks. To Benter, a twenty-one-year-old former Eagle Scout from a cookie-cutter suburb of Pittsburgh, it was simultaneously the most exhilarating and the most terrifying scene he had ever laid eyes on.

Atlantic City was within a six-hour drive for a quarter of the

American population. The first patrons of New Jersey gambling reflected the great diversity of the eastern United States, all squeezed together under one roof. There were dentists and teamsters, politicians and juvenile delinquents. They played slots for a nickel a pull or wrote checks for millions of dollars. The highest of high rollers included the owner of the Philadelphia Eagles, an international arms dealer, and a money launderer for the Medellín drug cartel.

Now standing awkwardly in their midst was Bill Benter with $200 in his wallet. He was supposed to be applying himself to his physics and philosophy college degrees like the good middle-class boy he was at heart. But like so many others, he'd read Thorp's *Beat the Dealer* and couldn't resist trying to find out if counting cards really worked. He had trained by dealing himself hand after hand at his kitchen table, keeping a running count in his head. His $200 bankroll had been scraped together from summer jobs working as a theater usher and warehouse security guard. He intended to make it last as long as he could.

The sheer number of gamblers crammed into the Resorts International Casino presented a problem, though. Every seat at every blackjack table was taken. Benter lingered nearby, trying to seem inconspicuous. It wasn't easy. He was much younger than most of the other patrons, skinnier, too, with a crown of unruly dark hair and eyes slightly too close together. His suit looked as though it had been borrowed from an older male relative.

Suddenly an empty seat appeared at a table where the minimum bet was $25. That was a day's wages for Benter. Not knowing what else to do, he jumped in. He tried to repeat what he'd practiced at his kitchen table.

Three of spades. Plus one. Jack of diamonds. Minus one. Remember not to show you are counting.

It was hard, given the din around him, but achievable with a bit of mental effort. The cards, however, were against him. The count never reached a point where he had a clear advantage over the dealer. Within moments, his entire $200 budget was gone. He stood up, nodded at the dealer, and walked back to his car to start the four-hundred-mile drive back to Pittsburgh.

Anyone else might have been discouraged. Not Benter. His mind fizzed with possibilities the whole way home. As an empiricist, he'd already satisfied himself that Thorp's method was sound. He intuitively understood the principle of expected value, which makes a single loss less important than overall strategy. And then there was that sign at the entrance. Why threaten to ban card counters unless they were taking the casino's money?

To fully grasp the power of expected value to an advantage player, it's useful to demonstrate it with something simpler than blackjack. Imagine, for example, a simple dice game wherein the players must bet on which number will be rolled. They have a one-in-six chance of predicting the right number, and they pay $1 per bet. Win, and they receive $6.

In this radically simplified version of a betting game, if a player bets ten thousand times, they should more or less break even, ending up with the same amount of money they started with. Over time, they would win on average one roll out of every six, making $6 for every $6 spent. But there's a catch: Nothing in life is so straightforward.

Imagine that the person running the game takes a 10-cent fee with each roll. This person represents the casino, or bookmaker. As in the real world, they will offer the game only if it makes them a profit, so they need a take (sometimes called the "vig," "juice," or "rake"). Barring that, they need the odds to be slightly in their favor, so that they will win more than they lose. Otherwise, why would they bother?

With this 10-cent fee, playing ten thousand times leads not to breaking even but to a loss of $1,000 for the player. That's the statistical reality behind all gambling. It's why the house always wins.

Now imagine that the player discovers that the paint used to mark the spots on the dice is unusually heavy, enough to weigh down the side with the most marks, the six. That makes rolling a one, the side facing up when six is down, slightly more likely.

The player feeds the data from thousands of throws of those dice into a computer, which calculates the *real* odds of rolling a one as more like one in five. But the person running the game hasn't realized it yet. All the player needs to do is repeatedly bet on one. Now they need to play only five times, on average, to hit the jackpot, spending

$5 to win $6. After ten thousand rolls, even with the 10-cent fee per roll, the player will be up around $1,000 (they pay $10,000 to win back $12,000, minus $1,000 in fees).

That is the statistical reality behind all advantage systems, the secret sauce that makes it all possible. It's not just about being right; it's about being right more often than the casino or bookmaker expects. Benter realized what really mattered: Celebrating a single win or cursing a single loss was wrongheaded. If a game played out as the casino intended and its odds dictated, eventually the random fluctuations of chance along with the house's take would erode any chance of making a profit.

But if Benter could find situations where the casino odds were off, as in our faulty dice example, that would be different. Thorp had already proven beyond a doubt that there were times in blackjack when the game favored the gambler. If Benter kept on playing correctly, he knew his advantage would tell. It was inevitable.

He'd just finished a year of study overseas in Bristol, England, where he'd discovered *Beat the Dealer* in a public library. He had also discovered something about himself: He craved adventure. Growing up in Pleasant Hills, Pennsylvania, his childhood had passed in the comfortable monochrome of suburban America. While studying in England, he'd taken time out to visit Marrakesh and Egypt, where he had seen the pyramids at Giza. Faced with the thrill of new sights and sounds, his shyness seemed less of a burden. He felt alive.

Back in Pittsburgh, he decided to take a break from college to travel, and he began dreaming up harebrained schemes to fund his plans. At one point, he seriously considered becoming a roaming peephole salesman, going from state to state with a hand drill, offering to install viewing holes in people's front doors. Now, despite his losses in Atlantic City, he felt confident that he could survive as a card counter. Maybe he could use the winnings to indulge his wanderlust. And there was really only one place in the world where a card counter could make enough money for international airfare. He gathered up as much cash as he could find, told his parents that college would have to wait, and boarded a Greyhound bus to Las Vegas.

ROB REITZEN

The car slammed into Rob Reitzen from the side as he was driving home from his job at Hamburger Henry's in West Los Angeles. The last thing he remembered was passing a green light on Sepulveda Boulevard and the sensation of his chest hitting the steering wheel with enough force to bend the metal spokes. After he came to, he tried to stagger clear of the accident, then decided to sit down and wait for an ambulance. A trip to the emergency room later, he was sent home to rest with cracked ribs and a bottle of painkillers.

The 1980s had just begun, and Reitzen didn't have much to show for his twenty-one years on the planet; no college degree or plan to make it big in a particular career. He'd taken a few extension classes at UCLA but clearly was not destined for academia, even without the dyslexia that scrambled the words on the pages of his schoolbooks. "I got Fs in every subject but math," he joked later. "I got Ds in that." Although he liked his job at Hamburger Henry's, it wasn't great for picking up girls, his most pressing ambition at the time.

Bored at home and woozy from pills, Reitzen asked his then girlfriend to buy him a book on poker. He'd been watching his hero Steve McQueen as the Cincinnati Kid in the 1965 movie and liked what he saw. The Kid was an ass-smacking bad boy who used mathematics to humble opponents at the poker table. Before the big showdown, McQueen is shown scribbling sums in a notepad under the heading "Practical exercises in rapid calculation." "He's a percentage player," a sidekick says.

Reitzen was unlike McQueen in most ways: He had buggy eyes and a thin mouth that sloped at the sides. Dressed like an overgrown teenager in an LA Dodgers cap and jeans, he had a sense of humor to match. But he could relate to the Cincinnati Kid's aptitude for playing the percentages. Words would always be a puzzle to him, yet the cadence of numerical sequences made sense. Whether it was chess, poker, or teaching himself to play the piano by memorizing the runic dots and dashes of sheet music and matching them to the sound of a Beatles song, Reitzen believed that he possessed something special; he just wasn't sure what it was.

The problem was convincing everyone else. He'd tell his friends about all the money he was going to make—then ask to borrow ten bucks. Employers at various dead-end jobs noted a distinct lack of seriousness when it came to work.

Reitzen's family tried to help. His uncle was a retired Hollywood director who'd worked with Errol Flynn, Elvis, and the Rat Pack. Through him Reitzen got an interview with the general manager at the Universal Studios lot. Reitzen got wasted the night before and arrived hungover and late. Enraged at being kept waiting, the executive sent him off to work in the greens department, moving plants around on set. That job didn't last long. He got fired from another for falling asleep.

Poker, on the other hand, got his blood pumping. He found it hard to articulate why. Lacking the patience to excel academically, perhaps he saw it as the best way to prove that, behind all the dick jokes, he had a remarkable mind. Had he been seeing a therapist, they might have pointed to the influence of his biological father, an actual rocket scientist, who had abandoned the family when Reitzen was a boy, leaving a void that any young man might seek to fill. As he fumbled his way through high school, Reitzen was reminded about his absent father's genius what felt like daily.

Ask Reitzen directly, though, and he'd give a simple answer: Poker was cool. He was cool, or wanted to be. His speech overflowed with profanity and California slang. Either you were a dude, or you were full of shit. "Jake" meant the situation was good. "Everything is Jake. The Jakest of the Jake." He seemed to view his life as the raw material for stories to tell at the bar, which made gambling a natural career choice.

The poker book Reitzen asked his girlfriend to buy was supposed to get him started. But she misheard him or couldn't find the right one, because she brought back a tome on card-counting techniques for blackjack. One of the successor titles to Thorp's *Beat the Dealer*, it was *Playing Blackjack as a Business* by Lawrence Revere, a former casino worker.

Like Thorp, Revere relied on technical analysis done on an IBM computer to calculate how advantage shifted back and forth between player and dealer. However, Revere claimed that his more complicated system improved the player's odds. Instead of counting up and down by ones, Revere's method scored each card on a scale from minus 3 to plus 4. According to the 9 billion simulations he had run on the IBM, it was a more profitable strategy.

At first, Reitzen was irritated by his girlfriend's mistake. Then he started reading. "If winning is your goal, this book is written for you," Revere had promised. That got Reitzen's attention. Unlike Thorp, Revere claimed to have made enough money from counting cards to do it professionally, all the while jetting around the world, eating in gourmet restaurants, and staying in the finest hotels. "You will not be gambling when you have learned the advantages set forth in this book. You will be in business."

That was the kind of book learning Reitzen could appreciate. After the car crash, he spent weeks recuperating at his grandparents' place, popping pills and thumbing through the strategy charts. When he'd recovered sufficiently, he dealt himself hands of blackjack to practice.

Revere's technique was trickier than Thorp's, "a bear to learn," in the words of one counter. The author advised keeping a separate mental log for aces, which have a special significance in part because you need one to get a blackjack (21), which pays out extra. Reitzen toiled over the cards, teaching himself basic strategy, then the Revere "fives" strategy, then the Revere "plus-minus strategy." Then he paid for the Revere "Advanced Point Count," another notch up on the migraine scale. He'd never studied harder.

The final stage in Revere's six-step plan was to take blackjack lessons, since "there are many points to learn that just cannot be explained in a book." Among the most important: composure under pressure. "I am cold blooded," Revere wrote, adding that he still practiced before playing to get into a blackjack frame of mind.

Reitzen found the perfect spot to hone his craft hidden in a drab roadside block out east in Anaheim. The Ungambling Casino got around California's punitive antibetting laws by marketing itself as a school and training ground for those not quite ready for the bright lights of Las Vegas. "You can practice your skills and have a ball in a friendly, relaxed Vegas-style Casino," a magazine ad promised.

For a five-dollar entry fee, Reitzen could play blackjack until his fingers were raw and his brain throbbed from the mental calculus. The staff didn't care if customers counted cards because there was no real money at stake. With his car totaled by the wreck, he talked his grandmother into driving him out there and picking him up several times a week.

After a month or so, one of the dealers noticed Reitzen with his mouth slightly open, concentrating hard. "You think you're a card counter?" the man said. "Check out that guy." He gestured to a figure at the next table. Reitzen went over and introduced himself. Sure enough, it was another young Thorp disciple trying to build up the courage to face a real casino. Until then, he was working in a furniture store.

Reitzen and his new friend played the next game together, counting silently, four decks, down to the very last card. If they'd mastered the system properly, it would allow them to predict the value of the last card in the plus-minus system and maybe even the card itself. The count had to return to zero. At least, that was the theory.

Reitzen was sure that the count was minus 4, which could mean only one thing. "It's got to be a five," he blurted out at the same time as his partner. They looked at each other, grinning, and turned to the dealer. Slowly, relishing the moment, the dealer overturned the last card. A 5.

INTERLUDE

AMERICAN GOMORRAH

When Nelson, Benter, and Reitzen took their first faltering steps as advantage players, they only dimly understood the shifting sands they were walking onto. Gambling was illegal almost everywhere, infested with criminals and condemned as a vice by campaigning politicians and religious figures.

Many Americans still regarded the practice as George Washington did in 1783: "It is the child of Avarice—the brother of inequity—& father of Mischief—It has been the Ruin of many worthy familys—the loss of many a mans honor—& the cause of Suicide."

At the same time, Americans embraced the spirit of the wager like nowhere else. The nation had been built by risk-takers who had chanced everything, even their lives, on the hope of a better future. In America, gamblers could be heroes: from the Founding Fathers, who had bet on horses and fighting cockerels, to gold prospectors, wildcat oil drillers, and Wall Street speculators.

By the late 1970s, gambling as a pursuit and a business was in flux, neither fully absorbed by the mainstream nor completely excluded from it—a refuge for outcasts, grifters, corporate predators, degenerates, and deadbeats. They met in Las Vegas, once a railroad stop with more snakes than people that had been transformed by legal betting into a dazzling American Gomorrah.

Casinos first appeared in seventeenth-century Venice as private playgrounds for the wealthy, who had to wear masks and three-pointed hats to gain entry. Around 150 years later, the invention of the roulette wheel in France helped spread the concept around Europe, but such amusements were open only to a fortunate few, mainly aristocrats and successful merchants.

Casino gambling as we know it today owes its existence to the

American West. The cowboys, sheepherders, miners, and railway men who flooded the frontier in the late nineteenth century worked rough, lonesome jobs so they could spend their money on whoring, drinking, and gambling. "The man whose tools of his profession are a hammer, a pick, and a pan, or a saddle, a bridle, and a horse, is at heart a gambler, a happy-go-lucky individualist, hell-bent for quick and easy money," J. B. Griswold wrote in *American Magazine* in 1938.

In that precarious environment, wagering became a mass-market activity quite unlike the private gaming clubs of old Europe. Gambling took place in full public view in "wide-open" venues from San Francisco to Dodge City. With intense competition for customers, saloon owners had to offer a better experience and were less inclined to cheat.

Games had to be refined so they would offer maximum excitement and longevity, which required a careful balancing act. The odds of winning had to be good enough to make patrons feel that they had a fair chance but finely weighted in the gaming house's favor to ensure its making a long-term profit. The economic model that emerged dominates the industry to this day.

Eventually the Wild West was tamed, and middle-class residents of wide-open gambling towns got sick of the violence and prostitution that so often followed the betting crowd. Reform movements flourished. Citizens pushed local legislators to rid their districts of vice. By the 1930s, open gambling was restricted to Nevada, where the law had never held much sway in daily life. Technically it was illegal even there, although there were gaming tables and slot machines in almost every hotel and gas station.

Then, in 1931, the Nevada legislature legalized wide-open gambling, alongside the quickie divorce, in an effort to drum up tax revenue as the Great Depression tore through the state. For $75 per month per table or $12.50 for a slot machine, anyone could get a casino license, even convicted felons. All the law required was that games be honest. In other words, they could be rigged only in the routine sense that the odds favored the house, not with loaded dice or sleight of hand.

Since gambling was still illegal everywhere else, the first people with expertise in running casinos tended to be criminals. Among the earliest Nevada proprietors was Anthony "the Admiral" Cornero, a former Prohibition rumrunner who'd operated illegal casino ships off the coast of Los Angeles and turned water cannons on government boats when they tried to stop him. Welcomed in Nevada, he died in 1955 at a Las Vegas craps table.

Benjamin "Bugsy" Siegel tapped his gangster friends to fund the construction of the Flamingo Hotel in Vegas, with its iconic hot-pink sign. "Come as you are to America's Monte Carlo," Flamingo advertisements invited, and come they did. Siegel, however, was gunned down in his Beverly Hills mansion in June 1947 after displeasing his backers.

Even casino operators who weren't mobbed up had outlaw reputations. Benny Binion, the Stetson-topped Texan behind Binion's Horseshoe, boasted about having killed two men during his casino license hearing. One had been self-defense, he explained; the other "just a n****r I caught stealing some whiskey." The Gaming Control Board laughed and approved him anyway.

Muckraking journalists and politicians occasionally tried to shake the underworld's grip on the casino business. Tennessee Senator Estes Kefauver, who ran televised hearings on organized crime in the late 1950s, warned that "hoodlums from the east and west coasts have invaded the legalized gambling setup." In the 1960s, the Nevada Gaming Commission created a black book containing the names and mug shots of individuals deemed too unsavory to run a casino.

The attention succeeded in driving criminals underground and in giving Las Vegas something else it could market to middle America: danger. "What this town needs is that scent of vice, a little sin," Bob Stupak, the owner of the Vegas World hotel and casino, once said. Throughout the 1960s and 1970s, Las Vegas continued to flourish.

Nothing seemed to stem the flood of betting dollars: not gangland murders, casino fires, or corruption scandals. When the military tested nuclear bombs in the Nevada desert, casinos held viewing parties for guests to watch the mushroom clouds blooming on the horizon while sipping on radiation-themed cocktails. Tourism actually increased.

By the time Nelson, Benter, and Reitzen set their sights on Las Vegas, it was the unquestioned capital of hedonism in the United States. Even religious critics seemed to have given up the fight. Billy Graham stopped there in 1978 on his Crusade for Christ. The famous evangelist and firebrand preacher announced that Sin City was "a nice place to visit." That year, 10 million tourists agreed with him, spending more than a billion dollars.

Las Vegas wasn't for everyone, however. There was the crime. The gangsters, now outnumbered by corporate interests, never really left. Throughout the 1970s, a diminutive sociopath, Anthony "The Ant" Spilotro, ran a gift shop at the Circus Circus Hotel while also fulfilling his duties as an enforcer for the Chicago Mob.

The author James Ellroy called Vegas "a shit hole. It's a testimony to greed and prostitution and exploitation of women and narcotics and the get-rich-quick fervor that is one of the worst aspects of America." The social critic James Howard Kunstler described it as "where American spirit crawls to die." But no one could deny that Las Vegas burned brightly; it was a place where people went to ignite stifled passions or surrender to temptation and be consumed.

PART 2

A FLAME IN THE DESERT

Las Vegas washes away your sins. It's like a morality car wash.
—Robert De Niro as Sam Rothstein in *Casino*

A flame in the desert that drew moths.
—"Jimmy the Greek" Snyder

BILL NELSON

After graduating from college, Bill Nelson shunned Wall Street and the moneyed future promised by the Goldman Sachs recruiter. He'd always known he would. Instead, he decided to try his luck as a professional card counter. It took a few months of bouncing between LA and Lake Tahoe before he felt ready to move to the epicenter of American gambling. One day in 1977, he packed his belongings into the blue Beetle and drove east. Once again, he had warm wind in his hair and the pleasant, weightless feeling of not knowing what was next.

The desert flattened out into a sun-scorched plain with a few twisted shrubs. On the fringes of Las Vegas, Nelson saw the first signs advertising motel vacancies, and some posted by church groups warning visitors about what lay ahead.

SIN HAS CONSEQUENCES. REPENT.

Closer to the Strip, the city began to unfurl its famous roadside welcome. Flashing billboards jostled for attention, overwhelming the senses. Las Vegas Boulevard and Fremont Street were ground zero for an avant-garde style Tom Wolfe called "electro-graphic car fantasy mobile architecture." Unlike cities in Europe and the eastern United States, where the metropolis was designed to project grandeur, Vegas had been built to catch the eye of people rolling past on four wheels. The effect was "wild enough and baroque enough to express the new age of motion and mass wealth," Wolfe wrote.

Nelson saw signs promising three-dollar steak, free beer and champagne. Casinos advertised loose slots and single-deck 21 alongside twenty-four-hour wedding chapels and Mr. Reed's Burlesque Go-Go, with its topless dancers. Circus Circus was serving a "Smorgasbord Internationale" dinner. He could only guess what that entailed.

Fleetwood Mac was playing at the Aladdin. Or if he preferred to dance, there was Dirty Sally's on the corner of Sands Boulevard, which boasted "the West Coast's most famous discotheque" as well as high-stakes backgammon. Nelson was glad to have put Los Angeles, with its traffic jams and polluted air, in his rearview mirror. He was struck by how small Vegas seemed in comparison. There were half a dozen casinos on the Strip and half a dozen more downtown. Behind the bright lights, it was a medium-sized town at best, he thought.

He rented the cheapest apartment he could find in the misleadingly named Enchanted Gardens, a squat, desert-colored complex within walking distance of the Strip. The room was tiny and bare, but he had few possessions and no intention of spending much time there. His first job was to scout out accommodating blackjack venues.

Nelson knew that table games such as craps and blackjack were patrolled by pit bosses, the sworn enemies of all card counters. A mongrel breed combining the character traits of nightclub doormen and butlers, pit bosses were employed to ensure that everything ran smoothly in their territory, typically half a dozen tables. Sometimes that meant bouncing drunks or collaring thieves who tried to pocket casino chips. Other times, they put on a friendlier face to glad-hand big spenders, offering meal vouchers or tickets to a show.

They also had to keep an eye on employees to make sure they weren't stealing or bungling the deal. In short, they were charged with making sure that the casino continued to vacuum up money in an orderly fashion. And it was the pit boss's neck on the line if, for example, a blackjack table started hemorrhaging cash. They seemed to take the presence of card counters personally, as if the act of winning were an affront to their profession.

In attitude and appearance, the warring tribes couldn't have been more different. Card counters were mostly bookish college graduates whose social skills might have placed them somewhere on the autism spectrum. Pit bosses had names such as Vinnie and Louie and wore black suits and pinky rings. They were a throwback to the old Vegas, schooled in the old ways. Outright violence was rare by the late 1970s, but it wasn't unheard of.

One card counter was punched so hard in a Reno alley that he needed reconstructive surgery on his face. Another had his arm twisted in a Vegas casino backroom until it broke. Nelson had heard the stories and knew the risks. But free money was free money. He had a job to do.

He scouted the dozen or so Vegas casinos for hours to find the right combination of good blackjack dealers, dumb pit bosses, and slack security. The older venues were best. The Sahara, with its neon minarets and plastic camels, was a favorite. So was the Aladdin, once the largest casino in Nevada, where Elvis had married Priscilla in 1967, lately reliant on funding from the Mob via Jimmy Hoffa and the Teamsters union pension fund. To stay invisible, Nelson played lower stakes, from $2 to $20 a bet, or $5 to $30 if he was having a good week.

Soon he began noticing other card counters. Sober young men, sipping sodas and staring at the cards—they weren't hard to spot. Mostly Nelson ignored them. They were his competition. But sometimes he would offer to buy them a coffee and trade war stories. In the jargon of the professional blackjack player, to be banished was to be eighty-sixed, as in "I'm eighty-sixed at the Mint." Gambling lore said that the phrase had originated from the rumored final destination of those who pushed their luck too far: eight miles out and six feet under. There was a security guard at the Horseshoe whom everybody knew as Gold Dust. He was in the habit of driving counters into the desert to deliver punishment beatings, or so Nelson's new friends told him.

Several other card counters were also renting at Enchanted Gardens, and they invited Nelson to join them in informal teams. Together, they could monitor more tables at more casinos to target the best games. After a long shift spent adding and subtracting numbers in his head, Nelson rarely felt like going out to enjoy the attractions of a Las Vegas night. Counting cards for hours on end was about as much fun as digging a hole in the dirt.

He and his new friends shared their apartment block with prostitutes who also worked the Strip, but the two professions seldom mixed. Even if they were the kind of men with the self-confidence to approach women, which they mostly were not, the card counters were so burned out that they normally went straight home to their unfurnished rooms to sleep. It was grueling, unglamorous work, but Nelson was hooked. He was his own boss, earning and living as he wanted, no corporate jackboot on his neck. Everything in Vegas was cheap—food, drink, and entertainment—all of it subsidized as a loss leader to entice people to the gaming tables.

One day, Nelson was scouting in the Paradise Hotel & Casino when he heard a commotion. A crowd was gathering around a smartly dressed man with unruly red hair and round John Lennon glasses. He was playing blackjack one on one against a dealer. Every time he got a winning hand, he jumped onto his chair and clapped his hands like a lunatic seal. His audience was eating it up and so were the dealers, despite the fact the flame-haired man had just made several thousand dollars at the house's expense. He'd persuaded them to raise the table betting limit just for him.

Nelson hung around and eventually caught the man's eye. He thought he saw a flicker of recognition and flashed a quizzical smile. After the gambler had finished playing and accumulated what seemed to Nelson like a monumental pile of chips, he approached Nelson and suggested that they go for a coffee. His name was Rusty London, he said, although he had several pseudonyms he used in casinos.

Nelson was in awe. He'd never seen a card counter win so much or in such flamboyant fashion. London was, he explained, a trained psychologist and an expert in the art of manipulation. The theatrics were part of his act, which was to play the part of an out-of-control big spender. Casinos were primed to spot intense young men who looked as though they were into mathematics, people like Nelson and his friends. But high rollers with no impulse control were their bread and butter.

"If you treat pit bosses as the enemy, that *makes* them the enemy," London told Nelson. Instead, London tipped liberally and bought them gifts. He showed them his cards and asked their advice on how to play. As a result, he was given free hotel suites and gourmet meals as often as he was barred. London offered to share some of his methods in return for a cut of Nelson's profits. Nelson, who thought London was the shrewdest gambler he'd met, agreed. A few weeks later, he drove out to San Francisco to visit London at his home.

The house confirmed Nelson's assessment. Compared to the prison cell ambiance of Nelson's apartment in Vegas, it was a palace fit for a movie star: six bedrooms plus a spacious gaming room with its own blackjack table. One side was entirely glass to showcase a stunning view of San Francisco Bay. London's blond girlfriend also looked as though she'd been dreamed into existence from a Hollywood fantasy. They invited Nelson to join them in the outdoor hot tub, which looked out over the Golden Gate Bridge.

"Oh, and by the way," London said, disrobing. "Everybody is naked here. You can join us. Or not. Your choice." Nelson let out one of his nervous laughs, a high-pitched staccato that hung in the air. What else could he do? He stripped off and joined them, hoping that the bubbles would protect his modesty. Nelson relaxed into the warm water and sipped from a bottle of beer. The guy was an eccentric creature; that much was obvious.

London's glasses were as thick as cola bottles. While he spoke with the methodical precision of a college professor, Nelson had never met an academic who appeared quite so relaxed exposing his genitals to a virtual stranger. But London also showed a clearer understanding of the economics of gambling than anyone else Nelson had yet encountered. He talked in percentage terms about how much of his betting fund he was willing to risk in any given circumstance. He'd survived for years; flourished, to judge by his home.

Unlike the card counters of Enchanted Gardens, London played without fear or shame. He had no desire to get one over on casinos or clash with pit bosses. He simply wanted the treasure they guarded. "Smart gamblers don't gamble" was one of his maxims. Nelson couldn't have agreed more.

Nelson and London fired back and forth in what passed for small talk among card counters, to the visible boredom of their blond companion. It didn't take long for them to get into a discussion about the finer points of their bible: Ed Thorp's *Beat the Dealer*. Thorp had predicted that winning systems for other betting games would emerge thanks to "the rise of fantastic new scientific tools" made possible by the computer. Until the late 1970s, only governments and large corporations could afford the thousands of dollars it cost to lease a single IBM mainframe. But as Nelson and London sat chatting in the hot tub, a new age had just begun.

In 1977, the Apple II was released, becoming the first genuine personal computer to go on sale to the general public. Hardly anyone bought it, and those who did had little idea what on Earth it was for. Resembling the bastard offspring of a vintage typewriter and a microwave, it came with four kilobytes of memory as standard, enough to store roughly two pages of ordinary text.

The earliest software could just about cope with basic games and accounting spreadsheets or niche tasks such as tracking biorhythms, a pseudoscience that creates wavelike cycles to explain human activity. Still, frustrating as it was to operate, the Apple II inspired a small community of hobbyists, who formed computer clubs to explore the technology's potential or just to have fun.

Nelson had sampled it already. His college roommate at UCLA had written a program to simulate blackjack. Running the software was what had persuaded Nelson that card counting was still possible, even after Lake Tahoe casinos had switched from using one deck of cards to four packs, shuffled together and dealt from a shoe. Virtual games had shown that card counting was mathematically viable even with multiple decks.

In *Beat the Dealer*, Thorp hinted that he'd developed a roulette system "in the basement lab of a world-famous scientist." The author said he'd managed to achieve something that even Albert Einstein had thought was impossible by predicting roulette using physics and mathematical models. It was the same principle that enabled NASA scientists to plot the trajectory of rockets, factoring in speed, drag, gravity, and other forces. If human beings could blast themselves to the moon and back, surely it should be possible to calculate the final destination of a plastic ball bouncing around a wooden wheel. Thorp claimed that the method worked, although when he described it in the 1960s, he admitted that "certain electronic problems" had prevented him from exploiting it for profit.

The prospect was tantalizing to any advantage player. Roulette was the ultimate challenge, virtually synonymous with unpredictability. No one would suspect that the game was vulnerable. "It will be even more fascinating when, sometime in the next few years, some of the few who possess the idea cash in on it in the casinos," Thorp wrote.

London told Nelson that he thought it was time to revisit roulette. He suggested assembling a team: one person to time the ball as it circled the wheel, another to clock the rotor. They could connect remotely to a third player wearing a computer to process the data. "One for the future," London suggested.

Nelson leaned back in the tub and pondered. He could already feel that counting cards might lose its appeal. As he saw it, he was only doing what dozens or maybe hundreds of other gamblers had done already. But roulette, that would be something new, something just for him.

"I'll think about it," he said.

BILL BENTER

Bill Benter arrived in Las Vegas a couple of years after Nelson, in the spring of 1979. The Bee Gees and Barry Manilow were playing on the radio. Gas prices were sky high thanks to the revolution in Iran, which had destabilized the whole Middle East. Vegas Mayor Bill Briare, meanwhile, was in a lather over a play featuring full nudity at the Jolly Trolley casino. "A convention city like Las Vegas just does not need this sort of image," he complained, radically misjudging his municipality's place in American culture.

Benter got off the Greyhound bus and went straight to the University of Nevada campus to search the message boards for notices seeking roommates. Technically, he was still a college student, taking a break to find himself, as twenty-two-year-olds often do. In reality, returning to the classroom was the last thing on his mind. Once he found an apartment, he got a job as a cashier at a nearby 7-Eleven, selling Slurpees to college kids for $3.10 an hour.

Benter planned to gamble all his wages at the blackjack tables. On his first outing he made a $13 profit and never looked back. He found his training ground on the faded carpets of the cheaper downtown casinos, away from the harsh glare of the Strip. He'd take the bus from his campus apartment and spend all day walking among the El Cortez, the Western, and the Four Queens. There his companions were blue-collar gamblers too rough looking or day drunk for the fancier venues uptown. On a good day he might earn $40.

Months passed. Benter worked nights at the 7-Eleven, days at the blackjack coalface. He made a few friends, fellow card counters, who formed little partnerships and talked about their systems. None of them dared play big enough to warrant being eighty-sixed. Benter proved to be a skilled counter. He kept winning, but with such a small bankroll he couldn't get out of first gear.

Benter's biggest concern wasn't casino security but a mathematical phenomenon called gambler's ruin. When betting against an opponent with effectively unlimited resources—a casino, for example—gamblers will always go broke first, even if the game is fair. Good fortune ebbs and flows. Keep betting long enough, and a run of bad luck will come along to blow away every last cent. Benter's bank balance wasn't just small compared to a casino's; it would have looked puny to the cheapskates drinking watery beer at the Western's $2 blackjack tables on a Tuesday afternoon.

All around Benter were reminders of the consequences of failure. Las Vegas was a boomtown with a flourishing homeless population. They lived in cardboard condominiums along the Union Pacific railroad tracks and slept under trees to avoid the blistering Nevada sun. Later, researchers found that roughly one in five reported having a gambling problem. Many wasted their panhandling dollars in the very same casinos where Benter was trying to make a living. You didn't have to look far in Vegas to find a gambler who'd fallen on hard times. Most of them had their systems, too.

After a year Benter was desperate enough for extra income to apply for a job as a night cleaner at McDonald's. While he sometimes doubted himself, he never questioned Thorp's teachings. Science was Benter's religion; statistics were his gospel. He had an unshakable belief that reality, even in the netherworld of a Las Vegas casino, was bound by immutable rules. Other card counters in his social group quit and moved home when the realities of the life sunk in. Benter stayed. His faith was stronger.

One afternoon, he was scouting downtown with his roommate, writing on a clipboard, when an older man approached. "Come on, boys, let's go have a coffee." Dressed smartly in a sports coat and dagger collar shirt, he appeared to be neither a casino worker nor a wild-eyed hobo, so Benter agreed.

The man's name was Will. He was in his forties, which in Benter's mind made him geriatric for a gambler. He'd picked them out as card counters and said he might be willing to sponsor them and share profits. Will took them back to his apartment and dealt them a few hands to make sure they could do what they said they could do. "All right, boys, you know your stuff," he declared and promptly handed them $1,000 each.

Benter had only ever seen so much cash on TV. The two young card counters took it back to their apartment, where they tossed it all over their moldering carpet and rolled around in it, laughing like children, trying to make snow angels in the scattered bills. Benter had the sense of passing through an invisible barrier. It felt good. It felt even better when they met Will again a week later to share their winnings and he handed over more.

Will had been in Vegas for years and knew most of the city's card-counting underground. Like other experienced players on the scene, he'd realized that his money could work harder if he invested some of it in new talent and invited them to split the profits fifty-fifty. There was always the risk of someone running off with his cash, but the type of people who took the time to learn the system and memorize strategy charts were not temperamentally inclined to outright theft. All it took was a handshake to bond their fates together.

Soon afterward, Will summoned Benter to share some news from the card-counting grapevine. There was a legendary blackjack team coming into town. Run by an Australian named Alan Woods, they circumnavigated the globe, milking casinos with ruthless efficiency. They had won so much money that they were known simply as "The Bankroll." Would Benter be interested in meeting them?

This is my ticket to the big time, Benter thought. He didn't hesitate to say yes.

In person, Alan Woods was lean and prematurely gray for a man in his thirties. Benter noticed an icy glint in his eyes. The younger men in the Woods group looked up to him as a kind of patriarch, and he led them with calm authority. He never got flustered by big losses or the threat of arrest. Benter heard that he'd managed to sneak through airport security in Manila with $10,000 stuffed into his underwear.

Woods didn't dress like a high roller, lounging in his hotel room in jeans and T-shirt, but he pursued the card counter's craft with iron discipline.

After Will vouched for him, Benter was in. There was to be no drinking on the job, Woods explained. The team pooled their resources into a shared bankroll, which paid out in proportion to how much a player had contributed as well as how much they earned at the table. Woods got the biggest cut by far. The Australian also insisted on having detailed notes from every session. Benter would have to submit them alongside a numerical record of his outlay versus profit. "Played Caesars, graveyard shift, main pit. Attention from the short, fat pit boss."

The Woods team managed their bankroll with a mathematical system called the Kelly criterion. Named for the Bell Labs physicist who had created it, John L. Kelly Jr., it was the antidote to gambler's ruin. Kelly, part of a clique of gambling scientists, had set out in the 1950s to find the perfect balance between risk and reward. Wager too much, and you risked losing it all to bad luck; wager too little, as Benter had been doing, and you missed out on the benefits of having an advantage.

Kelly succeeded in his goal. His method relied on complex equations, but in practice it was simple to execute. The best approach was to bet in proportion to your advantage over the house. For example, if a card counter worked out that their edge in a particular game of blackjack was 2 percent, they should bet 2 percent of their total funds. The bigger the edge, the bigger the bet.

Benter left the downtown fleapits behind and started playing on the Strip for $100 a hand, using the Bankroll's ample cash pile. Gambling the Alan Woods way yielded about $50 an hour in profit, he found. If he had a bad night, no one minded, least of all Woods; it was assumed to be a statistical fluctuation that would correct itself. After playing for a month in Vegas, Benter and his teammates took a road trip to Atlantic City, where they swarmed through the boardwalk casinos like army ants.

Benter learned more about his new boss, if that was the right word for the most experienced member of a gambling crew. Woods had been born in Murwillumbah, a small Australian town. In his twenties he had been an insurance actuary with a wife and two children. One day he'd decided that suburbia wasn't for him and left it all behind to become an itinerant gambler. From that moment, he'd willed a new life into existence.

Woods was in no hurry to spend the money he made. He groused about the cost of making long-distance phone calls. He wasn't interested in fast cars, luxury food, or any of the other trappings of wealth, although he loved the company of women. The only thing that seemed to worry him was the prospect of getting bored. He regarded the world with a cold, analytical gaze, as if it existed solely for him to mine for entertainment.

Six weeks after joining the team, Benter found himself on a plane bound for Europe. There, Woods divided the group and sent them to different locations around the continent. Benter and another counter were assigned to Monaco, the Mediterranean city-state popular with race car drivers and high-society tax dodgers. It was home to some of Europe's oldest gambling venues, the legacy of a French prince who had founded the Casino de Monte-Carlo in the middle of the nineteenth century.

Benter invested in a suit with coattails and tried to muster the savoir faire required to blend in with the minor aristocrats and celebrities who haunted the old casino. The venue itself was spectacular, the ideal on which Las Vegas imitations were modeled. The oil-painted murals and statues were a century old, not just faked to appear that way. The gaming rooms were as spotlessly clean and hushed as an art museum. No one in Monaco would be caught dead hollering and shouting over a bet.

At the blackjack tables, Benter imagined that he was James Bond as uniformed waiters brought him drinks on a silver tray. There were no pit bosses there. Surrounded by old-money eccentrics languidly sipping martinis, he felt even more invisible than usual. He suspected that the dealers had never heard of Ed Thorp. After a long shift, the James Bond fantasy evaporated. Benter and his partner were too timid to venture into Monaco's famous nightclubs, so they returned to their hotel to rest.

Their success in Monaco gave them a pile of bills to bring back to Woods, who acted as the group's unofficial banker. Back in Vegas, Benter quit his job at the 7-Eleven and moved into a nicer apartment. He abandoned the idea of returning to college. His parents trusted his judgment, though it led to some awkward conversations. "Bill's traveling right now," his mother would reply when family friends asked what Benter was doing.

Not that he told his parents, but Benter was certain he'd found his calling. His nerdiness, a handicap in other walks of life, was an asset in the card-counting community. He threw himself into studying the craft, reading books and papers on stochastic processes, Markov chains, and Boole's inequality.

Benter found other obsessives, too. A gambler who went by the nickname Little Dave was so committed to mathematical principles that he allowed himself to win only what he calculated was the expected return from his advantage. If Little Dave profited from a lucky streak, he'd stay at the tables without counting, losing until his winnings had shrunk to the appropriate size. To do anything else risked unbalancing the natural order of the universe, he felt.

The Woods team threw parties with other card counters, handing out bottled beer and plastic chairs around the swimming pools in their apartment complexes. Benter felt that he belonged. Little Dave and the rest were his people. They were fighting the same war against the same foe using the same tools. They could discuss things that were impossible for outsiders to comprehend. When told about card counting, relatives would often assume that it was illegal or cheating. Benter and his friends didn't see it that way; they were using talent and hard work to play the game better. The casinos were the real crooks.

Most of all, card counters shared a pathological aversion to the idea of getting a nine-to-five job, even if most of them, like Benter, had never been near one. Drones who sat in offices all day pushing paper were viewed with even more contempt than pit bosses. A member of the scene wrote a novel about gambling that described the attitude well: "You know you're alive. Isn't that worth something, knowing you're alive? A lot of people go through life without ever experiencing that, the quickening pulse, the heat of the blood. They're the ones—in my book—who are a little weird."

Around 1980, Benter was at a party in a Las Vegas apartment complex called Enchanted Gardens when he met a strikingly handsome card counter. His name was Bill Nelson. The two Bills had plenty in common and took a seat on a tattered couch together. Nelson explained that he'd been making money from blackjack for a few years already and was considering the viability of applying the same principles to other games. He glanced around to check that there was no one else within earshot. "I've been thinking about roulette," he said.

ROB REITZEN

Reitzen had to go. He made up his mind the second he heard about the Fifth National Conference on Gambling and Risk Taking. Some of the biggest names in card counting were scheduled to speak at Caesars Lake Tahoe in October 1981, including the man who had started it all, Ed Thorp. Reitzen figured that it would be the perfect place to meet like-minded gamblers. Plus, he could test his skills—for real this time—at the Caesars blackjack tables.

His new playing partner from the Ungambling Casino, the LA venue where they practiced with worthless chips, couldn't escape his shift at the furniture store but donated a few dollars for expenses in solidarity. "I'll come back with the knowledge," Reitzen promised.

Caesars Tahoe was shaped like two discarded cinder blocks, an ugly blot against a vista of mountains, snow, and sky. Inside, the new owners had spent $40 million revamping the place, outfitting more than four hundred hotel rooms and a convention center that hosted pro boxing bouts and comedy shows. The gambling and risk conference was originally created by the University of Nevada as a forum for casino executives and government officials to schmooze, slap backs, and invent new ways to profit from America's love of the wager.

The 1981 edition, however, attracted a new audience. They sat low in their seats, hats pulled down to hide their eyes. Some wore sunglasses indoors or unconvincing fake beards and mustaches. They had come not to support the casino industry but to learn how to squeeze it for every last nickel, so they were anxious for the suits not to see their faces. "If casinos wanted to put an end to card counting, I think one bomb in this room would probably do it," one of the moderators said early on; that got the biggest laugh of the morning.

Reitzen took his place in the conference hall, hidden under an oversized Dodgers baseball cap. He settled in to enjoy what one gambler would later call the blackjack generation's Woodstock. They weren't there only for Thorp. Also headlining were Peter Griffin, a mathematics professor at California State University, Sacramento, and the author of the book *The Theory of Blackjack*; John Gwynn, a computer science professor who specialized in running simulations of gambling games; and Ken Uston, who'd achieved something close to celebrity in the card-counting world by suing several casinos that had barred him because he "did not lose his money quite as fast as most people."

There were talks on the Kelly criterion and a mathematical analysis of the Chinese dominos game pai gow. A consultant had produced a statistical analysis of "early surrender," a blackjack rule change tested, then dropped, in Atlantic City that allowed players to forfeit in certain losing situations (great for card counters; it didn't last long). The conference planners had dug deep to tap into the groundbreaking scientific research taking place in the field and had inadvertently put on a card-counting convention.

Dr. Bill Eadington, the conference organizer, kicked things off by quoting the sociologist Edward Devereux. "Gambling is at once a major recreational institution, a minor vice, a large-scale industry, a powerful source of crime and political corruption, a perennial social problem, a fascinating psychological puzzle, and an intriguing pastime," he read. "We have a feeling that throughout this conference each one of those described will come under substantial scrutiny."

Thorp appeared during the lunchtime session on the first day. To Reitzen and other card counters it was as if Elvis himself had been hauled from the grave to honor the stage, such was Thorp's legend. Since publishing *Beat the Dealer*, he'd spent more than a decade running a hedge fund in California, trading stock warrants and convertible bonds. His speech was billed as "A Blackjack Player on Wall Street: How We Made 41 Million Dollars." But, as Thorp was quick to update his audience, it really should have been called "How We Made 54 Million Dollars"; the fund had earned an additional $13 million since he had submitted the title.

Thorp was playing in the biggest casino of all now, dealing in sums Reitzen could scarcely imagine. Yet he was still a card counter at heart, with the signature mix of awkwardness and defiance. He had a habit of stopping in midsentence to screw up his face and blink. "The stock market . . . [pause, blink, blink] is a game that I could beat."

The conference lurched on, a confusion of opposing agendas and viewpoints. First, a psychologist described the pathology of problem gambling, using the example of a priest who had wagered away his parishioners' money and ended up living in his car. Next, the card counter Ken Uston railed against the "insidious and powerful" casino lobby. He titled his talk "Does the Gambling Industry Have a Conscience?" Uston felt strongly that it did not. A Walter Funkenbusch from Michigan ummed and erred his way through a speech about a new casino game he'd invented, a roulette variant featuring "cyclic stochastic inequalities."

"Blue beats red beats green beats yellow, red beats green or yellow, and green beats yellow," Funkenbusch rambled. Reitzen devoured it all. During breaks, the Caesars blackjack tables thrummed with action. At one point, an attendee saw Ed Thorp standing engrossed in front of the Big Wheel, a type of giant vertical roulette wheel. The godfather of card counting watched the multicolored prize sections spin and spin, a pointer clicking against the spokes. Just another game to be beaten.

A recurring theme at the conference was how computers could process odds more accurately than had ever been possible before. Computers weren't yet in every home, but by 1981 they could be found in most universities. A mathematics professor with a European accent described using one to rank the various card-counting techniques by running tens of millions of simulated blackjack hands. Not only could he tell you that the Einstein system was more efficient than the high-low system, but he could tell you how much more efficient down to one-tenth of one percent.

By the ninth symposium Reitzen was ready to announce his

presence with a question. He raised his hand after a technical presentation by Peter Griffin, another math professor whose book *The Theory of Blackjack* was considered a classic. "Dr. Griffin," Reitzen began. "Why do you count eight as a positive integer when all the other counts give it a zero?"

He assumed that the inquiry would mark him as a budding blackjack scholar in front of a roomful of people with letters after their names. "Why? Why?" the indignant Griffin replied. "Because my computer told me to!" Reitzen sank back into his seat. Later, he was approached by an older guy who introduced himself as Wally Simmons. "I was asking myself the same thing," Simmons said. "You're a card counter, right?" Reitzen nodded. "Let's go get a drink."

As it turned out, both men were counters with a fondness for Scotch. Simmons was what Reitzen wanted to be a few years down the line. He'd just moved to Vegas after some profitable years in Atlantic City and was doing well enough to play with stacks of black chips, worth $100 each. A onetime all-American high school football star, his body and hair, combed over into a side parting, were just starting to surrender to middle age. After a few whiskeys, Simmons shared a little of his backstory. He'd acquired a taste for card games as a college student in Lexington, Virginia. Then, shortly after graduating, he had been diagnosed with terminal cancer. His parents had taken a chance on extensive radiation therapy, which had saved his life.

After that, Simmons had ricocheted from job to job, trying to find something that didn't feel like a waste of time. He had worked as a headhunter, which was so boring that he had spent all day practicing blackjack at his desk. He had done shifts at a logistics company where he had gotten interested in computers and taught himself Fortran, an early programming language. Then he had met a New Jersey dentist who'd also read Thorp. They had quit their jobs to start a blackjack team.

Reitzen decided that Simmons was a dude—the real deal. Simmons had a barrel chest and a crooked smile. Like Reitzen, he was as much attracted to the science of gambling as he was to the perks of the lifestyle: heady nights in a casino and the presence of glamorous women. Simmons, meanwhile, found his drinking partner hilarious.

Reitzen was the only other person he'd met who had been dogged enough to learn the headache-inducing Revere Advanced Point Count, the most technically challenging Thorp spin-off.

"Come on," the older gambler said to Reitzen. "Let's see how good you are." They went up to Simmons's room, where he pulled out a pack of cards. Counting down a deck was the standard test of mettle, just as it had been for Reitzen and his friend in the Ungambling Casino. The idea was to keep track of the score—plus 1, minus 3, and so on—for fifty-one cards, then use the count to predict the final card. Simmons dealt fast, and Reitzen was several whiskeys deep, but he managed it.

"Okay," said Simmons. "You're in. Want to join our team?"

"Fuck yeah," Reitzen replied. Simmons took his number and said he'd be in touch once they finished their current bankroll. Blackjack teams divide their work into lump sums in order to manage their finances. They might raise $50,000 together and with nonplaying partners, then gamble until they double their money and split the profits. That moment, known as "breaking the bank" in card-counting parlance, is the professional gambler's equivalent of a nine-to-fiver's annual bonus. If things go well, it is cause for much celebration.

Reitzen returned home to Los Angeles and waited for the call. As the weeks passed, his excitement turned to anxiety, then gloom, at the prospect of returning to the dead-end job market. Then one morning, the phone rang. Reitzen jolted awake and glanced out his window. It was 5:30 a.m. and still dark. He picked up the receiver.

"Rob, it's Wally." Reitzen could hear glasses clinking in the background. "You hear that? We broke the bank. We're drinking champagne!"

"Er. When do you want me?" Reitzen mumbled, his brain still sodden with sleep.

"Now, man! Can you get here now?"

Later that day, Reitzen drove to the furniture store to share the good news with his partner from the Ungambling Casino. "You're quitting right now," he said. "This is what we've been waiting for. It's real." They begged, scraped, and borrowed as much money as they could, then hit Interstate 10 and lit out for Vegas, headed for the allotted meeting spot, a Denny's.

Simmons was waiting for them. "How much have you got?" he asked. Reitzen and his friend unpacked $4,000, an amount equal to the entire worldly wealth of two Californians in their twenties, as well as gifts and loans from the relatives who hadn't dismissed them as crazy. "Put it all in," Simmons said. Card counters always needed to raise money to bet. By custom, they were paid both for hours spent at the table and a percentage of whatever they invested in the bankroll, he explained. Simmons believed that it was better for card counters to have skin in the game. Then he excused himself, saying he needed to "straighten out some team business," and disappeared.

An hour later, there was still no sign of Simmons. Reitzen started to fidget. It occurred to him that they had just given all their money to someone they barely knew and had no way of contacting. Reitzen's partner was convinced that they'd fallen victim to an elaborate con. After another hour, Reitzen was ready to believe it, too. He called his adoptive father from a pay phone outside. "I fucked up," he said. His father advised him to wait a little longer and offered to wire gas money if Simmons didn't show.

Half an hour later, Simmons breezed in as if nothing had happened. He produced a piece of paper with instructions on which casinos to play in and where to meet afterward. Then he handed over two thick bundles of cash. Ten thousand dollars. Each.

PART 3

THE WAY OF THE WIRE

The ultimate player would be a high-speed computer.
—Edward O. Thorp, *Beat the Dealer*

I must Create a System, or be enslav'd by another Mans.
—William Blake, *Jerusalem*

BILL NELSON

The idea of creating a roulette computer had been percolating in Nelson's mind. In the months after the conversation in Rusty London's hot tub, it came to him often. The late 1970s saw an explosion of computer hardware and software as mom-and-pop developers and campus nerds pushed the technology in new directions. Consumers began seeing computers in supermarkets, linked to barcode scanners, and in banks. The first generation of hackers was learning fast, too. In 1979, a group of students at UCLA broke into the college network to alter their grades.

Nelson pondered all that in his cramped apartment in Enchanted Gardens, in between long shifts of counting cards up and down the Strip. Microprocessors were revolutionizing communication, science, and business. What might they do for Las Vegas's growing population of professional gamblers?

As Nelson saw it, though, the challenge with roulette wasn't so much about computing power as it was about physics. Ed Thorp understood that. In 1969, seven years after releasing *Beat the Dealer*, he'd published a paper on the subject in an obscure scientific journal. "Our basic idea was to determine an initial position and velocity for the ball and rotor," he wrote. "We then hoped to predict the final position of the ball in much the same way that a planet's later position around the sun is predicted from initial conditions." Although a miniature computer had done the math, the equations came from Isaac Newton. Thorp built a contraption that would enable him to gather and process data, then became sidetracked by his career as a hedge fund manager. It ended up on display in the MIT museum: an exhibit, not a solution.

Nelson had studied physics at university, but every time he got as far as Newton's Second Law (force equals mass times acceleration), he felt the strong urge to sleep. Unknown to him, more serious scientists were grappling with the roulette question, too. In a beach house near the University of California, Santa Cruz, a group of hippie academics led by an astrophysicist had jury-rigged a computer to a roulette wheel and attempted to write software that could factor in all the forces influencing the ball's path. The program had four thousand instructions to follow, enough to fill fifty pages, and still didn't work properly. Tiny details made a huge difference, the academics discovered. The grade of plastic used in the ball, for example, or a minute change in atmospheric pressure altered the outcome significantly.

The problem was chaos or, more specifically, the emerging science of chaos theory. It revealed how small uncertainties multiplied, creating systems so complex that they were impossible to forecast. Mathematicians called the phenomenon "sensitive dependence on initial conditions." To everyone else, it came to be known as the "butterfly effect." A butterfly flaps its wings, creating a tiny amount of turbulence, which leads to still more turbulence, until, on the other side of the world, there's a hurricane. A ball glances off a one-millimeter metal divider on a roulette wheel and ends up on a completely different track.

Albert Einstein himself supposedly concluded that roulette was unbeatable after a visit to Las Vegas, where he was reported to have declared that the only way to win was to steal from the dealer. The quote was likely made up by a journalist, but it reflected the consensus. There were numerous betting systems for the game, from Oscar's Grind, which relied on wins coming in streaks, to Martingale, which required the gambler to double their bet after every loss. None of them worked. Casinos welcomed their practitioners with open arms.

Nelson was chewing all that over while having breakfast one morning. With him was an aspiring card counter who worked by day for the Environmental Protection Agency, an expert in mapping things such as toxic waste plumes in groundwater. Nelson described some of the challenges in using a computer to forecast roulette. His friend replied without looking up from his plate, "I would try regression analysis." A light bulb flickered on inside Nelson's skull.

Regression analysis turned the problem on its head. Instead of trying to account for the many forces acting on ball and wheel, Nelson could simply collect data and connect the dots. He didn't need to understand *how* the ball had reached a given pocket, just that it had. In the future, if the ball was traveling at a similar speed onto a rotor moving in a similar fashion, surely it would come to rest in the same spot or close to it.

Nelson took the idea to Rusty London, who told him to run with it and put up some funding for an experiment. A casino-standard roulette wheel cost about $8,000. Nelson found a manufacturer in Reno and had one shipped to an apartment he was renting in San Francisco. Roulette balls were available in the Gambler's Book Shop in Las Vegas. Nelson bought every variety of ball, synthetic and ceramic.

They didn't have enough money to buy a new computer, so Nelson had to make do with a Hewlett-Packard HP-55 programmable calculator, which came with a built-in stopwatch he could use to time rotations. The HP-55, designed to be simple enough for schoolchildren to use, had enough memory for fifty lines of basic code, not sufficient for complex modeling but enough for simple linear regressions.

Nelson talked one of his blackjack friends from the Bay Area into helping him. Their lives fell into a strange rhythm, synchronized to the rattling tempo of a ball dancing around a wheel thousands of times a day. One man would launch the ball; the other would operate the HP-55. By timing a full revolution of the central rotor, then a revolution of the ball around the perimeter, they could clock the speed and position of both. Rotor, rotor, ball, ball. Click, click, click, click.

Their hilltop apartment in San Francisco had no air-conditioning, so they left the window open all day, letting in the briny scent of the sea. To ease the hypnotic boredom, they played Fleetwood Mac's *Rumours* LP on repeat. "Never Going Back Again." "Don't Stop." "Go Your Own Way." It seemed to help. Summer faded into autumn.

A chill fog blew in through the window. Nelson put on a sweater and stuck to his task.

For simplicity, they divided the wheel into segments numbered one to eight. The calculator's job was to take all the recorded outcomes for a specific wheel and spit out the median result. Based on past data, if the most common finishing point was segment three, that number would flash up on the HP's display.

Nelson took quiet satisfaction in the work. Distilling the movements of a bouncing ball into mathematical equations appealed to his sense of order. Yet he could tell almost no one what he was doing. Bill Benter and his other gambler friends understood that he was deep into a roulette system involving a computer, but that was the extent of their insight. He clammed up when they pressed him for details. If that made him seem ruthless, it was a price he was willing to pay. Watching his father unravel at the family cemetery had taught Nelson early on that he could rely only on himself. The Darwinian battleground of casino gambling had reinforced the lesson. Only one thing horrified him more than failure: the idea of someone else getting there first.

After a couple of months, Nelson saw the first signs of progress. He kept a log of imaginary bets, selecting the twelve pockets closest to the HP's forecast, allowing a reasonable margin for error. Betting a pie-slice third of the wheel would cost more in chips but also increase the odds of hitting the correct number, which pays out at thirty-five to one in American-style roulette. Using some back-of-the-envelope math, he worked out that he and his partner would have made a 20 percent profit by betting the section around the HP's forecast had they been playing in a casino. The next day their advantage dipped a little, but it bounced back the day after and evened out at an average of 24 percent.

Now, confronted with evidence that prediction worked, Nelson allowed himself to get excited. The advantage seemed miraculous. Card counting typically yielded a percentage edge that could be quantified on one hand. Nelson had discovered something known to only a handful of gamblers anywhere: Roulette was not completely random.

Nelson surveyed the data. It showed the ball slowing gradually at first as friction, gravity, and drag impeded its progress. A speed graph would show a line arcing downward from launch. Then, as the ball made its final rotations before tumbling into a pocket, it slowed rapidly; the line on the graph shot almost straight down. Straight lines are predictable, even with a pocket calculator. The metal ridges and central cone of a roulette wheel added some random bounce and scatter, but apparently not enough to throw the HP off the trail.

Nelson went to see Rusty London to tell him the good news. "Fantastic. Let's go!" London responded. With proof of concept, they decided on a field test in a Las Vegas casino, the most challenging environment available. The best spot for roulette was the Horseshoe, which had the highest limits in town; they could bet $100 per number.

Unfortunately, it was run by Benny Binion, the confessed killer who'd bragged about gunning down those who crossed him. At around the same time Nelson had been working on his roulette computer, a Horseshoe customer had been shot dead after throwing a chair through a window. A casino guard had eventually pleaded guilty to manslaughter. Nelson knew that he and Rusty would be taking a risk by playing there. He convinced himself that the payoff would be worth it.

On their first outing, Nelson operated the HP-55, discreetly pressing the fingers of one hand against his opposite arm to signal which section to cover with chips. London put on his lunatic seal routine, jumping up on chairs and high-fiving dealers. Nelson was laughing so hard he could barely concentrate on timing. But the edge they had found in San Francisco was still there.

They were up several thousand dollars when a Horseshoe security operative carrying a level appeared and walked over to their table. Clearly, he was suspicious about why they were winning so often on the casino's most unbeatable game. He slapped it onto the wheel and squatted down to check the bubble. Nelson's sweat glands went into overdrive. Apparently satisfied, the man shrugged and walked away.

Nelson signaled to London to keep going for fifteen minutes, then get the hell out. They escaped with a nice profit. On other outings, they lost money. Roulette numbers don't appear in chronological order around the wheel, so it took some quick thinking to match the HP's chosen sector to the wheel before the dealer called "No more bets." Mistakes were costly. But as far as Nelson was concerned, they had proven that their system was viable.

He met London for a debriefing and to plan next steps. There were problems to overcome, both men agreed. For one thing, Vegas dealers spun the wheels so fast that it was difficult to record the speed of the rotor, which appeared as a blur. And the HP-55 was slow. It took five or six seconds to finish processing. By then the ball was already dropping out of its cycle. They discussed waiting for a more advanced model of programmable calculator to come out. But who knew when that would be?

"We need a faster computer," London said.

As it happened, Nelson had a friend from college who could help. Mark G., an electrical engineer who tinkered with computers in his free time, claimed that he could build something with a processing time of under a second. But he had a day job and no idea how long it would take, since he'd have to wire the circuit board himself. He'd never made anything like it before. Nelson wasn't sure anyone had.

Nelson, meanwhile, went back to playing blackjack and waited for news. Weeks stretched into months. Rusty London got so frustrated that he quit the project. "This is taking too long," he told Nelson. He went off to try his luck with a new trading system on Wall Street, where he fully expected to make the millions he felt he deserved. Nelson's friend and testing partner from San Francisco was also out. "I can't afford to take the risk," he said before returning to his old job at the post office.

Nelson refused to follow suit. "One thing I'm not is a quitter," he told them. He found new investors and playing partners. Nine months later, Mark G. called from Florida to say that the machine was ready. Nelson flew out to inspect it. The device was larger than he had expected, about the size of three paperback books taped together. Encased in metal, the inside looked like a jumble of wires pressed onto a bed of nails. Instead of buying a ready-made circuit board, Mark G. had used a technique called "wire wrap" to ensure that he could customize it as he wanted.

"Hey, that's pretty big," Nelson said. Then he thought: bell-bottoms. He could hide the computer in a sock concealed under flared pants. It would be a couple of years yet before those stopped appearing in Vegas. The timing switches worked fine. The output, attached by a long wire, was a small LED screen that flashed up a number in red, one through four for quarters running clockwise around the wheel. Nelson's friend was true to his word. Using tailor-made software, the computer could deliver its prediction in less than a second. Nelson asked what programming language he'd used. "Mark G. Basic" was the reply. He'd invented his own.

In January 1980, roughly three years after first discussing the idea in Rusty London's hot tub, Nelson was ready for the next stage of the plan—the part where they would all get rich. He assembled a new team, including a Polish gambler named Paul Prandecki who would take London's place as the main bettor, or "big player" in gambling parlance.

Paul had fled communism years earlier and embraced American decadence with the fervor of a man born again. Hustling his way around Vegas, he had no qualms about getting caught with a crew that used a roulette computer. He'd already used a mirror fragment glued to a paper clip to peek at blackjack dealers' cards.

Nelson decided not to hit the Las Vegas casinos this time, though. He and his friends were barred from most of them and the dealers were too quick, the pit bosses too wary. Besides, there were few roulette games at the time that were big enough to target without attracting attention. Roulette was seen as something husbands sent their wives to play while they got into the real action on the blackjack table. But in Europe, where roulette was invented, it was a different story.

Blaise Pascal, the seventeenth-century French mathematician, was credited with coming up with the idea for a perpetually spinning gambling machine. Betting on the contraption proved popular with the moneyed classes. Fyodor Dostoyevsky, the Russian literary great, was so obsessed with roulette that he nearly ruined himself with gambling debts. European roulette was classy.

Nelson decided to start in the Netherlands for no particular reason other than that he imagined it would be a friendly place to play.

He'd never been inside a European casino. The first Dutch venue had opened a few years earlier at Zandvoort, a beach resort popular with nudists. Others arrived soon afterward, including Scheveningen in The Hague, close to another nudist beach. It would be the first stop on Nelson's European tour.

It's said that casinos, like airport terminals, look the same the world over. That's partly true. Visitors can expect windowless halls with patterned carpets, dealers in smart uniforms, green felt, multicolored chips, and the familiar peal of electronic slot machines. But there were a few crucial differences in Europe, Nelson observed. Casinos there tended to be found in grand old municipal buildings, in contrast to the brightly lit Xanadus of Las Vegas. European patrons were wealthier and better dressed. The casino at Scheveningen required men to wear jackets and ties (or turtlenecks or neck scarves). Nelson sensed a less predatory atmosphere than in Nevada. The people losing money looked as though they could afford it. Most important: Scheveningen, like other casinos on the Continent, was owned by the state and run for the benefit of the taxpayer. The employees cared less about the bottom line, and there were no gun-toting proprietors to worry about.

By now each member of Nelson's team had drilled with the computer system enough to know what they were doing. Standing nearby, Nelson timed the rotor and ball with one hand hidden inside his pocket. Click, click, click, click. The computer, connected by wires running down his leg into a sock, flashed its predicted sector in red on an LED screen hidden inside a cigarette packet in his breast pocket.

Even standing right next to him, it would have been hard for a casino employee to see the screen, but Nelson stationed a female assistant to his left just in case. He used an adapted garage door clicker to remotely signal a vibrating earpiece worn by a teammate sitting at the table, sending between one and four short buzzes. After receiving the signal, the player would scramble to cover that section with chips.

No one in the Scheveningen casino paid them much attention, perhaps because they left a few hours later, having lost most of their bankroll. While the machine seemed to be working, the slow pace of play and small stakes made them vulnerable to statistical fluctuations. They had similar experiences at Valkenburg, near the border with West Germany, at Deauville in northern France, and in the hard-scrabble Belgian port city of Ostend. Their wins outweighed their losses but not by enough.

With travel expenses for half a dozen team members, plus days spent scouting for viable wheels, there wasn't much left over from the few thousand dollars they could earn in a good week. Operating the machine also took a physical toll on Nelson. He had to stand for hours at a slight angle to reach down to the clicker in his pocket, causing a cramp and later a twitch in his hand.

Even years afterward, Nelson's arm would hang limply at his side. Roulette arm, he called it. He christened the computer "Doomsday Machine," or DM for short. In Austria, Nelson's betting pool sunk so low that he had to ask a teammate to fetch the cash they'd set aside for airfare home. They made just enough to labor on.

Nelson began to resent his creation. The thing had cast him as Captain Ahab, trapped in a mad quest of his own design. He was stretched and irritable, under pressure to deliver from friends back home who'd fronted money for the project and expected a return. He started to question whether it was worth continuing.

They found themselves in Wiesbaden, West Germany. It seemed a fitting place for Nelson to turn things around. Dostoyevsky had gambled in the city's famed casino 120 years earlier. Going back even further, the Romans who had built the settlement had left behind a stone carving of the goddess Fortuna, whose spinning wheel could change men's fortunes, replacing bad luck with good.

Nelson was operating the Doomsday Machine as usual when a tall, gaunt German walked up to the table with an entourage trailing behind. He sat down, introduced himself as Klaus, then proceeded to throw chips all over the felt. Each one was the maximum bet, worth 200 German marks (about $100).

Klaus won on some spins and lost on others, tipping the dealer generously each time while barking orders at his assistants. When he finished, he'd accumulated a pile of chips worth the equivalent of about $100,000. Nelson was stumped. Was it pure luck? They watched Klaus for a few days. Somehow he kept winning. Nelson discovered that Klaus was well known in German casinos and had even appeared in newspapers.

They sent Polish Paul, the team's most gregarious member, to find out more. Klaus was one of two German roulette specialists in Wiesbaden at that moment, Paul learned. The other was Manfred, nicknamed "Money." Manfred played the same way as Klaus did and was also making huge profits. The two Germans appeared to know each other.

Nelson found Manfred at a hotel bar and struck up a conversation. He was burning to know their secret, so he did something he never would have considered before: He lifted up his pants leg to show the German his device. Manfred laughed. "You Americans and your computers," he said. Nelson gave him a brief description of the technique. "It's not easy, but it works. What's your system?"

"Come upstairs, and I'll tell you," Manfred replied. Nelson followed him to the most luxurious suite in Wiesbaden's most luxurious hotel. As he walked in, Nelson could see a row of identical gray suit jackets in Manfred's walk-in wardrobe. The man wore the same outfit every day. He invited Nelson to sit down and began to speak. "I look at the wheel. Then I look at the ball. I make my prediction and bet."

He's joking, Nelson thought. "There must be more to it than that," he said.

"It's a feeling," Manfred explained. "I watch the wheel and ball, and I think they are going to meet here." He said he'd first discovered the trick while gambling at a resort on the Baltic Sea. The roulette rotor had been unusually slow, barely moving, and Manfred had noticed that the ball would always drop from the outer rim and into the gently revolving pockets from the same spot. That had made it possible for him to guess which section of numbered pockets the ball was going to settle in.

They talked some more. This German must be some kind of savant, Nelson thought. But what about Klaus? What were the chances of two individuals possessing the same exceptional skill?

No, Nelson concluded, they weren't geniuses. Manfred and Klaus had simply uncovered a truth that he'd failed to consider. That night in his room, he stared at the ceiling, replaying the day's events in his head. Normally, he liked to think of himself as uncommonly rational, rarely allowing his emotions to surface. But as Nelson thought about the consequences of what he'd just heard, he felt like crying. He couldn't believe it. Years of his life spent pursuing an ingenious solution to the most unpredictable of all casino games. Months spent clocking a wheel in a drafty San Francisco apartment. Weeks working with Mark G. coding the software. The hours of testing, wiring, and concealing. Not to mention the thousands of dollars he'd spent. It was all for nothing. Two random German guys could do the same thing *in their heads.* And they didn't even seem to know how they did it.

Once he got over the shock, though, Nelson saw an opportunity. He was sick of the computer. If Klaus and Manfred could predict roulette without one, so could he. The next day, the team shipped out to Valkenburg in the Netherlands, where Nelson tried it for the first time. Manfred had encouraged him to watch the rotor, the inner part of the wheel containing the numbers, which was in constant motion. In the packed casino, Nelson strained and strained but kept missing the mark. He lost most of the team's remaining bankroll.

The next day, he tried again. This time he watched the ball instead of the rotor. It felt more natural. He'd spent so many hours timing the ball to configure the computer that he had a sense of when it was going to drop. Specifically, he knew roughly eight seconds before it happened. All he had to do was learn how many rotations the ball would make in eight seconds and take a mental note of the rotor's position. After that discovery, he started to win.

Playing with his eye, as he called it, was vastly easier than using the Doomsday Machine, which was put back into the suitcase. It was also safer. No one could accuse his crew of cheating by using their brains. They could bet the maximum amount per number, making $10,000 or $20,000 in an evening if Nelson was tuned in.

He continued using the garage door clicker, though, to signal the betting section to Polish Paul's earpiece, allowing him to concentrate on the wheel rather than on spreading chips on the layout. Paul bought a cream-colored suit and appointed himself the team's managing director of collecting attractive women from nightclubs. Having a female entourage and leaving thousand-dollar tips helped complete their transformation into roving high rollers, the kind of customer welcomed in casinos across the region.

One night in Valkenburg, Nelson and Paul hit the right number twenty-two times in a row, betting a third of the wheel each time, cheered on by a crowd of Dutch spectators. The chances of that happening by accident were approximately one in 30 billion. Nelson and his team flew to the Sun City casino in South Africa and made $100,000 in two weeks, then spent the cash on diamonds, which fit neatly into their hand luggage for the journey back.

As their success grew, Paul was finally able to persuade Nelson to stop obsessing about roulette for a few hours and join him on nights out. Photos from the time show the two of them in a succession of gilded restaurants and clubs, sipping wine from crystal glasses, always in the company of stylish young women. Nelson, who'd bleached his hair bottle blond, looks tanned and relaxed. Polish Paul wears the grin of a man who can't quite believe his luck. A few years earlier he'd been living behind the Iron Curtain, where tripe soup was considered a treat.

Handling the volume of banknotes they were collecting became an inconvenience. Nelson took road trips through the Alps to deposit their winnings in Swiss banks. Once, they were stopped by Italian police, who searched the car and found black garbage bags stuffed with millions of lire. They were escorted to the nearest station, where an English-speaking detective interrogated them. "How do we know you aren't drug dealers?" he asked. Nelson told him to call the casino. They were soon released. Anyway, most of the Italian officers seemed more interested in their blond companion, a former Miss Holland who was dating one of Nelson's teammates.

In Europe, casino executives were rarely hostile, even after Nelson took them for a small fortune. They were reduced to pleading with him to stop. "You can finish playing today, but it's probably time to take a vacation," a manager in Valkenburg said. Nelson took the advice—and headed to the United Kingdom. It was in Northampton, a backwater of a town nestled in England's industrial middle, that his success finally caught up with him.

On January 11, 1982, Nelson and Polish Paul were in the Rubicon

Sporting Club, playing roulette. It wasn't their first time in Northampton or in the Rubicon. Paul's younger brother, John, who was tagging along, insisted that they stop in the town so he could visit a nightclub called Cinderella Rockerfellas, which had beauty contests and a meat market vibe.

Nelson and Paul were just getting into their stride at the Rubicon's roulette tables when, at 6:10 p.m., two detectives appeared, flashed their badges, and invited them to come to the manager's office. Once inside, the police told them to open their jackets. They found the garage door opener wired to Nelson's pocket, as well as Paul's earpiece. "I am arresting you on suspicion of theft, namely that you have been cheating at roulette," a detective announced.

Nelson stared at him. "You can't do that," he said.

At the police station, Nelson and his partner's mug shots were taken, and their electrical gear was confiscated. He could feel indignation flaring up. He was certain that he hadn't cheated or broken any laws, yet the cops were treating him like a common criminal. "I want to make a phone call," he said.

"This is England, not America," the booking officer snorted in reply. They were led to a pair of holding cells, which smelled of the last occupants, regulars at Cinderella Rockerfellas to judge by the lingering scent of liquor and vomit. Later that night, a detective told him that they'd tested the wheel and found no signs of a fault that could explain how Nelson had done the seemingly impossible. After a few hours in a cell, he was still in an uncooperative mood. "I didn't cheat," he snapped. "I don't want to discuss it with you."

By the next morning, the reality of the situation had hit home. No wonder the police were suspicious, he thought. With his dyed blond mustache and the wires sewn into his jacket, he looked less like a casino cheat than a secret agent. He and Paul had checked into their hotel using false names—Nelson was Mr. Philips, Paul was Mr. Schultz—and officers had found a fake business card identifying Nelson as an assistant manager at the Tomar Travel Agency in Fort Lauderdale, Florida, which didn't exist.

His attitude softened further when a detective brought him a meal from McDonald's. "Look," he said, breaking his silence. "I've studied roulette with a computer. I used it to match the speed of the wheel and the speed of the ball and assume where on the wheel it would land." In the past, he'd worn a device, he continued, but he didn't any longer. And he could prove it. The computer was in his hotel room back in London with a dead battery. He didn't even have a plug adaptor to charge it.

The detectives drove Nelson down to London, and sure enough, there in a security safe amid piles of cash, was the computer, powered off. The police seemed baffled about what to do. They were under pressure from the Rubicon as well as casinos in London, where Nelson had made around $70,000 in the preceding weeks. The British Gaming Board, a government body responsible for regulating casinos, was also involved.

Nelson decided to make the detective an offer. "If I showed you how I did it, would you believe me then?" Deep down, he knew that a demonstration was probably a bad idea. But the cops had Paul and his younger brother in custody, and Nelson felt responsible for getting them out. He didn't know if there was some arcane British law that might put them in jeopardy.

On the morning of January 13, still in custody forty hours after being arrested, Nelson and Paul returned to the Rubicon to show what they could do. In front of the casino owner, security team, and several police officers, Nelson watched the wheel and shouted out his instructions to Paul, who placed chips as instructed. They hit the right number on twenty-one of forty-one spins. The casino proprietor seemed satisfied—though he refused to return the £5,000 worth of chips his staff had taken from Paul. He also declined Nelson's offer of double or nothing.

The cops were now treating the whole affair as an entertaining diversion from the usual car thefts and drunken assaults. After releasing the group without charge, detectives took Nelson to the local pub for a beer. Later, the supervising officer wrote in his official report that he was satisfied that Nelson could beat a roulette wheel with his mind. What's more, the detective said, he could appreciate Nelson's enmity toward "casinos who would appear to only want 'losing' customers."

A few weeks later, the story appeared in two British newspapers, apparently leaked by someone in uniform. None of the team members was identified, but the description of a "handsome blond American" with a "brilliant mathematical brain" would have been familiar to anyone who had witnessed the operation. "The Rubicon Sporting Club will never forget the day two Las Vegas gamblers hit town," the *Daily Mail*'s reporter gushed. Female staff at the hotel had apparently swooned over Nelson.

When contacted by the journalists, though, casino staff displayed an attitude markedly different from their agitation of a few weeks earlier. "They were just lucky," said Peter Halliday, the Rubicon's manager, with a shrug. An unnamed spokesman for the Playboy Club in London was even more dismissive: "We have heard it all before. People come with systems but they lose eventually."

Nelson, burned out from two years of almost constant roulette playing, sensed that this particular adventure might be coming to an end. As thrilling as it had been, roulette prediction was stressful—and risky. An entire team was relying on Nelson's talents and his ability to get them out of trouble. The burden grew heavier as the months passed. He was almost relieved when he got confirmation that the game was up in a South African casino, thousands of miles away from his troubles in Northampton but not far enough to escape his newfound infamy. He didn't even get near a roulette wheel before a security guard tapped him on the shoulder: "Are you William Nelson?"

ROB REITZEN

While Nelson was making headlines in Europe, Rob Reitzen was hard at work making a name for himself on the Las Vegas card-counting circuit.

Reitzen may not have had a college degree or physics lab experience, but he had qualities many of his peers lacked. They could see it in the way he moved, his southern California swagger, and hear it in the way he talked. One of his teammates had a speech impediment. Reitzen dubbed him Elmer Fudd and roared with laughter at his own joke.

With his show business pedigree, Reitzen was a natural performer. He was especially good at camouflage: disguising his gambling skills by playing the dupe. Card counting is hard if you're too mentally slow or inebriated to cope with the math. So, Reitzen thought, what better way to throw a pit boss off the scent than to act like a drunken idiot? It was a role he could execute with a Method actor's precision.

He'd sit down at a blackjack table, dressed in his usual baseball cap and a garish plaid jacket and shirt, unbuttoned to reveal a patch of chest hair. Demanding a Scotch and soda, he'd slur, "Hold the soda." He would proceed to play the dumbest blackjack imaginable. With an ace and a 9, a hard-to-beat 20, he'd ask the dealer to hit, waving hundred-dollar bills as he busted out. During breaks in play, he would replace his whiskey with apple juice in the restroom so he could down it in gulps in front of the pit boss while splashing liquor on himself to make sure that he smelled like an alcoholic.

Back at the table, though, when the count was good and his odds of winning were high, he'd bet as much money as possible, making thousands of dollars in a few minutes before stumbling away, propositioning the dealer, and knocking over his stool on the way out. "What an act," one of his partners said after watching Reitzen in full flow.

The 1980s were a good time to be a card counter, maybe the best time. In the tug-of-war between professional gamblers and casinos, players seized the advantage. There were believed to be more than a hundred full-time counters in Vegas, including a group of students from MIT who would go on to global fame thanks to several books, chief among them *Bringing Down the House*, which would be the inspiration for the Kevin Spacey movie *21*.

Some teams hired attorneys to draft profit-sharing agreements and accountants to square away their income with the IRS. One group acquired a toll-free 800 number so members could check in easily from anywhere. Casinos were quick to spend money on making player-friendly blackjack deals (free bets, or tweaks to the rules allowing gamblers to double down in more situations) if it would bring people to the tables, not so much on improving their security. A few counters joined the dark side to work as consultants, helping casinos catch their former brethren, but not many and not the good ones. "Our experts were better than their experts," as one of Reitzen's friends put it. "A lot of money was won."

America's culture and economy were shifting their axis. The "greed is good" era was coming, driven by bankers and corporate raiders, new elites who didn't give a damn about the old guard's disapproval. The effect was visible everywhere: from Wall Street to Main Street; from Las Vegas Boulevard, better known as the Strip, to Fremont Street's Glitter Gulch. Reitzen's generation of Thorp pilgrims was a product of the age.

Fast money was the ideal. No more sneaking around playing for $1 chips. No more settling for the scraps that casinos left on the table. Reitzen's cohort were unapologetic about their careers as gamblers and happy to provoke the industry that fed them. They saw themselves as Gordon Gekko and Robin Hood rolled into one, stealing from the rich to give to themselves.

Arnold Snyder, a buddy of Reitzen's and one of the scene's most vocal members, donned a gold-trimmed cape and bowler hat, anointing himself a bishop of the First Church of Blackjack. Thus attired, he hosted events and officiated weddings. He urged followers to "give greed a chance" from his pulpit, a stage at the Bally's casino theater. "I don't care if you've stolen. Maybe you have cheated on your taxes. Maybe you have cheated on your wife!" he shrieked. "I don't care what the other religious leaders say. I have . . . a vision! I see a dawning of the age of blackjack." Snyder dreamed of a future where schools would teach the three S's—standing, splitting, and surrendering—and where towering stacks of casino chips would line green felt streets. "You must give in to that one basic human emotion that has always led man to new heights of greatness," he said, lowering his voice to a growl. "Greeeeeed."

For the likes of Snyder and Reitzen, winning at casino games was more than just an interesting way to earn a living. It went deeper than that. Snyder told anyone who would listen that it was "un-American" for casinos to offer a game based on skill, then exclude those who played skillfully. One MIT team member argued that the industry's position—stupidity was permitted but not science or rational thinking—amounted to a crisis in human rights.

Reitzen delighted in poking his adversaries. The Barbary Coast Casino on the Strip was so hostile to card counters that Wally Simmons, the cancer survivor who led Reitzen's blackjack team, sent new players there just to get the experience of being barred. The two of them debated whether the Barbary pit bosses actually knew how card counting worked, or whether they just excluded anyone who had the look.

Reitzen suggested a prank. He visited the casino clutching printed sheets of meaningless numbers and took a seat at a blackjack table. Simmons perched nearby with the rest of the team to enjoy the spectacle. Reitzen made a great show of squinting at his page of random numbers. However, when the count was good, he reduced his bets, and when the count was against the player, he raised them. It was card counting in reverse, a strategy designed to lose money as quickly as possible.

The "Negative Bob" incident, as it came to be known, didn't last long. "You're done," a pit boss said, throwing him out in a fit of baffled rage. Reitzen had spent a few hundred dollars on losing to show that he was smarter than the Barbary goons, and he felt it was worth every cent. He enjoyed the rush of humiliating casinos as much as he enjoyed taking their money. He flew to Amsterdam to count cards in an underground joint, where craps tables competed for space with live sex shows. He came back with a stack of Dutch guilders and another story to tell.

Back in Vegas, Reitzen rented an apartment in—where else—Enchanted Gardens, the low-budget block popular with hookers and card counters. He bumped into Bill Benter at the Gambler's Book Shop, a source of reading material, supplies, and camaraderie for the city's blackjack professionals. The two became close friends, despite their contrasting personalities.

Benter, then playing with Alan Woods and his Australian team, was another rising star on the scene. They were both talented counters. Benter could watch three tables at once and keep track of the plus/minus score for each, allowing him to jump in when the count was good. Despite his shyness, or perhaps because of Reitzen's lack of it, they got on famously. Reitzen drove Benter around the Strip in a beat-up Buick, singing along to a cassette tape of songs from the musical *Camelot*.

During the evenings, Reitzen accompanied the gambler he called Elmer Fudd on missions to pick up women at an East Vegas joint called Alias Smith & Jones, which was popular with mobsters and off-duty showgirls, still in their stage makeup and fake eyelashes. The venue's happy hour, tuned to the nocturnal habits of its clientele, began at 1:00 a.m.

"All I want is to make ten grand," Reitzen told Wally Simmons when they first met. "If I make that I'll retire." The older man nodded sagely. He knew better. No amount of winning was ever enough for those who learned how to beat the house. Sure enough, the more Reitzen won, the more his ambition grew. On a typical day, the Simmons team would gather at Reitzen's apartment to fool around with technology. Ever since the Fifth National Conference on Gambling and Risk Taking in Lake Tahoe, the unofficial card-counting convention where Reitzen had met Simmons, they'd become convinced that the future of their craft was etched in silicon.

Simmons, who had taught himself computer programming in an earlier life as a nine-to-fiver, would sit smoking in front of an electronic chessboard that automatically moved pieces for his robotic opponent. To the uninitiated, it looked as if he were playing against an invisible man. He bought a Tandy TRS-80 microcomputer, a device so cumbersome that his team nicknamed it the Trash-80, though they used it to run millions of casino game simulations. It took around a week of processing time for the Trash-80 to break down a blackjack rule change and quantify how much it favored the player.

Simmons also dismantled and resoldered Sharp calculators to see whether they could make a gadget small enough to hide under a jacket. Reitzen, meanwhile, bought sex toys and toy train sets to pull out their vibrating mechanisms, which could be used to receive secret signals. As it happened, his estranged biological father, the rocket scientist who had been the phantom of his childhood, ran a successful semiconductor company in Arizona and might have had something to say about the venture if asked. But Reitzen hadn't spoken to his dad in years. If he wanted to spend his time tearing dildos apart, that was his business. Another day punching the clock in Enchanted Gardens.

When there was too much heat in Vegas, Reitzen took his big player routine up to northern Nevada. One night in Lake Tahoe, he found himself playing next to a stranger. The man was obviously counting cards. Reitzen, in the middle of a bad run, was down several thousand dollars. He went into the bathroom to take a break. The counter appeared next to him at the urinal. As usual, Reitzen tried to strike up a conversation. "The Big C, huh?" he offered—the "C" standing for "counting."

The stranger looked mortified. After a second it dawned on Reitzen that the player might think he was referring to a part of the male anatomy starting with a "c," a very different conversation from the one he'd planned. But then the counter grinned and lifted up his pant leg to reveal a bulge in his sock threaded with wires. "C" for "computer."

"You've got one on, too, right?" Reitzen insisted that he didn't. "No wonder you're making mistakes," the counter said.

Darrell Miers was a big Nebraskan with a dented nose like a wrestler, who'd been on his high school chess team. They got formally acquainted later, away from the prying eyes of casino workers. Miers came across as gruff and self-contained at first, with a gunfighter's hard stare. But Reitzen liked him. There was warmth there, too. Reitzen was also intrigued by the little blackjack computer Miers called "the Taft." He'd heard the name before and took the opportunity to examine it up close.

It was a remarkable piece of kit for 1982. A layer of red epoxy resin concealed a Zilog Z80 microprocessor containing 8,500 transistors that was small and versatile enough to power a decade of innovation, including the *Pac-Man* arcade game and the TRS-80 microcomputer. The Taft itself, no bigger than a pack of cards, was all the more impressive considering that it had been assembled in a makeshift laboratory in a garage extension at a residential address in Sunnyvale, California.

The property was home to Marty Taft, the lanky kid who had been arrested in Harveys Lake Tahoe in 1977, a few months after the overweight Elvis's last show at the Sahara, when casino security had threatened to plug him into the mains after finding Marty's blackjack computer. His father, Keith, was the machine's inventor. The Tafts were a deeply religious family, as well as being technological wizards. Whereas others looked at the ebb and flow of fortune in casino games and saw lucky or unlucky breaks, Keith Taft gazed into the vagaries of chance and saw evidence of the divine. He'd become obsessed with the mathematics of blackjack and, using his experience as a Raytheon Company engineer, had spent more than a decade building a machine that could count cards with godlike accuracy. He had christened it David, a miniature hero to defeat the casino's Goliath.

A series of setbacks in the 1970s, though, convinced Keith's wife that the Southern Baptists were right: Gambling was indeed a dangerous vice. Their son's arrest at Harveys was particularly alarming. Although Marty was released without charge, his mother was afraid that one day casino staff might make good on their threats. Keith pledged to stop using David and instead sell the machines to a handful of carefully selected customers for $10,000 each. Miers was one of the first buyers. A minister's son himself, he won the family's trust by singing hymns around the piano in their Sunnyvale home.

Up in Reitzen's Lake Tahoe hotel room, Miers demonstrated how the computer worked. He entered a dealt card's blackjack value from 1 to 11, using four switches hidden inside custom-made shoes. Right big toe up inputted a 1; right big toe down was 2. Left big toe up was 4; left big toe down was 8. That information flashed along a wire to David, which was tucked into a sock.

With such precise data, David could identify *exactly* which cards were left in the deck and therefore the odds of pulling an ace versus a 3, for example. If David calculated that a player's advantage over the dealer was 6 percent, it could advise on the mathematically optimal number of chips to risk based on the Kelly criterion. Finally, David delivered its guidance to Miers's crotch using a buzzer taped into a jockstrap.

Reitzen was awestruck by what Miers showed him. Compared to what the Simmons team was doing in Enchanted Gardens, David was space-age. They met again a few nights later. Reitzen was running low on bankroll. Miers, the disciplined preacher's son, fronted him some cash to get him back on track. They got to talking about their future plans. Miers had been planning to take David to Europe, but Reitzen talked him out of it. He suggested pooling their resources instead.

Miers had to admit that he was intrigued. He'd never met someone who combined a profane sense of humor with such a professorial knowledge of blackjack systems. He was astonished to see how comfortably Reitzen interacted with casino staff, joking with dealers and flirting with waitresses. At that moment they were sitting in Reitzen's luxury suite, comped by a casino boss who assumed that he was another high roller with cash to burn. Miers, meanwhile, was hiding away in a budget room and hoping that no one would notice him.

The more Miers thought about it, the more a partnership made sense. He agreed, and the two men started a new team. Reitzen called to break the news to Wally Simmons, who assured him that there were no hard feelings. It was disappointing to lose an effective player, but blackjack teams were fluid operations. Jumping from one bankroll to another was not unusual.

Operating David, Reitzen discovered, required a lot of practice and dexterous big toes. Clicking the buttons for hours left him calloused and limping. But once he'd mastered it, the Taft was worth the effort. It simply never erred. The little buzzer on his crotch would always let him know what to do and how much to bet.

What's more, the Taft could achieve feats of processing that defied belief. Keith Taft had spent months on another program to track cards after the deck was shuffled by the dealer. He called it "Thor." In blackjack, dealt cards are put into a special discard rack before being mixed together and redealt. Normally, the dealer's shuffle means doom for a card counter, resetting the plus/minus system. But by recording all the cards going into the discard rack, the Taft could identify clumps containing an unusual number of high cards that, even when shuffled with others, would tip the deck in the player's favor. The advantage created by the Thor upgrade was even bigger than that of David. "Like magic," Reitzen thought the first time he used it.

The new techniques were harder for casinos to spot, by virtue of being new, and the risks seemed relatively low. Gambling computers hadn't existed long enough for anyone to write laws preventing their use. As far as Reitzen and his friends were concerned, computers were only replicating what regular players did with their minds, using information made freely available to all casino patrons. They couldn't see how anyone would consider that cheating.

The main danger of using homemade wearable computers came not from casino security but from the new lithium batteries. In the 1980s, they had a tendency to overheat and explode if not powered off properly. While Reitzen and Miers never experienced it personally, they heard about a Taft customer whose device had self-destructed with a loud pop, splitting the metal case and spilling white powder over the floor of an Atlantic City casino. He had taken off up the boardwalk with security guards in hot pursuit. Another Atlantic City gambler felt a burning sensation on his leg at the table and realized with horror that the battery in his sock was leaking acid. He had to gather his chips as calmly as he could and make for the exit before running straight into the ocean. A severe burn wasn't enough to convince him to stop using the device, though.

The advantage delivered by the new generation of microprocessors was unprecedented. It was card counting on steroids. Casino games, invented in Wild West saloons or European casinos a century before the invention of the first computer, were not designed to be played this way. Other card counters were making the same discovery.

Reitzen's former partner Wally Simmons made his own breakthrough. His team created a wearable computer to track the shuffle in blackjack, much as Thor had done for Reitzen. Theirs was named "Butch" after Paul Newman's character in *Butch Cassidy and the Sundance Kid*. The Simmons team packed Butch into a suitcase and jetted off to hit casinos around Europe and the Caribbean.

There were moments when betting technology was so far ahead of the house, it seemed almost comically unfair. An aspiring casino tycoon spent years designing a new game with the perfect balance of randomness and accessibility: a bridge-blackjack hybrid in which players had to predict the color, number, or suit of two cards. The inventor proudly advertised its Las Vegas debut in a newspaper, which Simmons read. He ran the data on his TRS-80, and it took all of an afternoon to work out how the game could be beaten. The inventor watched, forlorn, as the Simmons team milked his creation like a prize cow. The casino withdrew it a few days later.

The future imagined by Ed Thorp two decades earlier was flickering to life. In *Beat the Dealer*, the godfather of card counting had foreseen computers one day playing superhuman blackjack, baccarat, roulette, and poker. "In the last part of the twentieth century there will be many new applications of scientific and particularly mathematical methods to the prediction of phenomena heretofore called 'chance,'" he wrote. "It will be exciting to see them unfold."

The casino industry's guardians, the men with thick necks and dark suits, didn't share Thorp's enthusiasm. They saw only a fraction of what was being soldered, wired, and programmed by advantage players, whatever they seized on the rare occasions a computer gambler was caught. It was enough for them to realize that their employers were facing a new kind of threat. In hindsight, a response by the house was inevitable.

BILL BENTER

Benter had never had a friend like Rob Reitzen. He was wild, unpredictable, uninhibited. He was, it was clear to see, everything Benter was not. Benter watched the drunken oaf routine and the Negative Bob prank with fascination and some anxiety. Although he would never be as brazen as Reitzen, Benter hoped he could absorb a little of his friend's intoxicating confidence.

By 1982, Benter was getting serious heat from the Vegas casinos where he earned his living alongside Alan Woods and the other members of the Australian team. It wasn't just his mastery of blackjack; with a math professor's fashion sense and a permanent look of wide-eyed surprise, he was the very archetype of a card counter. Even pit bosses who'd never seen him before barred him on sight, figuring he must be up to some kind of nerd mischief. Once he was chased out of the Stardust Casino thirty seconds after walking through the front door. Security guards pursued him down the street.

Benter set his mind to finding a solution. Why not come up with a convincing disguise and a whole new character, as Reitzen had? Wally Simmons had grown a hermit's beard to hide his features. Some of the costumes Benter saw were clumsy at best, such as that of the counter who used tape to pin back his eyes in the mistaken belief that it made him look Asian. Surely Benter could do better. The notion was daunting, but what was he doing in Vegas if not straining to escape the straitjacket of his introversion?

He decided to reinvent himself as a cocaine dealer, naming the persona "Neon Leon." The problem was, he had no idea what a drug dealer should look like. So he took his inspiration from Billy Idol, who'd just released his biggest hit, "White Wedding." He bleached his hair blond and acquired a black pleather jumpsuit with a zipper up the middle. To finish the look, he wore a tiny vial on a chain, of the type that might carry an illicit substance.

Neon Leon's first and only outing was at the Marina Hotel Casino on the Strip. Benter was playing blackjack, constantly ducking under the table to take ostentatious sniffs from the empty bottle around his neck. He'd lowered his voice an octave or two and affected his best impersonation of a coked-up punk. "Yeah, man, hit me. Gimme a hit." *This is perfect*, he thought. *No one's recognizing me.*

Then security guards arrived and took him to a back room. It transpired that they thought he was actually using, and probably dealing, cocaine. Leon was upsetting the other customers, and casino security was on the verge of calling the police. Benter was crestfallen. In his regular voice—soft with a hint of Kermit the Frog—he explained that the getup was just a disguise. They threw him out anyway.

While Benter had immersed himself in mathematical theorems, Arnold Snyder's "Give Greed a Chance" movement had pushed the card-counting community into an even more poisonous conflict with their casino adversaries. The cold war between the two sides heated up, bringing beatings and harassment. One gambler was taken out and kicked repeatedly by casino staff, who called the cops and had him arrested for injuring a security guard's foot. Card counters felt ever more persecuted and paranoid.

When Benter noticed a man sitting in a parked car at the end of his street, his mind raced with dangerous possibilities. Was it a casino mercenary stalking him? Someone from the Nevada Gaming Commission? A cop? A fed? It wasn't so far-fetched. Vegas was a casino town. Everyone knew the authorities looked out for the state's biggest industry. Even judges were assumed to be casino shills. Eventually, Benter found out the man in the car was a private detective hired to surveil not him but a cheating spouse.

The final straw came in 1984 when Benter, along with Alan Woods, earned a place in the *Griffin Book*. The book was produced by a firm called Griffin Investigations, which helped casinos keep cheats, pickpockets, and other undesirables off their property in return for a generous fee. The spread of video surveillance technology had made what had once been an impossible task much simpler. Cameras now dotted the ceilings of casino gaming rooms, recording suspicious play. Griffin's private detectives compiled a physical binder containing mug shots and descriptions of the worst offenders, as well as a searchable database.

The agency tried to distance itself from the strong-arm tactics used by casino staff against its targets, saying that the service was only a guide. The First Church of Blackjack faithful didn't buy it. Too many of them had been barred, threatened, or worse because of the Griffin list. Rumors circulated that the agency had been founded by a failed counter who'd switched sides out of spite.

One of Benter's friends got hold of a copy of the book. And there Benter was, a security camera snapshot of his face among pages of tattooed criminals, junkies, and con artists. The text described him as a "known card counter," as if keeping score in a game of blackjack were on a par with stealing purses or using counterfeit chips. A former Eagle Scout, Benter bristled at the association, but he had to accept reality. Once a gambler appeared in the *Griffin Book*, it became virtually impossible to play in a Vegas casino. His card-counting days appeared to be over.

Still brooding, he met Alan Woods to plot his next move. The Australian was a reliable source of gossip and moon-shot gambling schemes. He told Benter about some friends back home who were doing well betting on horses. They were taking advantage of the differences among various betting pools. If the same horse was three to one in Sydney and four to one in Perth, Woods's friends would take the more favorable odds. That strategy relied on at least one of the odds being *wrong*, which, as Benter and Woods both appreciated, was the single most important consideration for advantage gamblers.

Remember the example of the faulty dice game, which lands on one more often than it should? Gamblers need the odds being offered to be out of sync with reality. Otherwise, the occasional streak of bad luck and the house's commission on every bet will eventually wipe out a person's winnings. In blackjack, that mismatch comes from the casino's failure to adapt to the constantly evolving scenario of a shrinking deck, an imbalance that card counters capitalize on. In roulette, the house awards a static thirty-five-to-one payout on a single number, even if the ball is so close to its final destination that players such as Nelson and Klaus can effectively rule out half the wheel.

What about horses? Unlike those casino games, racing is not, strictly speaking, a game of chance. How could similar logic apply?

Woods explained his thinking. The odds at the track weren't set by the house but by a parimutuel or "tote" system—essentially, a market. All bets were pooled, and the odds were set by the proportion of wagers on each horse. That was why the odds could be different in Sydney's pool than in Perth's. Bettors' decisions were not coordinated or uniform. And as an average of human predictions about the future, they were fallible.

Benter pondered the idea. It made sense on a mathematical level. Say the market put a horse's chances of success at 20 percent (equivalent to betting odds of four to one). But the market was wrong, as it often seemed to be. The actual chances, considering all available data, were more like 25 percent. Benter would have to risk his capital only four times, on average, to get a fivefold return (the winning payout plus his stake back)—a 20 percent profit. And if he did that thousands of times, the profits might dwarf anything he could win in a casino.

There was a small challenge he'd need to overcome, though: He knew absolutely nothing about thoroughbreds. "You really think we can win at that game?" he asked Woods.

"Why not?" the Australian replied. He'd heard about giant betting pools in Hong Kong, where the two tracks, at Happy Valley and Sha Tin, were packed for races twice a week. Woods thought that they could probably beat the market by gathering data and rating each runner manually. They could do even better using a computer, he suggested.

Benter considered himself an enthusiastic amateur when it came to technology. He'd watched Rob Reitzen demonstrate the Taft and was aware that Bill Nelson was experimenting with a roulette computer in Europe. He'd seen Wally Simmons sitting in front of the robotic chessboard. They'd spent hours together fooling around on Simmons's favorite new toy, a Kaypro, an aluminum box the size of a carry-on suitcase with a lid that opened out to reveal a green screen and keyboard.

Billed as a "traveling computer," the Kaypro weighed as much as a standard car tire but was designed with simplicity in mind, whether for solving complex engineering problems or storing Christmas card lists. It was a step up from the Trash-80. Simmons ran blackjack simulations and processed roulette data on the machine. Benter had just upstaged him by spending $3,000 on the latest model, a Kaypro 10, which could back up files on a floppy disk.

Benter took the Australian to see Simmons, who, in addition to having been his friend Reitzen's early benefactor, had more experience with computers than anyone in their collective circle. Simmons agreed that the horse-racing idea had potential. If nothing else, it would be an intriguing technical challenge. The three men hashed out a plan: Woods would put up most of the funding; Benter and Simmons would work on a computer model.

From the start, the three gamblers understood that they were facing formidable odds. Not only were they building something that was, as far as they were aware, new to science; they would be competing against the most dedicated railbirds on Earth: Hong Kong's 5 million citizens bet more on horses than the entire population of the United States did.

Benter began his quest with a short drive north of the Strip to the shabby redbrick building housing the Gambler's Book Shop. Inside were thousands of tomes on blackjack, poker, sports betting, and casino management, as well as a fiction shelf featuring Vegas potboilers and Mafia dramas: a veritable Library of Babel for professional gamblers, containing the sum of all knowledge about betting.

He headed straight for the horse-racing section and found about a dozen titles. None looked remotely promising. Handicapping, the name given to the art of picking winning horses, attracted a particular subspecies of gambler. Mostly men, they could be found at every circuit in the country wearing short-sleeved shirts, pens tucked behind their ears, sniffing around for inside information. They followed their instincts, which they believed to be finely tuned to the wavelength of the turf after years spent watching horses, talking about horses, reading the horseplayer press, and screaming at horses in full gallop.

Benter found a book called *The Body Language of Horses*, which appealed to those who liked to inspect the runners in the show ring before the race, looking for signs of eagerness in the gait or a telltale weakness in the musculature. Other works promised that the future could be divined by a horse's speed out of the gate or by its parentage. The whole genre struck Benter as flimsy and unscientific. Many of the authors were journalists. He assumed that they wouldn't need to sell books if they had really unlocked the secrets of handicapping.

Benter struck up conversations with some of the customers lingering in his section. When he told them about his computer, they were dismissive. It took years of experience and human intuition to judge a thoroughbred, they solemnly advised. Such wisdom could never be attained from a glorified typewriter. Benter didn't argue, but he had a hunch that the opposite was true.

As he understood it, the gospel according to Edward O. Thorp was to ignore your instincts. Feelings were the product of a chemical stew flooding your brains and drowning your capacity for logic, a relic from the time when our species lived in caves and had no choice but to obey a nagging sensation in the pit of the stomach. A noise in the darkness might be a bear. A flicker on the horizon could be water. Act first, think later.

That mindset helped early *Homo sapiens* survive, but it was ill suited to complex analytical tasks. Benter knew that, and so did the gambling industry, which was built on a solid foundation of human folly. There was the Monte Carlo fallacy, the mistaken belief that twenty consecutive red pockets in roulette make a black more likely on the next spin. (They don't.) The idea of lucky streaks or winning runs? Pure fantasy. The phenomenon they describe is explained by statistical fluctuations and a cognitive bias called the "hot hand fallacy."

As for the dismissive horseplayers in the Gambler's Book Shop, Benter wasn't bothered by their skepticism. Men who chose to spend their lives at the racetrack seemed especially vulnerable to the tendency of people with low competence to overestimate their abilities—what would later be named the Dunning-Kruger effect after the sociologists who discovered it. If anything, their attitude made Benter more optimistic. It was evidence of an irrational market, one that could be beaten.

In search of real science, Benter went to the University of Nevada, Las Vegas. There, deep inside the library's special collection on gaming, he dug out a gem. It was an academic paper with the enticing title "Searching for Positive Returns at the Track: A Multinomial Logit Model for Handicapping Horse Races." Using data from two hundred races and equations borrowed from mainstream economics, the authors had come up with a basic model for a rider's winning probability. It looked like this:

$$\begin{aligned} U_h = {} & \theta_1\mathrm{LIFE\%WIN}_h + \theta_2\mathrm{AVESPRAT}_h + \theta_3 W/\mathrm{RACE}_h + \theta_4\mathrm{LSPEDRAT}_h \\ & + \theta_5\mathrm{JOCK\%WIN}_h + \theta_6\mathrm{JOCK\#WIN}_h + \theta_7\mathrm{JMISDATA}_h + \theta_8\mathrm{WEIGHT}_h \\ & + \theta_9\mathrm{POSTPOS}_h + \theta_{10}\mathrm{NEWDIST}_h + \epsilon_h. \end{aligned}$$

The model considered only a few factors, such as the winning record, the horse's average speed, and the jockey's historic ratio of victories, each one weighted by importance. Off the top of his head, Benter could think of dozens more that might affect a race, from a thoroughbred's diet to the quality of the trainer's facilities. Even so, it was a start.

Alan Woods, meanwhile, flew to Hong Kong and mailed back official results books, doorstops containing the records of thousands of races at Happy Valley and Sha Tin. Benter and Simmons hired secretaries to help input the data. Their Kaypros couldn't handle text and math at the same time, so they assigned numbers to each of the thousand or so horses on the Hong Kong circuit, doing the same for the jockeys.

Benter and Simmons spent hours hunched over the Kaypros' metal boxes, fiddling with their burgeoning statistical model. Exactly how significant was a jockey's skill to the outcome? What about the length of time since a horse's last race? Each factor had to be processed and weighted according to its power. Benter taught himself how to code. Simmons slept on the floor of Benter's Vegas garage. If insomnia struck in the small hours, he shuffled back to the Kaypros to feed in more numbers.

Nine months later, they were finally ready to test the system. In September 1985, Benter headed to Los Angeles for the daylong journey to Hong Kong. He stayed at Rob Reitzen's place for a night to get some rest. Before he had much time to consider what lay ahead, he was at the airport, dragging three bulky Kaypros in his wake. Then he was on the plane, contemplating his life choices.

As he strapped himself in for takeoff, it occurred to Benter that he might as well be flying to the dark side of the moon. He'd never been to Hong Kong, spoke no Cantonese, and had little money. He wasn't sure if his computer system—or any computer system—would work. And he still knew next to nothing about horses. Come to think of it, he'd never even set foot on a racecourse.

INTERLUDE

THE ELEPHANT AT THE TABLE

Cheating might seem like an easy concept to define, even in the competitive chaos of a gambling contest. But consider the case of Phil Ivey.

Ivey, a top poker professional, has won eleven World Series of Poker bracelets and shared a table with movie stars. He is also one of the few gamblers to have had an advantage system dissected in a court of law.

On August 20, 2012, Ivey made £7.7 million pounds at the Crockfords Club in London with a technique called "edge sorting," which he used to identify advantageous face-down cards in a baccarat spin-off called punto banco. The casino refused to pay, Ivey sued, and the two sides spent the next five years locked in a legal battle that went all the way to the UK Supreme Court.

The case was unusual because the judges had to consider questions of ethics and fairness, including the legal definition of cheating, as they pertained to a casino. Disagreements between gamblers and casinos are common, but they are rarely decided in public. Advantage players tend to view taking legal action against the house as a waste of time and money. Casinos prefer to avoid the bad press that comes from dragging customers to court.

Exactly how Ivey achieved his edge is difficult to explain and ultimately not that important. Suffice it to say that there are certain high-value cards in punto banco and it helps gamblers to know where they are. Ivey and his partner persuaded the Crockfords dealer to rotate the high-value cards 180 degrees before shuffling them back into the pack, citing some obscure superstition as justification. In reality, Ivey had noticed an asymmetric pattern on the reverse of the cards, which meant he could identify them from the back, even if their face value was hidden. That knowledge gave him a clear advantage.

Was Ivey cheating? The answer wasn't immediately obvious. Ivey believed that what he was doing was "a legal way to beat the house." Crockfords argued that the game had been "compromised" by his actions. Ivey countered that he'd never actually touched the deck. Both sides presented gambling experts at trial who touted opposing theories. One had carried out a survey of hundreds of people to get their opinions, which only added to the confusion. As the first-instance judge put it, "There is no commonly accepted view amongst those who play punto banco about whether edge-sorting does or does not amount to cheating."

If you gamble for a living, blurred lines like these arise at every turn. Of course, there are also age-old hustles so evidently dishonest that there was a time when their exponents risked being hung or shot. In the 1800s, professional gamblers along the Mississippi River had a habit of marking cards that could help them win. It could be done by scraping a sliver of paint off the side of the aces and royal cards. It's a simple trick, still effective today, and infuriating enough two centuries ago to have resulted in mass lynchings. A poker sharp called Gentleman Jack hid a tiny mirror on the inside of one finger so he could sneak a glimpse of his opponent's cards (not unlike the trick Paul, Nelson's Polish gambling compatriot, once used). Jack called it his "light," also known as a "glim" or "shiner."

Advantage play, for the most part, doesn't fall into this category. There is no rule of blackjack, nor any law, that prohibits card counting. But casinos are private property, and courts have upheld their right to bar whomever they wish. Those who refuse to leave can be arrested for trespassing. For practical purposes, the games belong to the house and the house gets to decide what's cheating and what isn't.

To the continued amazement of advantage players, casino operatives can argue with apparent conviction that card counting—essentially mental arithmetic—is a form of fraud. Andy Anderson, once a private detective for Griffin Investigations, demonstrated this remarkable feat of motivated reasoning in the 2004 documentary *The Hot Shoe.* He imagined a card counter playing at the same blackjack table as "Old Tommy over here from Kokomo, Indiana, [who] is coming to Vegas with his hundred-dollar bill." The counter knows that aces are coming. Tommy, lacking the same skills, doesn't. "Is it fair for Tom over here not to win, and you win?" he said. "I don't think so. I think it should be a level playing field."

Similarly, Steve Norton, a vice president at Resorts, the company that opened the first casino in Atlantic City, once told a reporter that the "law says that the casinos shall include games of chance. But when counters are allowed to play, it becomes a game of skill. There is no luck involved." This assertion strains logic and factual reality to the breaking point. Even regular players are supposed to use their judgment in blackjack; dealers encourage them to do so. And even the best counters are vulnerable to runs of misfortune.

In the gray zone between card counting and hidden mirrors, there are several entirely legal and morally dubious advantage plays that can get you thrown out of a casino. Spooking, for example, involves stationing a partner near a dealer. When the dealer lifts the top card slightly to check for a blackjack, a partner with good eyesight can catch a glimpse and signal to the player. Advantage players are capable of doing mental gymnastics to justify such actions. After all, casinos don't bother to make distinctions, labeling all winning systems as criminal. "Players on each side of this game often see the world with blinders on," wrote Robert A. Nersesian, one of the few attorneys who specializes in representing gamblers.

Supposedly neutral arbiters, such as the Nevada Gaming Control Board, historically haven't offered much help to the mistreated gambler. The control board is viewed as pro-industry and is reluctant to intervene on behalf of individuals. Bettors can file private lawsuits, since a wager is a contract between two parties. But such actions are expensive and unlikely to succeed. "The law is fickle, and especially mercurial, inconsistent, and unpredictable when it comes to gaming," Nersesian observed.

Phil Ivey learned that, to his cost. In 2017, the UK Supreme Court ruled that edge sorting was cheating because it *looked* like cheating, in the same way that an animal with big ears and a trunk is an elephant because it looks like one. "Dishonesty is by no means a defined concept," the judges wrote. "On the contrary, like the elephant, it is characterized more by recognition when encountered than by definition."

Ivey never received his winnings and was left with a large legal bill. A Crockfords attorney called the Supreme Court decision one of the most important rulings in a generation. Nersesian's partner in his Las Vegas law firm applies her own version of the criterion used by the British judges: If her grandma from Peoria can recognize an activity as cheating, it probably is.

The "smell test" approach to gambling ethics is a handy yardstick for casinos. However, it was of no use to Bill Nelson, Rob Reitzen, Bill Benter, and the other advantage players exploring new technology in the early 1980s. Gambling computers hadn't been around long enough to create legal precedents, let alone for the average person to form an opinion about their use. A grandmother in Peoria would likely have found it impossible to understand what the devices did, not to mention how they might be applied at the gambling table.

That put casinos into a difficult situation. Security guards would call the police whenever they frisked a player who was wired up like a suicide bomber. But they never managed to make charges stick. Marty Taft, the tall kid arrested in Lake Tahoe in 1977, was initially booked under "bunco steering" statutes, a vague prohibition on any action that changes the frequency of payouts in gambling. The law, written to punish confidence tricksters, had to be stretched thin to cover a wearable computer, and prosecutors knew it. The charges against Taft were quickly dropped.

Advantage players, meanwhile, had no difficulty defending betting machines. Under their moral code, anything that didn't physically interfere with the equipment or use information that was supposed to be hidden was fair game.

Ultimately, though, questions of law and ethics were a secondary concern. Nelson, Reitzen, and Benter were at war. They wanted victory and, almost as much, to see their adversaries humbled by defeat. The gambling industry's protectors viewed advantage players the same way. It made little difference what judges or cops or casino regulators or Peorian grandmothers thought. Both sides were prepared to do whatever they could get away with. Whatever it took to win.

PART 4

THE ABYSS

When you gaze long into an abyss, the abyss also gazes into you.
—Friedrich Nietzsche, *Beyond Good and Evil*

What good is honor if you're dead?
—Steve McQueen as Eric "The Kid" Stoner in *The Cincinnati Kid*

PART

BILL NELSON

Bill Nelson got married in January 1983 at the Candlelight Wedding Chapel in Las Vegas. Nestled between high-rise hotels and gas stations off the Strip, the Candlelight was a miniature replica of an old colonial church, clad in virginal white timber complete with a spire and high gables. Outside, a flashing sign advertised its opening hours—seven days a week until midnight—and its main purpose: the quickie wedding, that age-old Nevada tradition, as many as a hundred per day.

Nelson wore the same suit he'd used to blend in while playing roulette with the European glitterati. His new bride, Liliana, shimmered in a sheer frock paired with yellow daisies to match her flaxen hair. For the $45 package, they got a minister for fifteen minutes, enough time to say "I do" twice and sign a certificate. They were undoubtedly the finest-looking couple getting hitched at the Candlelight that day. Their only witnesses were Polish Paul's brother and his girlfriend.

The human tide flowing along Las Vegas Boulevard didn't pause for so much as a moment to mark this important milestone in Nelson's life. And why should they, with such gaudy delights to savor? Outside Circus Circus, a leering neon clown pointed down at the entrance of a candy-striped tent housing the city's most "family-friendly" casino. Inside, trapeze artists dangled from the roof, whirling and somersaulting above the quarter-dollar slot machines, while a boxing kangaroo named Boomer battled dwarfs in one-sided bouts, cheered on by baying tourists.

To have a Vegas-style instant wedding was partly a decision born of necessity. Liliana had been born in Poland, and her visa was about to run out. She and Nelson were also very much in love and planning to tie the knot eventually anyway. Besides, if the union didn't work out, there was another Nevada tradition to fall back on: the quickie divorce.

The couple had met in London a year earlier, just before Nelson's arrest in Northampton. Liliana had been working as a West End waitress, an exile from behind the Iron Curtain. On their first date, she asked about his job. Nelson hesitated.

"Black market?" she guessed.

"Gray," he replied.

She might have dismissed him as a playboy like his friend Paul, had he not been so nervous that night. Then she looked into his blue eyes. That sealed it.

At the time, Liliana had other suitors. A certain Carlos from Argentina came with a lustrous mustache and commitment issues. Nelson, by contrast, immediately asked if he could meet her sick mother. Liliana took great satisfaction in telling Carlos that she was moving to the United States to be with an American gambler. She wanted to travel. Though she didn't care for casinos herself, she didn't mind Nelson spending time in them. Something in his manner told her that he'd find a way to prosper.

After the tribulations of the roulette computer and the close call with British police, Nelson needed a break. He wanted to read, rest, and clear his head. He and Liliana futzed around Florida for a few months before the bugs and humidity got to be too much. Then Nelson looked around for inspiration and saw, in his mind's eye, the great homing beacon piercing the sky over the Nevada desert, the concentrated wattage of millions of light bulbs and miles of neon tubing calling all gamblers home to the City of Second Chances.

Liliana took some convincing before she agreed to relocate to Vegas. He promised that if she hated it, they would stay for only a year. Nelson was going back to where he had started his career, and the earnings from his European trip were dwindling fast. Hoping for a new challenge, he sought out his gambler friends to see what kind of advantage they were now pursuing.

While Nelson was away playing roulette in the Old World, one of his old Las Vegas partners was thriving. Mike Kent had once been a computer engineer at Westinghouse in West Mifflin, Pennsylvania, writing programs to test the integrity of nuclear reactors. In the early 1970s, that involved pushing punch cards through a reader connected to a mainframe computer. Although Kent was overweight and asthmatic, he was fiercely competitive and proud of his spot on the Westinghouse softball team.

Around 1972, Kent decided to use the company computer to rank the strength of teams in the corporate softball league beyond their simple win-loss ratio. He didn't ask his bosses for permission to use what was then a state-of-the-art machine. He just did it, mostly because he was extremely bored. Later, he did the same with college football and NFL games, entering performance data into his own algorithm using thousands of Westinghouse punch cards. By calculating a power rating for each team, the system told him who was most likely to win a matchup and by roughly how many points.

Soon he began comparing the computer's predictions to the odds offered by "Primo" and "Bobo," his black-market bookmakers in Pittsburgh. Sports betting was technically illegal in every state apart from Nevada, but the authorities tended to turn a blind eye. Kent, a die-hard Steelers fan, already enjoyed making the odd wager. He thought the computer might help him do better.

If, for example, his program calculated that Notre Dame would beat Georgia Tech by 7 points and Primo was taking bets on Notre Dame at minus 3, Kent put money down with Primo. He assumed that the bookmaker didn't use anything like a rigorous scientific method to set the line and had underestimated Notre Dame's chances. If Kent was right, and he mostly was, Primo would have to pay up.

At first, Kent's ranking system wasn't particularly sophisticated. He fed it with data on wins and losses, weighting the recent results as more significant and adding a handful of obvious considerations such as whether a team was playing at home or away. Since no one else in the market had access to a computer, the analyses produced were sophisticated enough.

Kent started out by betting a few dollars, gradually increasing the stakes as his confidence grew. When Primo and Bobo realized how well he was doing, they cut him off. Kent persuaded colleagues and family members to bet for him instead. By 1979, he was spending twenty to thirty hours a week honing the program.

That year, he quit his job, stuffed $100,000 into a brown paper bag, and moved to Las Vegas, the only major American city where it was legal to gamble on sports. Bill Nelson was one of the first people Kent met. They both played on the same tennis courts. Nelson was curious about his opponent, a chubby, bearded guy with tinted aviator glasses who just couldn't stand to lose at anything. Kent wouldn't even let his five-year-old nephew beat him at chess. While watching his beloved Steelers, he was known to tear at his clothes in frustration when the other team scored.

On the other hand, his scientific credentials were undeniable. His work on nuclear reactors at Westinghouse had been sensitive enough to require security clearance from the federal government, something to do with "finite element analysis," he told Nelson. After learning about the sports-betting system, Nelson agreed to help Kent get started in Vegas, even as he was about to depart for Europe with his roulette computer.

In 1980, wagering on sports was a world away from the corporate money gusher it would become decades later. Instead, it was "the odd, slightly uncouth child of the gambling family," the journalist Albert Chen wrote in his history of the trade. Only a few casinos ran sports books, and the specialist venues were foul-smelling ratholes. At Leroy's Horse & Sports Place, the TV hanging on the wall had to be replaced after a customer known as Crazy Kenny pulled a gun and shot holes in it.

The idea of carrying cash around Vegas in such circumstances didn't appeal to Nelson. He took Kent to seek counsel from another sports bettor whose opinion he respected. Ivan "Doc" Mindlin knew every power broker and hustler on the Strip, a legacy of his years as the on-call doctor for various casino hotels. Mindlin's medical background, elfin frame, and neat gray suits were deceptive. He was a creature of the Sin City underworld, the kind of man who did favors and expected favors in return. Compared to his time as an orthopedic surgeon, gambling felt like "riding high on a rocket exploding into the Las Vegas night," he wrote years later.

It was a Sunday, NFL game day, when Nelson and Kent showed up unannounced at Doc's Las Vegas home. He invited them down to a basement office and asked them to wait while he attended to some business using the two phones on his desk. "Give me the Giants, minus five-point-five," Doc said into a handset. "Yeah. For fifty thousand." After he was done, he asked how he could help. Nelson described Kent's computer program, and how difficult and dangerous it was running around the sports-betting parlors, making cash wagers over the counter.

"No, no, no," Doc said. "There are plenty of ways to get a bet down over the phone."

"Well, isn't that illegal?" Nelson asked, genuinely curious. The FBI occasionally raided bookies who had ties to organized crime, but Nelson couldn't remember law enforcement ever targeting their customers, the folks making the bets.

Doc Mindlin responded with a wry chuckle. "I can get you down," he said. That was all they needed to know.

Three years later, when Nelson returned from Europe, he found Kent and Doc's partnership flourishing. They'd accumulated a million-dollar betting pool and expanded into basketball, both college and pro. Doc had taken charge of the betting alongside Billy Walters, a swaggering former car salesman from Kentucky who'd been wagering on sports since he was nine years old. The three of them had built a slick, lucrative operation.

Walters and Mindlin recruited dozens of runners, or "beards," to work the phones and visit betting counters to put money down on Kent's picks. At first, they relied on friends in Vegas. Then they went nationwide. Chicago Gary ran a crew of thirty for Walters. The New York outpost employed a Harvard alum with a degree in Japanese studies and a Brooklyn chef. A real estate agent in Baltimore installed three phone lines and allowed her home to be used as a betting hub on evenings and weekends. "There was no shortage of needy gamblers willing to put in long hours in exchange for a few hundred bucks a week and the inside scoop on the games we told them to bet," Walters recalled later.

At first, Mike Kent rented server time from a company in Rockville, Maryland. Then he invested in his own computers. A whole network depended on their predictive power. Freed by Doc and Walters from the burden of dealing with bookies, Kent could concentrate on sharpening his program. One day he had a hunch that longer-than-average journeys to away games might hurt a visiting team's chances. It was the kind of detail that was hard to quantify unless you had a powerful computer. Kent ran the numbers from a few years of results and confirmed that every five hundred miles of travel cost about a point on game day. That and other factors, such as injuries or new coaches, were absorbed into his model, which improved with every season.

Nelson got back in touch with Kent soon after his wedding at the Candlelight Wedding Chapel. "I'm burned out from roulette," he said. "Can I do something in sports? Can I get back in?" Kent and Doc had the largest share of the profits from the various betting pools, with 30 percent each, followed by Walters. As the creator, Kent had the final say on new partners. He granted Nelson a 2 percent stake and put him to work placing bets over the phone with the Stardust Resort and Casino in Vegas.

Nelson didn't know the name of the individual whose account he was using. All he had to do was call the Stardust and read out a customer number and a list of games. Occasionally he helped Kent collect his share of the profits from Billy Walters or from the cashier's cage at one of the casinos: always in cash, always in hundred-dollar bills.

Neither Kent nor Nelson was sure how Walters and Doc did it. They oversaw up to half a million dollars in wagers each day, spread out among hundreds of bets made by a small army of beards. In 1984, the team bet a total of $21 million on college football alone.

The phone bill ran to hundreds of dollars each month, a considerable sum at the time. Profits after paying off the runners and other expenses routinely hit six figures for a season. Still, Nelson didn't ask questions, and Walters and Doc didn't seem keen to share details. The need for secrecy was obvious enough to remain unspoken, and not just because they were operating on the black market.

Their success was possible only because the computer's predictions were more accurate than the line being offered by bookmakers, just as Bill Benter's horse-racing software produced more precise odds than the Hong Kong market. That made Kent's tips extraordinarily valuable. He was the secret sage of American sport, able to divine a future no one else could see. Winning so much was bound to attract attention, especially among gamblers who were used to losing. Back when Kent was still placing bets himself, he started to notice people lingering near the counter copying out his picks into notepads.

With Doc and Walters at the helm, Kent no longer had to show his face to potential copycats. He didn't even have to leave the house; Doc could access the computer rankings from his own terminal. Even so, the beards were instructed to use code names over the phone, not revealing anything that might tie them to a coordinated effort. Walters was "Bones." Doc was "Piano." There was a runner known as "Triple" and a "Mrs. 406" in Texas. A nickel meant $500; a dime was $1,000. Small bills were referred to derisively as "grocery dollars."

Despite those precautions, by 1984 rumors had started to leak out about the mysterious outfit using technology to dominate national sports-betting markets. Bookies and their regulars spoke in awe of the "Computer Group" or "Computer Team" whenever there was a spike in betting. The runners had to hit the phones simultaneously, across several time zones, so bookmakers would have no time to adjust their own misjudged odds in response. Sometimes Walters would back the wrong side initially, just to move the line in his favor, then pile in on the computer's prediction at improved odds.

All of it required haste and precise timing. The beards used automatic dialers that connected calls at the push of a button. If a bookmaker's line was busy, they would keep bashing away until they got through. Walters, the Kentucky brawler, relished the challenge. "We're gonna roll over them like water over low land," he'd say before opening the floodgates to release a wave of gambling dollars.

Despite the subterfuge, it was a happy time for Nelson and his new wife, Liliana. His 2 percent stake in the country's biggest gambling syndicate yielded a steady flow of cash and left plenty of leisure time. The couple joined Mike Kent on trips up to Lake Mead, staying overnight on a houseboat. Kent bought a Vegas McMansion with garages for his car collection, including a Porsche, and got a cat to keep him company. Nelson and Liliana were regular dinner guests.

Across the nation, sports gambling was booming in lockstep with the growing popularity of televised games. Despite being a potential criminal offense outside Nevada, everyone seemed to be doing it. Pundits on NBC's pregame NFL show offered their view on the point spread, and at least eighty regional newspapers published betting lines. An Oklahoma Sooners coach reportedly stopped going to cocktail parties after overhearing a prominent businessman refer to him as "that bastard who cost me $5,000."

When Kent quit Westinghouse, his monthly salary had been $2,000. In January 1985, when he flew up to Doc Mindlin's ski lodge in Colorado to deliver $200,000 in cash, he was well on his way to making his first million. Kent's sports-forecasting machine was influential enough to move the odds for millions of gamblers across the United States. He was probably the single most powerful player in a market worth anywhere from $30 billion to $70 billion annually, though no one could be certain of the exact figure as the majority of the action was illegal.

It's not clear exactly when the Mafia first heard about Kent's computer. A presidential commission on organized crime in the 1980s found that gambling was second only to drugs as a source of revenue for the loose affiliation of crime families known as "Cosa Nostra." Outside Nevada, underground bookies, the likes of Primo and Bobo, often answered to wiseguys. Another Mob money-spinner was the "numbers racket," a kind of back-alley lottery popular in the working-class neighborhoods of New York, Boston, and Chicago.

In Las Vegas, the Mafia had its tentacles in virtually any enterprise that turned a profit, legal or not. There were eighteen crime families operating in the city, involved in arson, escort services, pornography, loan-sharking, narcotics, unions, and street crime. Raids on suspects as far away as LA yielded stacks of Vegas casino chips. The Stardust, where Nelson placed phone bets for Doc Mindlin, was suspected by the FBI of being a front for the Mob, which skimmed off a portion of the torrent of gambling dollars flowing in daily.

That information was available to anyone who read the newspapers. It was something everyone knew and no one talked about. Nelson himself had met one of Sin City's most infamous gangsters. He had been out for dinner with a friend, a well-known poker hustler, when a guy in a shiny suit had approached their table. "Bill, this is Tony," the poker player had said. Nelson had immediately recognized Tony as Anthony "The Ant" Spilotro, a Mafia enforcer for bosses in Chicago.

At five feet and change, including a pompadour of gray-streaked hair, Spilotro radiated the concentrated menace distinctive to truly violent men. He ran an off-Strip jewelry store and the gift shop at Circus Circus. According to the FBI, he was also a suspect in at least a dozen homicides. A decade later, he would achieve something like immortality as the inspiration for Joe Pesci's character in the Martin Scorsese classic *Casino*.

At the time, Nelson shook the man's hand and thought little more of it. He'd been in Vegas long enough to know how things worked. What he didn't yet realize was that Spilotro and his pals knew all about Mike Kent's sports-betting machine. The FBI, which was tapping the Mob's phones, knew something about it, too. Agents had heard Spilotro talking about what he called "the Computer" with Dominic Spinale, a Boston crime family member with a long rap sheet for illegal gambling.

Spinale was getting the computer's picks ahead of time from two sources in the Kent network, the FBI learned. One was Glen Walker, a runner working for Billy Walters in Vegas who gave Spinale instructions on which teams to bet and how much to risk. The other source Spinale referred to as "Doc." The FBI believed that Doc was none other than Kent's cofounder Ivan Mindlin. On a call intercepted by the FBI in 1984, Walker talked about Doc being "treacherous."

"He can't be with me," Spinale replied. "He needs me for, for favors, you know?" Agents were also aware that Spinale had a betting account at the Stardust containing $270,000—the very same account that the oblivious Bill Nelson was using to place his phone wagers, on Mindlin's instructions. (Mindlin says that he didn't know Spinale well and had no formal relationship with him.)

It's easy to imagine what the feds thought as they sat next to a whirring tape recorder, listening to these conversations on their headphones. Here were mobsters talking about a secretive network they called "the Computer" that was moving "big money" on the sports-betting market, a known sanctuary for organized crime. Doc ran gambling profits through a commodities-trading company that didn't trade commodities. Walters used an office rented by a collections agency that was not a collections agency. To law enforcement professionals, it must have looked like every other Mafia racket, the sort of predatory blight they were determined to eradicate from American society.

Bill Nelson kept on using the Stardust account into 1985, the group's most profitable season yet. He had no idea that Doc Mindlin's friends had put him, and everyone else in Kent's syndicate, in the FBI's crosshairs.

BILL BENTER

Bill Benter landed in Hong Kong in September 1985 and instantly felt a long way from home. Flying into Kai Tak Airport was an experience in itself. The Cathay Pacific jet dropped through the clouds to under five hundred feet, then banked into a forty-five-degree turn to make a narrow approach between high-rise apartment buildings. Looking out of the plane window, he saw television antennas and bamboo scaffolding rushing past at eye level.

Then there was that famous skyline, rivaling Las Vegas's in fluorescent power. Benter stepped off the plane, taking in the humid air and the view. A cluster of skyscrapers—some topped with corporate logos, some as yet unfinished—sprang up from the Pearl River Estuary, the only patch of land flat enough to build on, enclosed by mountains and the South China Sea. Hong Kong's 5 million souls were piled on top of one another in tiny apartments in one of the most densely populated places on Earth. At night, the buildings' illuminated windows looked like a constellation of fallen stars.

Alan Woods was renting a flat in the Causeway Bay neighborhood. Benter headed there to check out his new lodgings. He found the Australian on the ninth floor of Pearl City Mansion, an odd name, he thought, for more than five hundred microscopic dwellings cemented together above a polluted shopping district. He could hear the neighbors talking loudly in Cantonese and smell what they were preparing in their kitchens. There were strange stains on the walls. The view might have been spectacular had it not been blocked by the side of another grim high-rise.

Benter deposited the Kaypro computers on the living room table, which, it was decided, would be their office. Wally Simmons, Benter's programming partner from Vegas, arrived a few days later. The racing season had just begun, and all three men were eager to see what the model could do.

Woods set up a television in the corner with live coverage from Hong Kong's two racecourses, Happy Valley and Sha Tin. He sat chain-smoking in front of a pile of newspapers, looking at the form guides. His job was to act as a sanity check against the computers' tendency to spit out wild predictions that needed to be corrected by an experienced horseplayer.

Benter and Simmons, meanwhile, couldn't have named a single one of the horses or the jockeys they were betting on. On the Kaypro screens, they saw only numbers. If Woods was satisfied with a prediction, they called the Hong Kong Jockey Club's dedicated phone betting line. "Account number 18752, passcode 6524. Three thousand on horse three to win."

Sometimes they backed an unexpected winner, hitting the jackpot. Just as often they lost. With the stoicism typical of card counters, they showed no emotion either way. Success could be considered an advantage only if it happened over and over, hundreds or thousands of times. Luck, good or bad, was a distraction.

For the first few weeks, the three of them barely left the apartment, relying on the McDonald's down the street for sustenance. Pearl City Mansion was a half-hour walk from Happy Valley. Benter thought he might as well take a look. There was a one-mile running track along the length of the inside rail, so he took his sneakers.

Jogging around the course, Benter could appreciate why the place was a mecca for horse-racing fans. The view was as striking as any in Hong Kong, the concrete metropolis framed by a jade mountain canopy and endless sky. The spectator stands, empty at that moment, would be packed to the rafters on race night with tens of thousands of people from every corner of the city, bank executives standing cheek to cheek with cabdrivers, millions more watching on television.

The British started racing horses at Happy Valley in 1846, a few years after seizing the territory, in an attempt to import some semblance of order to the patch of steaming jungle they had claimed in Queen Victoria's name. So it was that a pristine ring of turf straight out of the English shires appeared in the middle of a bustling port on China's southern coast.

The Hong Kong Jockey Club was formed in 1884—members only, naturally—but over time it evolved into an important cultural institution, donating funds to public clinics, parks, and schools. The venue turned professional in the 1970s, shedding some of its elitism to embrace the patronage of the local Chinese, who made up more than 90 percent of the population and whose passion for betting on horses was unmatched. It quickly became clear that Happy Valley wasn't big enough to meet the demand. A second track was built at Sha Tin with room for thirty-five thousand spectators; it was swiftly expanded with a new grandstand that doubled its capacity.

It still wasn't enough. The top jockeys of the 1980s were rock stars, their faces pasted onto billboards downtown, unable to take the metro without being mobbed by autograph hunters. The territory's residents wagered some $2.7 billion a year at the two tracks, as well as in a network of off-site betting parlors, the highest per capita rate of any country in the world. The club, a nonprofit run for the benefit of the state, provided a sizable chunk of the territory's tax revenue, thanks to the 17 percent commission it skimmed from the betting pool.

That commission, as Benter knew, made the computer's job harder, since it was taken directly out of the winner's pot. Therefore a small betting edge wouldn't be enough to make a profit. The team would have to be nearly a fifth more accurate than the consensus in this city of horse-racing fanatics. On the other hand, the betting pool was so large that surely no one would pay any attention to a single gambler, no matter how much they won. It was the main reason Benter was there.

Hong Kong throbbed with the chaotic energy of a city in flux, caught in the space between its colonial past and an Asian future. Great Britain was due to return the territory to China in 1997 after more than 150 years of rule. The knowledge cast a long shadow in what was already a place of extremes. At one end of Benter's block, chauffeur-driven Bentleys ferried the finance industry crowd around the department stores to shop for Yves Saint Laurent and Chanel. At the other, the Chinese Merchandise Emporium flogged cheap textiles from the mainland and grandmothers sold *da siu yan*—a curse on enemies—for a few dollars from street stalls.

After a few weeks glued to the Kaypros, Alan Woods persuaded Benter and Simmons to join him for a night out in Wan Chai, a red-light district teeming with expat businessmen and much younger Filipino and Indonesian immigrant women who danced behind velvet curtains. Thousands of miles from home, untethered from their families and social networks, the behavior of those businessmen was eye-opening, even to a longtime Vegas resident like Benter. Woods, a committed hedonist, thought it was paradise. He'd left his wife and children behind for a reason.

The silver-haired Australian was particularly interested in the Filipino bar girls, handing out drinks and cash until a crowd of them gathered around. He introduced Benter. "This is Bill," he said. "He's a very smart guy. Not as smart as me, but very smart."

Wally Simmons, the all-American high school football star, wasn't convinced by the unfolding scene. He'd heard about the Wan Chai girls from a navy friend who'd taken shore leave there decades earlier. "Those girls he was talking about, the same ones are still here," he observed. Many of the women looked bored or exhausted by the merry-go-round of leering Westerners.

By the small hours, Benter, too, had seen enough. He watched Woods saunter off in the direction of a massage parlor, part of him wishing he were cocksure enough to do the same. Gambling professionally could be a lonely existence. The constant travel, the need for subterfuge and fake identities, the lies and disguises, all of it chipped away at a person's sense of self. The feeling was even more acute in Hong Kong, this neon fantasy of a town on a distant shore.

Years of card counting had already taught Benter to be cautious with strangers. A curious acquaintance at a bar could be a rival trying to steal their advantage. A potential girlfriend might be a casino mole. Gamblers had to depend on one another for both emotional support and professional success. Consequently, relationships among teammates could become insular and strained. When they broke down, the intensity of the split was closer to a divorce than the end of a business partnership.

For months the win rate of Benter's software ebbed and flowed. By the end of the racing season, however, the results were clear: The team was not doing well. They'd lost $50,000 and were down to their last $30,000. Woods and Simmons argued about why. Wally thought the Australian's interventions were the problem, since he overruled the computer whenever he saw fit. But Woods knew only one way to do things: his way.

In the end, Simmons decided to leave the team and fly back home. He was sick of Woods and craved familiar comforts. He liked American Chinese food more than Chinese Chinese food, it turned out. Benter, however, could envisage the computer's predictions getting better and better. They needed more data, more factors. In the summer of 1986, he, too, flew to Vegas, not to retreat but to fine-tune the horse-racing software and attempt to raise more bankroll from friends. "Next year is going to be a winner for sure," he told them. They politely declined to invest.

Benter was back in Hong Kong in September, no better off in terms of funding but energized by the break. "We're making great progress," he told Woods, who was worried about their dwindling funds.

"I've got some money on the outside," the Australian said. "But if we use it, I want a larger share."

"How much larger?" Benter asked.

"Ninety percent," Woods said.

"That's not fair. That's not acceptable," Benter said. He was outraged. The older man, as he saw it, had broken the sacred code binding advantage players together as equals. He was trying to screw him. "This is crazy," Benter pleaded. "It's my computer system."

He went away fuming—and powerless. It was time to play hardball. He'd spent two years building the thing. He wasn't about to give up without a fight. He powered up the computers and wrote in a line of code that would stop it functioning after a given date, then returned to Woods with an ultimatum. "If we can't reach some kind of agreement," he said, "I'm not going to let you play with my software."

Woods never blinked. He was immovable. Their partnership was over. There was nothing more to say.

Benter spent the flight back to the United States ruminating. He recalled the Australian's icy expression as he had expelled Benter from his own venture. The stop code wouldn't hinder him for long. Woods might lack technological skills, but he could easily find a software expert to defuse Benter's time bomb. Benter was sure that his former friend and partner would continue using a computer to bet on horses. So as his plane left Asia behind and raced across the Pacific toward a new day, Benter resolved that he would, too.

ROB REITZEN

Reitzen was driving the familiar route out of Las Vegas on Highway 15, casinos in his rearview, urban sprawl on either side, desert ahead. Darrell Miers, the Nebraskan who'd introduced him to wearable blackjack computers, was in the car. So was John Wayne, Reitzen's best friend from Los Angeles.

Everyone knew Wayne as "The Duke," the alias used by his namesake, Hollywood's most illustrious cowboy. The Duke was the newest member of their betting crew. He was also—and this was almost as unusual as his famous name—a black ex-soldier in a community populated by white nerds.

As he drove, Reitzen noticed a car behind them, close enough to catch his eye, too far back for him to see who or what was inside. It was painted yellow, a sickly shade that Reitzen was sure he'd seen before. Now that he thought about it, maybe the car had been tailing them for a while. "Hey, I think we're being followed," he said.

It was 1984. The three men were heading home after another incursion into Vegas with their gambling machines. Reitzen had been trying out a new ruse with the Tafts, the God-fearing family who had created the world's first card-counting computer. The latest system involved hiding a tiny camera inside a player's belt buckle. Outside, in a truck with a communications dish bolted to the side, teammates could pause its footage, zoom in, and see the blackjack dealer's hidden card for a split second as it was placed face down on the felt.

Keith Taft and his sons had provided the technology. Reitzen,

Miers, and the Duke took it into casinos. Was it cheating? Probably. Players weren't supposed to know the dealer's so-called hole card. Keith, a devout Baptist, labored to justify their actions. The lens was no more than an extension of the human eye, he told himself, just as David, his card-counting machine, was an extension of the human brain.

Reitzen simply didn't care. Casinos played dirty, why shouldn't he? And the advantage gained from knowing a dealer's face-down card was damn near unbeatable. Still, he and his team knew that they had crossed a line, and it made them itchy. They hadn't even told their wives and girlfriends about the cameras. Reitzen was on the alert for anything that might spell danger, such as strange cars tailing them on the freeway.

Miers suggested making a right turn. The yellow car disappeared, but another one tucked in behind. When they rejoined Highway 15, that car did, too. "Okay, we are definitely being followed," Reitzen said. He pulled over into an old airstrip, abandoned and blown over by desert grit. They all sat in silence, wondering what to do next.

Then Miers spotted a vehicle parked nearby. A man was watching them from inside. He appeared to be drinking a bottle of beer. Leaning closer, Miers realized that the beer was in fact a pair of binoculars, and he saw the man slide down in his seat in a cartoonish attempt to stay out of sight. Miers, with his pugilist's nose, could be intimidating when pushed. With a flash of rage, he jumped out and walked over to bang on the hood. "Hey!" he yelled at the occupant.

He didn't have time to say anything else, because within moments several cars skidded to a halt around them and there were police officers pointing guns and ordering them to the ground. They shoved Miers face down in the dirt and cuffed his hands behind his back. As Reitzen got out of the car with his hands raised, he glanced at the plainclothes female officer aiming a pistol at his face. Her hands were shaking. She looked terrified.

Down on the tarmac, he caught his best friend's eye. The Duke gave him a look that asked, "What the hell did you get me into now?" A couple of years earlier, the Duke had been working a steady job as a color technician for a film company. He had been doing fine until

Reitzen had returned from a gambling trip flaunting a Cartier watch and an exotic gadget called a Sony Walkman.

"You're still working at that place?" Reitzen had said. "Quit. Just quit. I'll teach you how to play."

With the Taft machines it was easy, and the Duke was a quick study. Gambling with his buddy was the coolest job he'd ever had. But being arrested on an abandoned airfield was not cool, even if Reitzen tried to make it seem that way when he told the story later.

The three men were taken to the station and booked on charges of assaulting an officer and resisting arrest, apparently thanks to Miers putting his hand on an unmarked police car. The charges were later dropped without explanation. Reitzen never discovered exactly what had gone down at the airstrip. He was convinced that the Nevada Gaming Commission knew about the computers and had persuaded the police to open an investigation. That would explain the tail and the undercover officer with the binoculars. Whatever was going on, it felt as though a net were tightening around them.

Around the same time, Ted Taft, another of Keith's sons, was arrested at the Marina Hotel and Casino in Vegas wearing the belt camera. A security guard stumbled across the truck in the parking lot and found it rigged up like a mobile television studio, with a live feed from groin level at the blackjack table.

Taft and his partner were prosecuted under generic cheating statutes and convicted by a Vegas jury. They served three months in prison, including a month in solitary confinement. Even Reitzen, the barstool bard, couldn't spin that one as a screwball caper. Soon after, the Duke only just made it out of the Vegas World casino after a guard saw wires protruding from his outfit from the gear he was wearing, and started yelling about a bomb. Each bust was a warning shot. The house was fighting back.

On May 10, 1985, Sam McMullen stood up in front of the Nevada Senate judiciary committee to talk about a grave threat to the casino business and, by implication, the economic health of the state. McMullen, a lawyer and lobbyist for Harrah's Casino, warned lawmakers of "a problem that is surfacing very graphically in the industry right now."

He was talking about the Taft and other machines like it. "A computerized device is strapped onto the body," he explained, or hidden inside "dingo boots." It could count cards, analyze odds, and tell a player when to up their bets or back off. Casinos already had the power to ban people using computers, but existing legislation wasn't enough. "These things should be outlawed," he urged. "Make sure that there is no question as a matter of law that they are, and that their possession with intent to use is also a crime."

An official from the Nevada Gaming Control Board, Michael Rumbolz, stood alongside McMullen. The state regulator supported the move, he said. In fact, Rumbolz argued, the language in the bill should be as broad as possible to "cover devices that may be created in the future which could be used in other games." No one spoke up to question the consequences of such a prohibition. There was no debate about what constituted cheating in a game of chance.

Twenty days later, on May 30, 1985, Nevada Revised Statutes, Chapter 465, was approved by the governor and written into law with the following amendment:

> *It is unlawful for any person to use, possess with the intent to use or assist another person in using or possessing with the intent to use any computerized, electronic, electrical or mechanical device, or any software or hardware, or any combination thereof, which is designed, constructed, altered or programmed to obtain an advantage at playing any game in a licensed gaming establishment.*

The statute banned devices that could predict the outcome of a game, track cards, measure odds, or guide strategy. Its phrasing was so nebulous that using a pen and paper to scrawl out sums in a casino might be considered a criminal offense, punishable by up to ten years in prison and a $10,000 fine. Some attorneys claimed that the new law was unconstitutional. But this was Nevada. A court challenge seemed unlikely to succeed in a state where so much power emanated from casinos' overflowing coffers.

Faced with the prospect of being outsmarted at its own game, the house had simply changed the rules. There was outrage in some corners of the gambling community. "There's no bottom with these pricks," one advantage player grumbled. Reitzen, however, was philosophical. It was the nature of the career they'd chosen, a cat-and-mouse conflict between two rival forces. Besides, there were other advantages to be found, not to mention locations where Nevada law didn't apply. His home state, for example.

California's weird patchwork of gambling regulations prohibited most of the games Reitzen knew how to beat, with one notable exception. It happened to be his favorite. "Poker is where the money is," he told friends. "Poker is the future."

Poker appealed to Reitzen for several reasons: It was the most defiantly American card game, especially in the country's western half. Cowboys played poker, as did movie stars and presidents. Harry Truman, Dwight D. Eisenhower, and Richard Nixon had been serious players. Poker was also a blend of probability and strategy, two things Reitzen felt were in his sweet spot.

The game's many variants were built around the same concept. The winner had to accumulate the strongest combination of cards from a shuffled deck. The randomness of the deal made the contest more exciting and worked as an equalizer. A bit of luck was all it took for a novice to beat the world's best player. There weren't many games where that was possible. But the promise of good fortune was misleading.

Ultimately, skill was decisive. The outcome was influenced by choices: when to fold, check, raise, or go all in. Since the participants could see only their own hands, it was possible to come out on top with lousy cards by bluffing, manipulating, and intimidating everyone else. Over a long session, talent would outshine luck.

Reitzen was already a handy competitor. As a younger man, he'd had a great time taking money from campus jerks who'd thought their college degrees made them invincible. Now in his late twenties, he had years of advantage play under his belt. He'd taught himself how to ride the shifting probabilities in a deck of cards for blackjack. And he knew that the best way to track those odds was with a computer. He imagined himself as Steve McQueen in *The Cincinnati Kid*, the coolest poker player ever to grace the silver screen. "I'm gonna win this game," the Kid had promised. "And I'm gonna win it my way."

McQueen made it sound so simple. At the end of the 1965 film, though, the Kid fails, bested by a more experienced rival. Poker was always a tough way to make a living. The standard in California's popular card rooms was brutal. High-stakes tables swarmed with sharks: people who, if they weren't playing poker, were watching poker, talking about poker, practicing poker, or studying poker books.

Below them in the poker hierarchy were pros who were good but not quite good enough. There were plenty of players who'd lost everything to the game and had been left to haunt the card rooms with defeated eyes, eking out a meager income. Another rung down, hometown champions—the best players from Goober Hill or Fairchance or Moose Lake—were the biggest victims of all, easy prey for the sharks. They didn't last long.

Reitzen's idea was to grind down poker the way advantage players had beaten blackjack: with computer simulations. He hired a freelance programmer, an MIT graduate who'd worked as a consultant for the Rand Corporation. The man's fiancée wasn't thrilled when he agreed to halve his normal hourly rate to work on card games, but Reitzen could be persuasive when he was passionate about an idea.

Poker was full of marginal decisions, creating both a challenge and an opportunity for Reitzen. Let's say he was dealt a weak pair—two 6s, better than nothing but not by much. How likely was that to be the best hand at the table? There were 2.6 million different combinations of five cards. With three players, the number of potential variations topped 4 trillion. And that was just the starting point, before any player had access to new cards, which most poker formats allowed after a first round of betting.

No human mind was able to parse a data set that huge. A computer could, though. Reitzen's MIT-trained freelancer wrote a basic program to replicate hands of poker, generating random cards and a range of strategies for the other participants. It may well have been the world's first automated poker solver. (Earlier efforts by math professors in the 1970s had been found to contain fatal flaws because of the authors' lack of poker experience.)

It's hard to imagine, looking back now, how big a leap this was in 1986. There had been chess computers as far back as the 1950s at the Los Alamos National Laboratory, the birthplace of the atomic bomb. IBM machines had been playing checkers by the 1960s. Backgammon software was still in its infancy in the 1980s. Poker, however, was vastly more complicated than any of those. For that reason, serious academic research on the game didn't begin until the mid-1990s.

When Reitzen got started, the most popular game permitted in California was lowball, a kind of upside-down poker where the aim was to get the worst possible hand. In some cases, a winning strategy would be obvious. The best hand in lowball is 5, 4, 3, 2, and ace, known as a "wheel." If Reitzen got those cards, he'd bet as many chips as he could.

In many situations, though, the optimal approach was hidden by a cloud of swirling possibilities. That was where the computer came in. The software could run the same hand thirty thousand times, generating different cards and bets for virtual opponents. At the end, there would be a plus or minus dollar figure next to each possible course of action—bet, fold, check, raise—reflecting the total money won or lost over thousands of simulations. The highest number was the best move. The math didn't lie.

To reduce the processing load on their ponderous home computers, Reitzen and his partner removed the worst hands from consideration. California card room regulars were skilled enough to avoid them, so they didn't need to waste time simulating scenarios in which opponents acted irrationally. Even so, it took a few hours to get a definitive answer for a single combination of cards. Sometimes they'd have to run the software all night.

Reitzen took comfort from the fact that they were seeing the game as no one had before. The machine decreed, for example, that a king, 8, 5, 4, 3 set wasn't good enough to stay in the game in lowball poker. With that hand the player should fold at the first opportunity. But king, 8, 5, 3, 2 *was* a playable hand, worth betting on. No mere mortal could reach such precise conclusions.

To fund their work, Darrell Miers spent his weekends using a wearable blackjack computer in Atlantic City. New Jersey, like California, had no equivalent of Nevada's new antidevice law. Miers could earn $20,000 on a good trip, keeping a third for himself and handing over the rest to Reitzen for poker research. Every time the computer finished running the numbers for a given combination of cards, the team added it to their charts and took another step closer to perfection.

And perfection was Reitzen's goal. He printed the charts onto flash cards and tried to memorize them. He also paid a contact to build a wearable computer just like the Taft. All Reitzen had to do was input his cards using the toe switches, as before. Then the microprocessor consulted its ever-expanding database of optimal moves. The buzzer on his crotch would tell him what to do.

When Reitzen first took the machine to try it out in LA card rooms, he noticed that its guidance often defied conventional wisdom. He'd played enough lowball poker to know that the best regulars played a tight game, taking few risks. The poker software, however, was ferociously aggressive at unexpected times. Occasionally it paid off, but when it didn't, Reitzen would watch his entire bankroll disappear in an instant.

The busiest card room in LA was the Bicycle Club in Bell Gardens, a neighborhood better known for drive-by shootings. The club's interior was hardly more inviting. On the ceiling above 120 felt tables, filtration units fought a losing battle against clouds of cigarette smoke so thick that it was hard to see one end of the room from the other. The place smelled of a thousand future workplace exposure lawsuits and despair.

One of Reitzen's teammates recalls seeing a frail older man connected to an oxygen tank by tubes hanging from his nose. He had his cards in one hand, a lit cigarette in the other. Another regular had terminal cancer. She spent her last weeks in the club, saying it was the only place she could escape the pain. Patrons rented their seats from the club, the club paid a portion of its revenues to the city, and the city provided police officers to stop the patrons from being robbed in the parking lot by Bell Gardens' teenaged gangbangers.

There was no sign there of the joyful abandon of a Vegas casino. Instead, the atmosphere was thick with the intense concentration of several hundred people trying to bankrupt one another. Competitive poker is "hours of boredom followed by moments of sheer terror," wrote Tom McEvoy, a Poker Hall of Fame inductee. Reitzen would fold hand after hand, waiting for one the computer deemed worthy; then it was all on the line.

After eighteen months, the team was still bleeding money and the stress was mounting. "I can't take it," Reitzen told Miers. Ever the loyal partner, the big Nebraskan talked him down. Sure, there were problems. They would solve them together, as they always had. "Thirty more days," Miers said. "We'll make a million, or we'll go broke."

Slowly, inexorably, the tide began to turn. Using a combination of the wearable computer buzzing its guidance and late-night study sessions poring over printouts, Reitzen could feel the game's mysteries unraveling. Miers joined him in the card rooms. He didn't consider himself a particularly strong player, but with the computer he didn't need to think. After a while he stopped wearing it. He'd been shown the correct moves often enough to remember them. If he came across something he hadn't seen before, he'd make a mental note to run simulations on the computer overnight. By the morning, he'd have an answer.

One afternoon, Miers was in the Bicycle Club chatting with an old pro. In front of them was a sea of poker, the click-clacking symphony of hundreds of plastic chips being twirled, stacked, and rolled across knuckles. Miers was complaining. He'd been working on poker for years, he said, and was only now breaking even. "Buddy," the old pro responded, gesturing out over the tables, "most of them would give a body part to be breaking even."

Losing to robotic poker was a new experience for the regulars at the Bicycle Club, not that any of them really understood what was going on. The style recommended by the computer wasn't dramatic. It presented as a series of moments during which Reitzen and Miers appeared to get lucky. Being on the other side could be confusing and disheartening. How did it keep happening? The answer, unknown to their opponents, was that Reitzen and Miers were repeatedly putting themselves onto the path of victory, where the odds were—demonstrably, quantifiably—in their favor.

Danny the Marine was a familiar face at the Bike, as it was known. A veteran with a roomful of poker trophies, he earned enough from his retail business to spend his free time gambling. He was an old-school player, looking for weaknesses around the table. A telltale facial twitch, or a clumsy raise, Danny believed, told him enough to spot a bluff.

Miers, though, was playing a different kind of game. Thanks to the computer, he could gaze into thousands of potential futures and grasp the single best decision it was possible to make. It didn't matter to him what Danny the Marine said or did. All that mattered was that the computer could simulate more games in two hours than a club player could grind out in a lifetime.

Danny stared at his dwindling pile of chips. "Kid," he said, "I used to have three liquor stores. I lost two of them to this game. If I lose the last one, I'm going to have to kill you." He was smiling—a bitter joke.

Miers looked down at his cards. He had the second best hand in lowball poker, a certain winner. "You've still got one store," he said. "Let's raise."

PART 5

FORBIDDEN FRUIT

Your eyes shall be opened,
and ye shall be as gods,
knowing good and evil.
—Genesis 3:5

BILL NELSON

As Ronald Reagan began his second term as president and Apple unveiled its brand-new Macintosh, Mike Kent's computer team was enjoying its most successful season. The software was purring, guided by a decade of data and the former nuclear reactor engineer's singular genius. Whether it was basketball or football, Kent's system was winning so much that by the end of 1984, moving the proceeds became a chore.

Two of the team's beards complained bitterly about the burden of delivering cash to an investor brought in by Doc Mindlin. It took them two hours to count out nearly half a million dollars in hundred-dollar bills at the investor's Las Vegas penthouse. In all, there were about twenty betting pools for different sports and leagues. Various friends, business partners, and family members were getting a cut, including Bill Nelson. All of them were benefiting from Kent's golden touch. In the six-week period around Christmas, the group grossed $1.6 million, with $558,000 of profit to be shared around.

Yet Nelson sensed something poisonous in the air. Doc and his partner Billy Walters, the Kentucky brawler, were not getting on well. The two most important managers in the betting operation also possessed the biggest egos. Walters was a gambler of the most aggressive kind. His aim, he wrote later, was to "drain you dry before you drained me." He didn't trust Doc and wasn't shy about saying so.

Doc felt the same. Once Walters asked him to team up on some casino venture. "Billy, if you can find two people who have a nice word to say about you, I'll do it," Doc recalls saying. The plan never happened, and the two men settled into a working relationship that seemed to get more strained as the profits piled up.

Walters decided to move his side of the operation to Florida for a while. He was worried about his phone in Vegas being tapped, he told the team. Doc asked Nelson to go along. He was certain that Walters was skimming off profits, making side bets for himself, and he wanted Nelson's eyes on his partner on game days.

Nelson wasn't sure that Doc was right but agreed to do his bidding. He knew the boom-bust cycle of advantage gambling too well to be complacent. Periods of great success could be the most dangerous of all.

On Saturday, January 19, 1985, Nelson arrived at Walters's Fort Lauderdale house early. It was a busy period for the team. Super Bowl XIX was hours away. A battle between two of the game's greatest quarterbacks—Miami's Dan Marino and San Francisco's Joe Montana—was sure to attract an extraordinary level of action. The college basketball season was also in full swing. There were maybe sixty games to get money on.

Walters and a handful of beards were burning up the phones, getting the line from bookmakers on the Redmen of St. John's University at Boston College; Southern Methodist at Texas Christian; and the Kansas Jayhawks at the Oklahoma Sooners. Nelson watched the clamor of bets being made without taking part. He was under strict instructions from Doc to stay off the phones and monitor what was going on.

A loud bang jolted him out of his vigil. Suddenly the room was full of people wearing helmets and waving guns, yelling, "THIS IS A RAID!" Their blue jackets were emblazoned with three letters that made Nelson's heart sink into his stomach: FBI.

The agents told Nelson and the others to remain seated while they fanned out through the house, taking what they wanted. They swiftly gathered up all the paperwork they could find, plus cash from the safe and the computers. Walters glowered. "You won't get away with this," he said.

"Why aren't you guys doing something useful like busting drug dealers?" Nelson snapped.

Just as quickly as they had appeared, the feds were gone. "Well, boys, it looks like we're shutting down for a while," Walters announced. Then he, too, disappeared.

Nelson was left to ponder what had just occurred. His first thought was of Dr. Ivan Mindlin. Only Doc could be involved in something shady enough to have gotten onto the FBI's radar; Doc, with his secrets and favors and guys with Italian names calling his office to talk about God knows what. "Fucking Ivan," Nelson thought.

At the same moment, two thousand miles away, federal agents arrived at Doc's ski lodge in Vail, Colorado. They started kicking at the door. "What are you doing?" asked Mike Kent's brother, who was standing by the porch. "It's open. Just turn the handle." Kent himself, who liked to take ski breaks at Doc's place, was inside watching TV as agents poured in. They grabbed Doc and made him open a briefcase full of cash they found, then confiscated the contents. As men in uniform rifled through his files, Doc spotted a bundle of cashier's checks worth at least a million dollars and slipped it into his back pocket. There was no way the feds were getting that without another warrant, he thought as he hurried outside.

Doc found Mike Kent standing in the snow in a state of shock. He and Walters had largely shielded Kent from the messy business of wrangling beards, dealing with bookmakers, and moving cash. Kent's only brush with the law had come years earlier when he had been arrested by Pittsburgh traffic cops because the muffler on his car was too noisy. He couldn't understand what the FBI was doing there. "What did we do wrong?" he asked Doc over and over.

The FBI raided forty-five locations across the country that day. Agents searched C&B Collections Agency, the front business used by Billy Walters in Las Vegas, as well as Doc's medical office. They took betting sheets from under the bed of one beard and seized a Dungeons & Dragons game from another's twelve-year-old son, presumably because it included dice.

Afterward, Doc rushed back to Vegas, cleaned all the old records out of his house, and left them in a dumpster. He wanted to make the government's job as difficult as possible. Kent, meanwhile, was worried about his beloved computers. He drove to Pittsburgh to download his data onto a friend's machine in case the FBI came back.

The Bureau was leaning hard on anyone who did business with Kent's outfit, a list that included wives and siblings who'd opened betting accounts or deposited cash. Billy Walters blew his top when an agent visited his wife and told her it was unfortunate that her family was being dragged into the matter.

Bill Nelson decided that the best policy was silence. He didn't want to worry Liliana, so he downplayed the investigation when they discussed it at home. It was just a bunch of bureaucrats trying to make a name for themselves, he explained. They didn't have anything. The FBI soon summoned him to the Las Vegas field office for an interview. The agent in charge reeled off a list of names and aliases, some of which Nelson recognized. Tony "The Ant" Spilotro was one of them. They also asked about Dominic Spinale, the owner of the Stardust betting account he'd unwittingly been using. Nelson kept his mouth shut.

"Mr. Nelson," the agent said, "are you willing to cooperate with this investigation?" Nelson said he wasn't, and he meant it. Last time he'd checked, wagering on sporting events was legal in Nevada. Yes, they'd used black-market bookmakers. So had a large portion of Nevada's judges, politicians, and police officers, Nelson imagined, along with perhaps half the adult population of the United States. It got under his skin to hear the FBI suits using ominous terms such as "organized betting," as if there were something wrong with doing it well.

Billy Walters, meanwhile, managed to provoke the government further by hiring a defense lawyer named Oscar Goodman. Goodman was well known as the Mob's attorney-of-choice; his client list included Tony Spilotro. It took a while for Walters to realize what kind of signal that sent to the FBI. In the meantime, Spilotro, Goodman's most infamous client, got wind of what was going on. He demanded a meeting with Walters at Goodman's office and explained that Doc had been giving him the computer's numbers. Now that Doc was no longer reachable, Spilotro expressed his desire that Walters should do the same. Walters would later recall looking into the gangster's eyes. "Empty. Dead."

"I'll get back to you on that," Walters said, with no intention of doing so. Later, he was playing poker at the Golden Nugget when one of Spilotro's associates approached him in the restroom. "The little guy wants to see you." Walters feigned ignorance. "You know who I'm talking about," the man insisted. Walters asked for time to finish his game; then, as soon as the coast was clear, he fled the casino, leaving a pile of chips on the table. He took his wife on the next available flight to Kentucky and stayed there, hiding out at a house rented in a friend's name.

Mob bosses in Chicago and Kansas City seemed to think that Kent's computer possessed some sort of magic. But Spilotro was pushing the limits of Mafia tolerance, sauntering around Las Vegas like a little emperor, robbing, extorting, and terrifying everyone he met. Something had to give.

The Ant had been collecting enemies for years. He had earned his nickname after telling a federal agent who was tailing him to go fuck himself. The agent had thereafter referred to him as "that little pissant" in conversations with the press, which picked up the more publishable half of the epithet. Before Spilotro came to Vegas, the Mob was making so much money from loan-sharking, bookmaking, and skimming that its enforcers oversaw a kind of uneasy peace. The few murders that occurred took place in the desert, far from public view.

That wasn't Spilotro's way. He was constantly in the newspapers, waving at reporters outside court after beating another murder rap or in the gossip pages for having an affair with a casino executive's wife. The FBI was coming down hard all over the country, tapping phones and flipping low-level hoods. Wiseguys were getting assassinated just for knowing enough to snitch. Many of them turned to the government for protection from their own kind.

Spilotro's temperament didn't help his cause. "He dared you to murder him," recalled one federal agent. Finally, in June 1986, the Ant's luck ran out. His nearly naked corpse was found buried in an Indiana cornfield. He'd been so badly beaten that he had to be identified by his fingerprints. While the murder was never solved, Spilotro's final resting place, a few miles from property owned by a Chicago don, was its own explanation.

The bad omens kept coming for the computer team. Doc Mindlin's wife died in strange circumstances due to an anaphylactic reaction to medicine he'd given her. Within weeks he was spotted out in the company of a much younger woman. It was his way of coping with his extreme grief, he would later explain.

Kent was buckling under the strain, arguing about the defense strategy with Doc, who told him that his lawyer was a "schmuck." When Nelson went to check on Kent, he noticed that his friend had broken out in a rash from the stress and his asthma was playing up. Months passed. The FBI still hadn't indicted anyone, though it was clear that its investigation was ongoing. Kent's legal team advised that it was safe to fire up the software again, as long as the gamblers limited their activities to the legal sanctuary of Nevada. (The antidevice law passed in 1985 applied only inside casinos, so it didn't cover Kent's computers.)

But Kent and Doc quickly fell out over money. The FBI had released about $600,000 in cash and checks seized during the raids, and Kent claimed that he had never gotten his share back from Doc. Then he demanded that Mindlin pay a flat fee of $700,000 for the continued use of the system. Doc said he couldn't agree, and Kent filed a lawsuit against him in federal court. By 1987, the two men were communicating only through lawyers.

Bill Nelson thought the lawsuit was ridiculous. He couldn't forgive Doc for the business with the Mafia. He was mad at Walters for taking so many risks in pursuit of an ever-bigger payday. The whole enterprise had sunk into a toxic sludge of competing self-interest, and Nelson wanted nothing more to do with it. "I'm out," he told Kent.

Nelson got a new job working for one of Bill Benter's friends in Australia. The Australians had a horse-racing syndicate, but they couldn't find a way to get television feed showing American and Canadian fixtures. Nelson subscribed to the channels, connecting to a server in his closet that the Australians could access remotely from the other side of the world. They paid him several thousand dollars a month for what amounted to a few hours of work.

Meanwhile, Nelson poured his energy into starting a family with Liliana, the one person in his life he could count on not to let him down. They'd been trying for years, spending a fortune on three rounds of in vitro fertilization. In 1989, the couple adopted a baby girl. She was two days old when she arrived, tiny, perfectly formed, and utterly helpless. Nelson was smitten. He watched her sleep, scarcely able to believe that she was real.

A few months later, he was at home when he got a phone call from Mike Kent. Although no longer working together, they'd stayed friends. "You and me go way back," Kent told Nelson over the phone. "I need to tell you something. You're going to be indicted tomorrow."

Nelson was too stunned to speak. It took him a few seconds to gather himself. "How do you know?" he asked.

"Because I'm turning state's evidence," Kent replied.

Nelson listened as Kent laid out what he'd done. He'd agreed to testify for the government against Walters, Doc, Nelson, and eleven other defendants in the computer group. In return, he had been granted immunity from prosecution. Nelson's mind raced. He remembered his share of the last season's profits before the raid: a lousy $28,000. Kent had made at least a million. Now Nelson was being indicted, and Kent was off the hook.

He felt like tearing into his friend for what he considered a breathtaking betrayal. But he didn't say anything. What would be the point? Instead, he did what he'd always done. During his childhood at the cemetery, through his father's drug use and depression, he had developed the ability to retreat into a more logical part of his brain, ignoring the limbic impulses to weep or lose his temper. With his frontal cortex fully activated, he'd found he could endure most hardships and think clearly about possible solutions.

Kent's actions, in that light, were rational. He was a good Catholic who used to work on secret government projects. He couldn't bear to be on the wrong side of the law. Besides, boiling with rage against Kent wouldn't help Nelson out of what was now a very serious situation.

The next day, federal agents arrived at Nelson's house and took him away in handcuffs to be charged at the courthouse. Liliana watched him go. As her husband was marched down the driveway, she was struck by the lack of emotion on his face. If he was scared, he wasn't showing it. His lips were pursed, his features a mask. It looked almost as if he felt nothing at all.

BILL BENTER

Bill Benter went home to the United States nursing a bruised ego. The rift with Alan Woods in Hong Kong had been a setback, but it also provided a jolt of motivating energy. He would have to prove to everyone, above all himself, that he could succeed in horse racing without help from the man who had once been his mentor.

He needed a new bankroll, probably a couple of hundred thousand dollars, before he could go back and pick up where he'd left off. Still barred from every casino in Las Vegas, he returned to the place where his gambling career had begun.

Atlantic City had changed in the decade since Benter had lost his theater usher's salary while trying to count cards at Resorts International. The floodlit ramparts of several new casinos illuminated a longer stretch of sandy shore, making the foaming surf glow in strange pastel shades. The city's expansion during the 1980s was largely down to a New York real estate investor with a big personality and an even bigger name: one Donald J. Trump.

Trump blew into AC in a now familiar whirlwind of self-promotion and other people's money. He bought two casinos in New Jersey, loaded with debt, and had his eye on buying more. Patrons could buy books written by Trump at the Trump bookstore while enjoying a four-by-five-foot window display of Trump. His wife Ivana flew in from Manhattan by helicopter a couple of days a week to run the Trump Castle casino complex.

Trump's superyacht, *Trump Princess*, was moored in the marina.

After its maiden voyage in 1988, Trump disembarked at Trump Castle, waving to the crowds like a visiting monarch. "Be our next president," someone shouted. Anyone who still hadn't gotten enough Trump could take in a stage show, where the performers changed song lyrics to name-check the owner.

Benter had no interest in corporate pageantry, but he had to admit that Trump's presence made Atlantic City an excellent place to play blackjack. His two casinos competed against each other, and the whole boardwalk competed against them. In the mad scramble for customers, there were even deals that seemed to be specifically for card counters. The Claridge was promoting four-deck blackjack, down from the usual eight. The only real benefit was for a player trying to keep track of the cards left in the shoe.

Benter formed a team to take advantage of a glaring weakness in the casinos' defenses. They were desperate for high rollers, the deep-pocketed gamblers who kept profit margins fat. Anyone who looked the part got a license to do whatever they liked. The "big player" routine, honed to a fine art by card counters in Vegas, was perfect cover. Benter and his scouts could keep a low profile, betting minimal amounts until the deck turned hot. Then they'd give the signal, normally by standing up. At that moment a teammate would sit down and immediately throw down enormous wagers with the odds in their favor.

A big player needed to look like the kind of person who didn't mind risking huge sums at the blackjack table. Benter recruited a hulking athlete who'd been on the roster of the Philadelphia Eagles. The man liked to saunter around the casino floor with a girl on each arm. There was a Japanese guy called Rocky who played an Asian businessman, the highest of high rollers.

It took two years for Benter to earn what he needed—two long years of bouncing between Las Vegas, where he lived, and New Jersey, where he worked. Two years of counting and saving and scheming and wishing he were in Hong Kong building the world's most advanced horse-racing algorithm.

Benter heard from mutual friends that Alan Woods had debugged his software, hired a team of programmers, and was doing well. There were rumors of millions of dollars being made. He imagined his former partner in some neon dungeon of a nightclub, drinking cocktails and celebrating another successful night at the track. The thought made him work even harder.

The 1988 horse-racing season at Sha Tin began at 1:30 p.m. on September 17. Any earlier in the year, and the humidity and threat of summer typhoons would put the horses at risk. The animals spent their off months in air-conditioned luxury, relaxing in swimming pools after a run, listening to soothing music piped in through personalized sound systems.

Benter was back in Hong Kong. Thanks to the lax security of New Jersey's casinos, he had funds in hand. And he had a new partner, an American software developer he had met in an elevator in Atlantic City. Together, they rented an apartment on Wong Nai Chung Road, so close to the Happy Valley racetrack that Benter could see the floodlit stands from his window. Their shared living room became an office, fitted out with secondhand desks, a couple of boxy computer terminals, telephones, and teetering piles of racing newspapers and results books.

Benter needed new inputs to sharpen his algorithm if he was going to catch up with Woods, who had a two-year head start building on what Benter had created. The original software accounted for basic factors such as straight-line speed and recent results. Benter knew that there were thousands of other data points to consider when rating a horse's chances. But his only practical experience of the track was jogging around Happy Valley. He'd have to use trial and error, married to common sense.

Perhaps, he thought, there was wisdom to be found in the aggregated predictions of professionals. In financial markets, stock pickers and analysts published reports that served as guides for all kinds of successful investors. The closest equivalent in racing was the tipster pages in the local press. There were eleven dedicated racing newspapers in Hong Kong, with around fifty pseudonymous experts offering their forecasts.

Most were written in Chinese, which Benter didn't understand, so he had to painstakingly match the symbols in Professor Wong's Pick of the Week to the numbers in the English form guides. It was no use. The professor and his peers did nothing to improve his win rate. After a while, he stopped inputting their tips.

Sometimes he hit paydirt without understanding why. The total number of races on a horse's record proved to be significant. Whether the effect caught old nags too broken down to go flat out, young colts too inexperienced to last the course, or both, he was never quite sure. He suspected that the race total worked in combination with other variables, acting as a kind of corrector. But the reason didn't matter; statistical truth was all he required.

Benter's computers, connected by modem to a digital feed, updated the market odds every twelve seconds. He and his partner found that they could make six to eight bets a minute by calling the club's Telebet service. They were normally still on the phone when the starting pistol fired. That first season, Benter made a profit of around $700,000. It was less than he'd heard Woods was earning but encouraging nonetheless.

The next year, the team hired six phone operators, Filipino women from Hong Kong's army of migrant workers. With their help, Benter could place hundreds of bets on each of the eight or nine races on a race card, adding up to thousands per day. The computer software proved especially adept at predicting exotic wagers such as the quinella (the first and second finisher in any order) and the tierce (first, second, and third in the correct order).

Locals loved the exotics, pumping in money until the jackpots swelled to lottery size. They were famously hard to win. In a nine-horse contest, there were 729 possible combinations for the tierce. That kind of analysis was beyond even the most dedicated student of racing forms. Benter's system, though, was made for it.

In the 1989 season, his second using the new software, he lost a little overall. He attributed the shortfall to a statistical quirk and plowed on. Around that time, he convinced himself that certain horses preferred specific temperatures. Hong Kong's climate was relatively stable, ranging from warm to swelteringly hot. Still, Benter thought the theory was worth testing.

He found out that the British Meteorological Office operated a weather station in the territory, so he flew to England and boarded a train to visit a dusty regional archive. There, a librarian led him down to the basement and sat him in front of several large binders. Benter scribbled the data into a notepad, excited at the prospect of unearthing quantitative gold. When he fed the numbers into his computers, however, he discovered that horses didn't seem to care whether the temperature was 60 degrees or 90 degrees. It made no difference to his model.

The 1990 season was his first big winner. At least HK $23 million (US $3 million) in betting revenue poured in. Benter hired more phone operators and moved into a fancy top-floor office. His software was evolving daily. The most telling innovation was to incorporate market odds into the model. At first, he had opted to ignore public sentiment, assuming that his math would be more reliable. But while Hong Kong's millions of punters were fallible individually, the combined weight of their knowledge was surprisingly prescient. It provided an effective starting point for the software's more advanced calculations.

Benter even learned how to adjust for superstition. In Chinese culture, four is the unluckiest number because of a phonological fluke: It sounds like the word for "death." The symbolism had such power that many Hong Kong skyscrapers lacked a fourth floor, or a fourteenth, or a twenty-fourth. Elevator panels simply skipped the offending digit as if it didn't exist.

Benter's data showed that people were just as unwilling to be tainted by death when it came to horses, which were allocated a number to make them easier to identify on betting tickets. Thoroughbreds with the pedigree to be favorites consistently got longer odds because the market was put off by the number four on the saddle.

That was precisely the sort of underpriced bet Benter was looking for. The expected value was positive—repeated thousands of times, he could win more than he'd invested in wagers. He shared a philosophy with value investors in financial markets, figures such as Warren Buffett. Possible future success wasn't a good enough measure if the invisible hand of the market had already priced in that potential by buying and selling shares at their proper value. For a stock to really take off, the market had to have misjudged it. In the same way, Benter profited from horses that were underestimated by the betting herd.

In the middle of the 1991 season, Benter got a phone call out of the blue from the Hong Kong Jockey Club. When the English-accented voice on the other end of the line started talking about "high turnover," he winced, remembering the heavy hand of the Las Vegas pit boss on his shoulder. But the blow never fell. "You are one of our best customers," the club's representative said. "What can we do to help you?"

Unlike in a casino, the club wasn't on the other side of Benter's wagers. It made money by taking a 17 percent commission, give or take a few percentage points, out of the pools. After expenses, the funds went to the state in taxes and to local charities. The club was telling Benter that it wanted *more* of his business.

He asked if there was a way to bet electronically from his own office. Soon afterward, technicians arrived from the club to install customer input terminals. It was a simple matter to wire them to the computers. His operators could now bet with the click of a button. Every second counted. Rival bettors watched the odds moving live on screens at the track. A sudden swing in the price was their signal to get behind a new favorite, potentially wrecking Benter's edge. With the customer input terminals, he could wait until thirty seconds before the race started and still get all his bets in before other bettors had time to react. Now he wasn't just smarter; he was faster, too.

Now that he had the tools he required, he began an epic winning run. He was making so much money that it was almost embarrassing. His system was probably the first of its kind anywhere in the world. It used more than eighty data points to generate accurate odds, comparing the prices to those available in the pools. The software selected hundreds or thousands of wagers where the mismatch was big enough to be worth the risk. Finally, it placed the bets with the Jockey Club. The whole process was automated, with only minimal supervision by an operator.

As far as Benter knew, his only real competition was the Alan Woods syndicate on the other side of Happy Valley. He and the Australian had reached the top of an ecosystem remade by their computers. Viewed up close, it would have looked something like this:

A taxi driver, let's call him Mr. Chau, took his tips to the offtrack betting parlor in Kowloon. He always bet the tierce since the jackpot was big enough to change his life. Dr. Ding the pediatrician did the same at the counter at Sha Tin, spending a few dollars on the last race of the night, a quick thrill after a long day at the hospital. So did Nigel, a British bond trader, who called the Telebet service from his twenty-second-floor office in the central business district. So did thousands upon thousands of others across the metropolis. All that money flowed into a special tierce pool managed by the Jockey Club, which would later extract its commission.

At the end of the night, Mr. Chau, Dr. Ding, and Nigel were disappointed but not altogether surprised to discover that they hadn't picked the right finishers in the right order to win the tierce. Because they were making a single selection out of thousands, the odds were always stacked against them. But in a top-floor office overlooking Happy Valley, a computer had algorithmically processed the hundred most likely combinations. One of them was correct. The total cost of placing all the bets was $1,000 (Hong Kong). The jackpot: $200,000.

Typically, Bill Benter wouldn't have watched the race that had won him the prize. If he had, he wouldn't have celebrated. A quick glance at the screen displaying the system's tally for the evening was enough. Then his thoughts would turn to the next fixture in the calendar and how the software might be tweaked to perform even better. The betting population of Hong Kong continued as they always had, oblivious to the new reality Benter helped create.

The Hong Kong Jockey Club remained a bastion of Britishness in a fast-changing city, all brass buttons and bristling mustaches. The chief executive, Major General Guy Watkins, played cricket and went to the ballet. It wasn't the sort of place Benter would have wanted to spend his free time in, even if he hadn't been worried about the club changing its mind and shutting down his accounts for winning so much, which he was.

Where, then, could he enjoy his newfound success? Hong Kong's society had many layers reflecting the wealth, status, ethnicity, and habits of the city's diverse population. There was the high-finance set: bankers in contrast collars and suspenders. They favored cocktail bars with million-dollar views. "Cocaine respectable" was how one British observer described the scene.

Across the harbor in Yau Ma Tei, elderly Cantonese speakers met in mahjong parlors to play the ancient board game and gossip, interrupted by periodic gangland shootings involving the city's Triads. Conversely, the beachside community of Repulse Bay had an upmarket, suburban vibe, with spaces for wealthy locals to play golf, soak in a spa, or take afternoon tea.

Somewhere near the bottom of the social hierarchy was the Wan Chai gambling crowd. They were rowdy, unkempt expats who drank all evening in Joe Bananas or the Crazy Horse Club, pubs that reminded them of home. At the end of the night, they migrated to the hostess bars and strip clubs of the red-light district. They were Benter's people, for better or worse. It was them or solitude.

Wan Chai was within stumbling distance of Happy Valley. Technicians and data professionals who worked for Benter or Woods often socialized there after work. As members of the only two computer syndicates in town, most of them knew one another. Some even defected from one team to the other. An Australian employed by Woods bought a bar with a pool area and a soundtrack of rock staples that became a favorite haunt.

Benter, though, was still too sore to talk to his rival. When he saw Woods on a night out, he would nod politely and walk away. Their respective staffs were mystified by the tension. "What happened with you guys?" one employee asked. Benter refused to say.

Woods was also thriving; that much was obvious. He bought a Rolls-Royce he never used and moved into a vast penthouse in the shadow of Mount Cameron, with lush forest views on one side and the bright lights of Wan Chai on the other. His parties were the stuff of legend. One attendee remembers arriving to see two naked women writhing on a glass coffee table. "Are you decadent?" Woods would ask his guests, which was his code word for sexually liberated polyamory. The invitation to his "Flirtation Fantasy" bash was decorated with an oil painting of nude torsos embracing. The dress code was "sensual," though the Australian appeared in jeans and a T-shirt as usual. Benter was not invited and would have been mortified by the spectacle anyway.

Woods gambled the way he partied: no boundaries; no consequences. During the 1994 soccer World Cup, he placed a million-dollar bet with a black-market Asian betting syndicate. He watched the game on his television in the company of heavies from the outfit who were keeping an eye on their investment. He seemed unfazed by their presence, impassively smoking a cigarette as the twenty-two players on the pitch determined his fate. In a back room, a handful of Chinese employees bashed away at computer terminals to keep the horse-racing operation humming.

Bob Moore was a regular at the Woods penthouse. A manic New Zealander who devoured MDMA tablets like jelly beans, he was a video specialist. He rewatched race footage to find moments when a horse was bumped, blocked, or otherwise hindered by bad luck. That was useful data for computer models, and Moore worked for both Benter and Woods at different periods.

He was also a volatile braggart who broke a cardinal rule of advantage gambling by talking to the press. Publicity was known to be a hex. Once an advantage is shared, it can be copied until it disappears. Alternatively, those losing out can raise hell until it's banned. Nothing good came from being in the limelight. They all respected the code—apart from Bob Moore.

He boasted about the betting power of computers to the Chinese language press, which dubbed him "The God of Horses." Moore's behavior grew so erratic that even Woods avoided him. He flew to the Netherlands and came back with hundreds of ecstasy pills. Gripped by dark moods, he faxed death threats to his colleagues, accusing them of incompetence. "You should be bashed and killed," said one such missive.

Benter was horrified to see Moore brawling with the bouncers at

Joe Bananas. Things got so bad that he would stay home if he heard that the Kiwi was going out. Benter felt increasingly estranged from the Happy Valley social scene, preferring to spend his free hours reading academic papers on probability or computing. He invested in a vineyard in Bordeaux. It felt good to do something so far removed from the drugs and sleaze of Wan Chai.

When he did hit the bars, he was often seen seated alone or talking quietly with a friend. He was never visibly drunk. Employees of the two rival syndicates noticed an aura around Benter. It wasn't the kind of confidence they saw in Woods, holding court in the Neptune II nightclub surrounded by a crowd of young women and hangers-on. Benter's was an unspoken gravitas. People sought him out rather than vice versa. They listened not because he spoke loudly but because he knew what he was talking about.

His system was the most advanced, the most profitable, and the most professionally run. Everyone knew it, even Alan Woods, though he refused to say so.

ROB REITZEN

GOOD MORNING, GOOD MORNING. I HAVE A TRADE FOR YOU. I HAVE A TRADE FOR YOU.

Reitzen's sleep was interrupted by a robotic voice emanating from his computer.

GO LONG S&P500. GO LONG S&P500.

The voice was Klaatu, Reitzen's newest piece of homemade gadgetry. He'd patched together some software to monitor stock prices, scraping the market for buying opportunities. For reasons that made sense only to his closest friends, he had connected it to a Texas Instruments speech synthesizer. It was like having Stephen Hawking for an alarm clock. The idea was eventually to have a fully automated trader working day and night so Reitzen could focus on more important matters, such as goofing around or dreaming up new poker strategies.

Like many of his other schemes, however, Klaatu turned out to be more entertaining than practical. It was named after the alien messenger in the film *The Day the Earth Stood Still.* Originally, he had wired the machine to his telephone and had it make daily calls to his stockbroker in Chicago, until the guy had begged him to stop.

When Klaatu fell silent, Reitzen forced his eyes open, propping himself up on his elbows. His girlfriend, Kathryn, lay next to him in bed, still asleep. Outside, the morning traffic was grinding along

Santa Monica Boulevard. The 1990s had just begun. A police siren screamed somewhere nearby. It wasn't the most glamorous neighborhood, deep in the smog and noise of West Hollywood, but Reitzen didn't plan on living there forever. He liked to let his imagination soar, looking up at the hillside mansions high above the city. He had a dozen madcap gambling ideas. Any one of them could get him there, up among the infinity pools and celebrities, in the rarified air of real success.

Kathryn, a slender brunette, had a similar vision. They had met at a poker table in the card room where she was working as a dealer. Reitzen wasn't like the other sharks, she noticed. He had a lighthearted, bumbling demeanor, blaming his slow play on dyslexia, saying he struggled to read the cards. Whenever he won a pot, he shrugged. "I just had a feeling." His opponents didn't know what to make of him. Yet within a couple of years, he and his Nebraskan partner, Darrell Miers, had become two of the best lowball poker players in California, which made them two of the best lowball players on the planet, since the upside-down version of the game wasn't popular anywhere else.

Reitzen and his unconventional mind grew on Kathryn. His first marriage, to a Las Vegas blackjack dealer, had just ended amicably enough after the birth of a baby daughter. The advantage gambler's life, seesawing between the flush of victory and the hardship required to achieve it, wasn't for everyone. But Kathryn, newly in love, saw only potential.

She called Reitzen "my bobo," short for Bobby. When his computers generated new poker strategies, he tested them against her experience as a dealer. She even tolerated early-morning wake-up calls by Klaatu. As she began to stir, she found Reitzen sitting bolt upright in bed. "I think I've solved the unequal contest," he announced.

Reitzen was obsessed with poker. Even in relatively simple variants, like lowball, the complexity seemed to stretch off into infinity, multiplying into fractal patterns that mesmerized him. At the same time, it *was* possible to gain a genuine advantage. In the late 1980s, the game was mired in its "primordial soup phase," as the poker professional and statistician Nate Silver described it. The top players relied on gut feelings and experience. Virtually none of them knew the percentage odds of a specific set of cards being strong enough to claim the pot, let alone the best betting strategy for optimizing the return from that hand.

Reitzen had already glimpsed the future by using his lowball simulator. He knew from the computer's calculations that professionals were making obvious mistakes, which made them beatable. However, he and Miers were still battling to turn their advantage into cash. On a good day they might make $10,000 at the high-stakes tables in the Bicycle Club, the LA card room they frequented. Or they could just as easily lose that much.

One problem was variance, otherwise known as luck. A shuffled deck delivered good and bad hands at random. Even the most talented players struggled to overcome a lousy run of cards. Earning enough to eat was basically a coin toss, even for the 1 percent good enough to do it full-time. In Hong Kong, Bill Benter could overcome randomness with scale, firing off a thousand bets on a single horse race to get closer to the expected value of his advantage. But in poker, it took much longer to see results. Playing a thousand hands might take two solid days.

Another problem: Not all poker was alike. California's incomprehensible gambling regulations were constantly shifting. Throughout the 1980s, card room operators won a series of lawsuits striking down restrictions on different versions of the game. In 1991, state legislators finally eliminated one of the last remaining prohibitions on something called stud-horse poker, a variant so outdated that no one could remember the rules. The move was a legal milestone of sorts, effectively decriminalizing poker across California.

Lowball fell out of favor and was replaced by more modern and exciting games: pai gow, a Chinese spin-off played with dominolike tiles; and Texas Hold'em, the most popular incarnation of all.

Each presented different statistical challenges, and Reitzen hungered to solve them all. Nothing less than mathematical purity would do. Someone gave him a book on poker by Dr. Norman Zadeh, a visiting professor at various top-tier universities and the son of a famous mathematician (his father had introduced the world to an important modeling concept known as "fuzzy logic"). "There's quite a bit of math in there," Miers said when he saw the book. "I'm saying this as a friend. It might go over your head."

Reitzen read Zadeh's work over and over, thumbing through the pages until the edges frayed and the equations started to make sense. After wearing out several copies, he felt confident enough to contact the author. They arranged to meet at a singles dance in LA—Zadeh's choice of venue. Reitzen wanted Zadeh to join his team as a consultant and help computerize the principles in the book. He tried flattery, telling the mathematician how important his work was. But Zadeh's attention was obviously elsewhere.

Zadeh, bald and bespectacled, was fixated on women. He'd developed a rating system to score their appeal when he was just four. To his lifelong frustration, he found numbers significantly easier to understand than the opposite sex. At their next meeting, Reitzen took Kathryn along. Her youth and attractiveness had the desired effect. Zadeh was besotted. He agreed to work with Reitzen mostly in the hope of seeing her again.

Recruiting Zadeh was a coup. Zadeh treated life's challenges as if they were fieldwork for a dissertation. He used to wear a motorcycle helmet while driving his car, afraid of damaging his most important research tool. He was particularly fascinated by the logistics of competitive play, from backgammon to professional sports.

Game theory, one of his interests, had begun as a rebel branch of mathematics, then spread across the scientific world, revolutionizing economics, biology, philosophy, and politics. It all started with poker. The founder of game theory, John von Neumann, was a polymath who worked on the Manhattan Project, tried to predict the weather, and, in the 1950s, influenced the American doctrine of nuclear deterrence. In between it all, he enjoyed a game of cards.

While playing poker, von Neumann noticed how traditional economics failed to reflect real human behavior. Economic models treated people as if they were Robinson Crusoe, living on a remote island, making self-interested decisions in a vacuum. Poker wasn't like that, and neither was real life. People competed for the same resources. Their decisions affected the behavior of others.

Take a game of rock-paper-scissors, the simplest of contests. If you pick scissors, you should have a one-in-three chance of winning. But if you pull out scissors every time, your opponent will notice and change their strategy to crush your scissors with a rock. You will lose until you change your strategy. This battle of wits is the wellspring of game theory.

Von Neumann sought to understand and improve decisions using mathematical models that could identify the optimal choices. He invented a radically simplified version of poker for the job. "Real life consists of bluffing, of little tactics of deception, of asking yourself: what is the other man going to think I mean to do," he said.

Von Neumann's math quickly gets into Greek alphabet territory, but in essence he played out the various options (high bid, low bid, pass, fold) for a range of situations to find out which led to the most profit. He proved that bluffing was all-important because it confused opponents and forced them into making decisions they could otherwise avoid. The best strategy of all was to bluff regularly, at random intervals, even with the weakest hands. Von Neumann's vision of poker was as much about misdirection as it was about playing the odds.

But his stripped-down model was too basic to be useful to actual poker players—until Zadeh picked up the baton in the 1970s. Zadeh spent six months calculating, by hand, the optimal moves in real poker scenarios. His book *Winning Poker Systems* was full of charts showing players what calls to make in the marginal situations that render poker such a difficult game to predict.

Leaving bluffing aside, what was the weakest hand worth betting on in an eight-player game of draw poker? Zadeh's book had the answer, which was different for each player at the table depending on their position in relation to the dealer. The number of chips in the pot also mattered. A small bet for the chance to win a huge pot was a risk worth taking, even with a mediocre hand.

What about how often to bluff with a nothing hand against four opponents? Zadeh calculated that number, too, to be delivered at random intervals using von Neumann logic. His work was precise and methodical, a world away from the pseudopsychology employed by top poker professionals at the time.

But the study of game theory as it related to poker was still in its infancy in the 1980s. Computers were not yet powerful enough to cut through the complexity of any but the most basic contests. The range of scenarios in games people actually wanted to play—Texas Hold'em, for example—multiplied exponentially. Not only were there millions of possible card combinations, but every player also had to make choices, each of which affected the other players' choices. Game theorists liked to imagine these decisions as branches on a tree, splitting at inflection points into new branches that divided into still more branches, reaching up to a vast canopy of potential futures.

Without seeing all those scenarios, it was nearly impossible to plot the correct path. In rock-paper-scissors or in von Neumann's simplified poker model, the number of branches was small enough to work out by hand. But in Texas Hold'em, with no limit on bet size, the branches grew so numerous that they escaped the boundaries of language and comprehension. There was no easy way to represent the number of variations in a game of multiplayer no-limit Texas Hold'em. Billions or trillions didn't get close; it was greater than the number of atoms in the universe.

Reitzen, though, was nothing if not a dreamer. He began driving up to Zadeh's house in a hillside gated community overlooking Hollywood to pepper the author with questions. Zadeh's young female employees would be milling around (he hired them as assistants in his investment business or to do his shopping—any excuse to be in their company). Reitzen and Zadeh would spend hours discussing the mathematical foundations of Texas Hold'em. Reitzen and his programmer would then go away to run simulations on their computers.

Zadeh's best idea came straight out of the von Neumann playbook. A player should act, he said, as if their opponents were always using good strategy. For instance, if a player two seats down from the dealer bet into the pot, it was safe to assume that they had at least the minimum competitive hand: an ace-9 or better. If they didn't and were making anything less than optimal decisions, they would simply lose faster, so there was no need to compute the possibility. That had the effect of trimming the tree of potential scenarios down to a more manageable size, thus allowing the computers to work their magic.

Reitzen's curiosity was insatiable. He wanted Zadeh to help produce mathematical proofs for semibluffing, bin betting, and sandbagging, all the tricks he'd picked up playing marathon sessions at the Bicycle Club. Sometimes he took his young daughter with him to his programmer's house, where they worked until three in the morning.

It was during that period that Reitzen developed Klaatu and had his morning revelation about a solution to the unequal contest. He jumped out of bed to call Zadeh with the news. The unequal contest was an arcane but important mathematical quandary related to having insufficient information about an opponent's range of cards. It had been on Reitzen's mind for months. But Zadeh didn't seem to care. "That's great," he mumbled.

Zadeh's lack of interest was in part explained by his lack of faith in Reitzen, whom he considered highly intelligent but lacking in formal education. He was also hopelessly in love with Kathryn, who was about to become Reitzen's second wife. Zadeh even tried to change her mind. "If for some reason you need an alternative to Robert, that could be me," he told her. It made no difference.

Reitzen married Kathryn in 1993. She wore a chiffon minidress. He donned a dinner jacket and bow tie, his tousled black hair freed, for once, from the confines of a sports cap. For most of the guests present, it was the first time they'd seen him in a suit. When the party got underway, Reitzen dropped down onto the seat of his pants to break dance, pinwheeling around like a spinning top.

Reitzen's poker research wouldn't have been possible without a new generation of computers, which continued to become smaller, cheaper, and more powerful throughout the early 1990s. However, the fastest processors remained less capable than the average five-year-old at any task that required imagination, such as basic communication. While programming nerds were hard at work trying to prove otherwise, most people still viewed computers as unthinking robots, as mindlessly efficient as a mule pulling a cart.

Chess became the battleground of an era of man-versus-machine rivalry. Computer performance in strategy games was improving steadily, albeit hamstrung by sluggish loading times. In 1991, it took a supercomputer at the Los Alamos National Laboratory five hours to work out how a bishop, rook, and king could defeat a king and two knights. The world's best player, Garry Kasparov, had crushed an early version of IBM's Deep Blue chess system, then a few years old. Afterward, Kasparov was dismissive about his electronic rival's skill. "I was puzzled, because there was no opposition," he said.

Reitzen read the media coverage about the rise of intelligent machines and saw an opportunity to have some fun. He and his friend John "The Duke" Wayne were chess enthusiasts who'd bonded over the game years earlier. It was how they had first met. The Duke had posted a flyer, inviting challenges against "John Wayne, chess champion and arm-wrestling champion." Reitzen had responded, setting the tone for a relationship built on competitive pranks.

Reitzen had been experimenting with chess software for years. It was in some ways a simpler challenge than poker. All the information required in chess was on the board, with no hidden cards or opportunities for misdirection. A chess computer needed only to propose strong moves, then simulate each one to its conclusion to see which worked out best. The number of branches in the tree of potential chess futures was still huge, but Reitzen knew from his poker research that those branches could be cut down to size with a few astute assumptions.

In 1993, he decided to test the strength of his software at the World Open chess tournament in Philadelphia. Reitzen, the Duke, and a suitcase full of computing equipment took a flight together to the City of Brotherly Love. There, the Duke signed up for the tournament in disguise, wearing fake Rastafarian-style dreadlocks and brightly colored clothes. On the entry form, he wrote the name John von Neumann. "As in . . . the father of game theory?" a skeptical official asked. Wayne nodded. The official raised an eyebrow, then put him into the draw.

Reitzen, meanwhile, checked into a hotel suite and powered up the computers. As well as central processing units, he'd brought along a Taft-style wearable device. Though it had originally been used to process blackjack probabilities, Reitzen had modified it to communicate remotely with his chess software. The Duke could input an opponent's moves by entering grid numbers on the board using toe switches in his shoes. Reitzen, hidden nearby, could beam back a countermove to a buzzer concealed in Wayne's pants.

The top prize for the unrated section of the World Open was a few hundred dollars, barely covering their airfare. Darrell Miers had tried to talk Reitzen out of going, telling him he was insane. Their partnership was already low on cash, and that was before Miers injured his back, leaving him unable to play blackjack, their main source of income. Reitzen ignored him. He lived for moments like this.

The 1993 Chess Open began on July 1. The Duke wired himself up, testing the buzzer and the toe switches and putting on a pair of headphones to secure his wig. Reitzen stationed himself in front of a bank of monitors in their hotel room. The two friends looked at each other, Reitzen grinning. This was it—their shot at chess immortality.

The event was held in the conference suite of a sprawling hotel complex. For the most part, the crowd was male, pale, and nearsighted. Its members squinted at the Duke. A square-jawed military veteran, he'd have stood out even without the fake dreadlocks. In the first round he got a bye. In the second round he drew a grand master, Helgi Ólafsson, a former child prodigy from Iceland.

Wayne sat down at a long dining table, where dozens of chessboards were laid out in rows, each with a digital clock to one side. Players had no more than two hours to make their first forty moves, with the total duration of each game limited to six hours. Wayne became increasingly aware of the timer as he carefully lifted and lowered his big toes to signal Ólafsson's moves to Reitzen, then waited for the buzzer to assign a response. It was taking much longer than he had expected.

The minutes passed in awkward silence. Wayne passed the time by staring at the ceiling. But somehow it was working. The rattled Ólafsson made an error. Then, a few moves later, the machine lost radio signal. Wayne waited what seemed like an age for a vibration that never came. With little other choice, he played out the later stages himself. Finally Ólafsson offered a draw and held out his hand. "Von Neumann" had pulled off a remarkable upset, competing on level terms with a world-class player.

"I was sure I was playing a complete patzer," Ólafsson told journalists afterward. "He had no idea about the game, and I even thought he was on drugs. He took way too much time to reply to obvious moves and he was very strange." Von Neumann marched on, to Reitzen's undiluted joy.

In the next two rounds, the coms link failed again. Wayne was delayed so long that he forfeited both games. In between matches, he amused himself by marching into a recreation area where attendees were playing speed chess. He slapped $500 onto the table. "No clock. Three minutes a move," he offered. There were no takers.

In the following days, the Duke won a couple more games, was timed out of others, and began to attract a crowd of curious spectators. Everyone wanted to see the mysterious Rastafarian with the somnolent playing style who had come from nowhere to draw against a grand master. He was on track to win a sizable chunk of the prize money for unrated entrants when a tournament organizer appeared at his table.

There had been some complaints about his play, the man explained. Did he have any identification? When it became clear that Wayne didn't have any, the official said he needed to explain himself to the event director. "I can't," Wayne replied. There was a long pause. "My wife is having a baby." He hurried out, escaping follow-up questions.

Back in their hotel room, Reitzen wasn't ready to end the caper. They'd done enough to deserve a reward, he argued. "Dude—go back!" But the organizers were now so suspicious that when Wayne returned, they insisted that he play another game on the spot to prove he wasn't getting assistance. Wayne refused, accused them of being racist, and stormed out. The brief and inglorious chess career of John von Neumann the Second was over.

Reitzen, at least, was happy. He'd succeeded in raising a middle finger at the chess establishment. He'd also collected what would, with the usual embellishments, turn into one of his better bar stool yarns. And, in a way, he and the Duke did earn a place in chess history. *Inside Chess* magazine gave them top billing in its report a few weeks later. "The Von Neumann Affair Rocks the World Open," screamed the front page, alongside a cartoon of a shadowy dreadlocked figure.

The magazine correctly guessed that Wayne had been receiving instructions remotely from someone using a computer, though it wrongly assumed that he had received them through his headphones. Tournament organizers would only say that a competitor had been denied his share of the unrated prize because of alleged cheating. Decades later, the incident would be recorded as one of the first examples of technological cheating in chess. Reitzen and Wayne's role was never made public.

In the summer of 1993, though, *Inside Chess* could only speculate about the future. "If computers become strong enough to be of genuine assistance to top players," the magazine warned, "then watch out!" A few pages back in the same issue, an advertisement seemed to suggest that a new epoch had already arrived. The Chessbase training program promised expert insight into openings, middle games, endgames, and such exotic delights as hedgehog structures and the Benko gambit. "10 WAYS TO IMPROVE YOUR CHESS USING YOUR PERSONAL COMPUTER! (Requires MS-DOS 2.0 or higher.)"

Chess made for an entertaining diversion, but it would never occupy Reitzen's mind the way poker did. Luckily for him, a new era of high-tech poker was beginning, too.

INTERLUDE

THE AMERICAN WAY TO PLAY

Donald Trump's reign as the casino king of Atlantic City didn't last. Managed by his relatives and assorted cronies, his venues overspent on luxuries that did nothing to improve the bottom line. Using a gilded pan to sweep up cigarette butts, as the cleaners in Trump Castle reportedly did, did not persuade customers to wager more at the craps tables.

Throughout the 2000s, Trump's companies filed for bankruptcy or were taken over, leaving behind unpaid contractors and abandoned boardwalk properties. The future president pulled off a rare business feat: He lost money running casinos. His legacy, however, persisted. Trump was one of the first gambling entrepreneurs, along with Steve Wynn, to tap the booming market for cheap debt. In the 1980s, casinos sold $5 billion worth of junk bonds.

The influx of cash supercharged an industry that had previously been restrained by its association with the criminal underworld. The FBI finally broke the Cosa Nostra's hold on gambling with the 1986 convictions of Chicago overlords Joseph J. Aiuppa and John P. Cerone. At trial, witnesses testified that the Mob had siphoned $87 million from the Teamsters union pension fund to invest in casinos. While that might have sounded like a lot to a jury, it was pocket change compared to what Wall Street's junk bond peddlers could deliver. The Mafia era of Las Vegas was over; the megaresort era had begun.

The house's new owners were legacy corporations—the likes of Hilton, Holiday Inn, Caesars (Eldorado Resorts), and Steve Wynn's Mirage Resorts. They employed hordes of marketing professionals who "successfully repackaged the popular view of gambling, selling it as just another form of recreation by making it appear to be free of either moral of financial worries," wrote the journalist David Cay Johnston. "America Inc. bought out Murder Inc."

A Reagan-era television ad showed off the new face of Las Vegas, a place of horseback rides, golf, and waterslides. Jay Leno made a cameo, reading a newspaper, as did Joan Rivers, perched on a grand piano. "It's the American way to play," the jingle declared as the sun set over the desert and a saxophone soundtrack squealed in the background.

Other states looked on with envy as Nevada and New Jersey raked in millions of dollars from gambling taxes. Residents of Deadwood, South Dakota, where the outlaw Wild Bill Hickok had been shot in the head over a game of poker a century earlier, voted to bring back card games and slot machines in 1989. Legislators in Colorado, Illinois, Iowa, Louisiana, and Mississippi followed soon afterward. Casinos sprang up on tribal lands in Florida, California, and Connecticut that, thanks to Indigenous nation sovereignty, had a degree of immunity from state law.

Legal betting did indeed deliver funds to cash-strapped municipalities—at a cost. Communities that welcomed casino business saw rising bankruptcies, crime, suicide, and divorce, according to the 1999 National Gambling Impact Study. Many of the negative consequences were hidden, since "it is difficult to quantify the emotional damage and its long-term impact on families and their children," the final report's authors warned. ". . . It is currently impossible to obtain even a rough approximation of a true cost-benefit calculation concerning the economic impact of legalized gambling."

In Atlantic City, for example, casinos were supposed to rebuild a city in decline. "Instead, they have transformed it into the place where the South Bronx meets Las Vegas-by-the-sea, where heroin and hookers are readily available and armed robbery is a constant danger," Johnston wrote in the 1990s. To get to the boardwalk, visitors had to drive through blocks of urban decay so severe that buildings reduced to rubble were left to fester as dumping grounds for trash and playgrounds for bored teens. Unemployment remained high. Casino jobs tended to be low paid, unstable, and closed to the minority communities that needed them most.

The same story played out in other municipalities hoping that gambling's silver bullet would solve their economic problems. In 1996, Donald Trump opened a showboat casino in Gary, Indiana, a former steel town plagued by violent crime. "Too many guns, too many drugs, too few jobs," then mayor Thomas Barnes diagnosed. Trump, who flew in by private jet, pledged renewal. "Gary has had some rough times over the years," he said. "This is really the beginning of the end of those rough times." A few years later, the project collapsed in a mire of bankruptcies and lawsuits. Jobs that Trump had promised for the city's majority black residents never materialized. (His lawyers argued that his commitments had not been legally binding.)

Still, no one could deny that the new generation of megaresorts delivered spectacle on a scale the nation had never seen before. Opened in 1989 at a cost of $600 million, Wynn's Mirage in Las Vegas set a new standard. The complex boasted a fifty-foot-tall man-made volcano that periodically spouted flame, a quarter-mile-long pool, and a pair of white Siberian tigers. Other breathtaking follies arrived in the 1990s. An obsidian-black pyramid shot a beam of light ten miles into the desert sky. There was a mock medieval castle with four thousand hotel rooms. Today, the Vegas skyline is a testament not just to vice but to the power of modern American capitalism.

As for Donald Trump, he emerged from his failed casino ventures stronger than ever. While investors in his enterprises lost more than $1.5 billion, he drew millions of dollars in salaries, bonuses, and other perks, such as the ability to shift his personal debts onto his corporations. "Atlantic City fueled a lot of growth for me," he said in May 2016. "The money I took out of there was incredible."

PART

6

THE GARDEN OF FORKING PATHS

Time is forever dividing itself toward innumerable
futures and in one of them I am your enemy.
—Jorge Luis Borges, "The Garden of Forking Paths"

BILL NELSON

The Foley Federal Building and U.S. Courthouse on Las Vegas Boulevard was a drab fortress protected by a concrete grid facade like the bars of a cage. Outside, the Stars and Stripes hung limp under a steely sky. The morning was unusually cold, enough to make a mockery of the row of palm trees leading up to the security checkpoint.

A steady stream of visitors trudged up the steps, some of them wearing gloves and hats to ward off the chill. Among them were attorneys, clerks, reporters, probation officers, social workers, and defendants, a procession of beleaguered souls entering the grinding maw of the American criminal justice system.

Anthony "The Ant" Spilotro had once walked the same path, smirking in handcuffs, ready to bat away another indictment. So, too, had the German-born illusionists Siegfried and Roy on their way to take the oath of US citizenship in one of the building's faded, leak-prone courtrooms. As had Reuben Sturman, America's most prolific pornographer, whose videos of incest and bestiality a Las Vegas jury had found insufficiently shocking to convict him on obscenity charges.

Today, it was Bill Nelson's turn.

The trial of the Computer Group began on January 7, 1992. In the seven years since the FBI's nationwide raids on properties linked to the team, Nelson had never wavered in his defiance of the federal government. In a deposition before prosecutors, he hadn't bothered to hide his disdain. "Oh, come on," he'd said at one point, dismissing his interlocutor's interest in "trivial junk." In response to a leading question, he'd snapped back: "How long have you been beating your wife?"

After being indicted in 1990, Nelson had visited the University of Nevada law library to read up on the relevant statute: the Wire Act, Title 18, United States Code, section 1084. The FBI had long since given up trying to link the Computer Group to organized crime. In fact, the team's defense attorneys had succeeded in striking out taped evidence from intercepted calls between Mafia figures discussing "the Computer," on the grounds that Spilotro and his friends were so infamous that their voices alone might prejudice the trial. The jury would never hear them. Instead, the prosecution had proceeded on the more technical charge of using a telephone to transmit betting information from state to state.

Nelson was dismayed when he read the vague language in the legislation. Apparently, it really was a federal crime to be "engaged in the business of betting or wagering" using a wire communication facility. "Fuck it," he thought. "I'm guilty." His lawyer, however, was hopeful. "It's all political," he said. "They are trying to come up with a way to get out of this case without getting egg on their faces."

Nelson didn't share any of that with Liliana, his wife, nor did he allow himself to contemplate the thought that he might be separated from their adopted daughter, who was still a toddler and couldn't have comprehended what was happening. As far as he was concerned, he'd done nothing wrong. If the feds were going to convict him, at least he could walk through the prison gates with his head held high, knowing he was in the right.

On the first morning of the trial, Nelson set his jaw and walked into the courtroom to find his former teammates in huddles, conferring with their separate legal teams. There was Ivan "Doc" Mindlin, dapper in a blue suit, and Billy Walters, back from Kentucky now that Spilotro was no longer around to shake him down, who looked strung out and angry. The two men were not on speaking terms, their mutual distrust having blossomed into open loathing. Near the back, ten former employees who'd made phone bets for the group congregated with their own attorneys.

Mike Kent, the mastermind behind the computer program and the government's star witness, sat apart. He was the only member of the team who'd agreed to help prosecutors. Nelson avoided his gaze. They hadn't spoken since Kent had revealed that he would be testifying for the state.

Finally, prosecutors occupied the prime real estate in front of the judge, wearing government issue dark suits, led by Jane Shoemaker from the U.S. Attorney's Office. The proceedings began with housekeeping: legalistic squabbles over this or that piece of evidence and how it might be used. The veteran judge dealt with each matter briskly, then summoned the jurors. Shoemaker began the government's case. "The sole purpose of this venture was to profit as much as they could by any means, whether through legal sports books here in Nevada or illegal bookmakers throughout the United States," she explained. "The group was so successful that they became known nationally to those involved in the gambling business, and they were often referred to as 'The Computer Group' or 'The Computer' because they used a computer program to calculate the odds and to determine the amounts of the bets to be made."

She spoke of millions of dollars in profits, front companies, beards, and code names: Cowboy, Piano, and Bones. The Computer Group were not "mere bettors," she concluded ominously. "They engaged in the business of betting and wagering."

The defendants' response, delivered once Shoemaker was done, could be boiled down to two words: "So what?" In his opening, Doc's lawyer told the jury that the group's members were guilty only of winning, something all gamblers tried to do. He called their success a "great American story." Kenneth Hense, an attorney for one of the team's runners, argued that the law had been intended to punish black-market bookmakers, those *accepting* sports wagers. They were the real bad guys, supporting their business with predatory loansharking and enforcing it with violence, he said. "It's really a case of David and Goliath. Mr. Kent, through the computer, and Dr. Mindlin, who was able to set up the organization, was finally able to beat the line. And there is no crime in that."

The prosecution's first and most important witness was Mike

Kent. His testimony, however, served only to reinforce the impression that the Computer Group had been engaged in clever technological wizardry, not a criminal conspiracy. Kent described his time as a Westinghouse computer technician, moving to Vegas, meeting Bill Nelson and, through him, Doc Mindlin. He explained why they had gone through periodic losing spells, even though the software gave them an advantage over the rest of the market.

"So this was a risky venture?" he was asked.

"Oh yes," Kent replied. "It's called gambling."

As the hours dragged on, the government's case looked increasingly bureaucratic and petty. The defense, meanwhile, joked with jurors as if they were old friends. Toward the end of Kent's testimony, an attorney named Tom Pitaro turned to the witness with one last question, evoking the television detective Columbo.

> Pitaro: And one other case that has been burning in my mind and I want to just say. Are the Red Sox going to win in 1992?
>
> Kent: I don't do baseball.
>
> Pitaro: Neither do they.

There were hearty laughs from the jury box. Nelson's lawyer leaned over to Nelson to whisper a confirmation of what everyone in court could see: The prosecution was flailing. Nelson even noticed some of the jurors winking at him.

Special Agent Thomas Noble, the lead investigator, fluffed his lines when he was cross-examined by the defense about wagering logistics such as the line, the spread, lay betting, and the vigorish (the bookmaker's fee, more often simply "the vig"). "I am not a gambling expert," he protested.

There was a telling moment when he was asked to read out a section of the FBI's training manual advising on when to investigate gambling crime. He mumbled a reply, his eyes downcast.

"I can't hear you, Mr. Noble."

"A mere bettor does not qualify," the agent repeated.

Day after day, prosecutors played wiretaps of the Computer Group's members talking about betting, presented spreadsheets showing its betting profits, and called witnesses to testify about bets being made, all in the service of an endeavor that the Bureau's own guidelines said did not warrant investigation. An FBI analyst who had reviewed audio of approximately ten thousand conversations reached the unsurprising conclusion that Kent's team was a "large wagering operation." Yet when he was asked on the stand whether the act of making a bet across state lines was illegal, he didn't know the answer.

Of the Computer Group's most senior members, only Kent agreed to testify. Doc, Walters, and Nelson let their lawyers talk for them. Still, the rift between the founders of America's most successful sports-betting syndicate was clear to everyone in the courtroom.

Doc's lawyer accused Kent of running to the government out of spite. "Michael Kent after a period of time got very angry with Ivan Mindlin," he told jurors. "And what were they angry about? Often happens with friends: Money." Kent, in turn, trashed Doc's own attempts at computer programming as a costly failure.

Kent's system had turned both Doc and Walters into millionaires. But instead of keeping it secret, the evidence showed them sharing it all over town, either for their own benefit or as a favor to friends and associates. The software's picks were valuable precisely because the outside world didn't have access to the same information. That value decreased with every wager made in the same direction, pushing the market to catch up with the computer's more accurate predictions.

Alongside his Mob contacts, Doc had been giving tips to a prominent Vegas businessman, who had passed them on to the president of a local bank. Walters would later call Doc "one of the most conniving people I've met in my life." Doc's suspicions about Walters proved to be correct: He had been front-running all along, making wagers for himself and not reporting them to the team. The Kentuckian would call his own man first before giving the go-ahead to the Computer Group beards.

The whole business made Nelson sick. As he sat there listening to the mounting evidence of betrayal and greed, it occurred to him that he was one of the only members of the syndicate who hadn't broken the gambler's code of silence. Loose lips will kill an advantage stone dead. And sure enough, the Computer Group had engineered its own destruction.

Most shocking of all, Doc found out that Walters had been acting as a confidential informant for the FBI before he had been indicted. He'd tried, unsuccessfully, to use that status to escape prosecution, according to a sworn statement by Special Agent Thomas Noble. In Doc's world, snitching was a mortal sin; his friends from the underworld were apt to deliver a bullet to the brain as punishment. Doc and Walters stared daggers at each other across the courtroom.

To a Las Vegas jury, though, living in a town built on bets, it was the state's case that looked shady. The government had been so determined to get a grip on sports betting that the Internal Revenue Service had run an undercover sting operation in an attempt to ensnare gamblers. The "Marcus Sports Book" had grown from nowhere into one of the largest black-market bookmakers in Vegas, grossing an estimated $2 million a week and welcoming anyone with cash to spend, including the Mob and the Computer Group's beards. Then, one day, it had disappeared. What none of its customers had realized was that it was an IRS front. As part of the same law enforcement strike force, the FBI had known about the ruse, Noble confirmed. When the defense team cried foul, saying its clients had been entrapped, the FBI claimed that the material it had received from Marcus had been lost or destroyed.

In his closing argument, Walters's lawyer painted the whole case as a textbook example of federal overreach. The FBI, he said, "latch on and they're like a dog," and not the nice kind. "These are pitbulls. Right here." He gestured to a point on his leg where an imaginary hound was gnawing away. A few jurors chuckled knowingly.

Another defense attorney went further, comparing prosecutors to the Nazis. "Our society cannot allow tyranny to surface," he argued. "Is that what this country is all about? Educated, good people from the walks of life sitting here because they got a better idea?"

In the end, it took the jury three days to reach a verdict: acquittal on sixty-four counts. It was unable to decide on the remaining charges. "This was just a terrible waste of money," the forewoman told the *Las Vegas Review-Journal* afterward. One of the jurors, a casino security guard, had turned up in court wearing a jacket with dice and cards embroidered on the back. "These guys were betting, and I bet every day," he told reporters.

"Even coming from liberal Las Vegas, the resounding not guilty verdict in the trial illustrates the nation's changing viewpoint towards gambling on ballgames," a *Review-Journal* columnist concluded a few days later. Kent, Walters, and Doc, all smiles for the photographers outside court, buried the hatchet for long enough to go to the Strip for a party at the Horseshoe Casino. The Computer Group, however, was finished.

Bill Nelson didn't feel much like celebrating. He wanted to get as far away from his codefendants as possible. The government had held his passport for years to stop him fleeing the country. Now that he had it back, he decided to take a trip, of the kind he used to make regularly: He booked himself on the next flight to Australia. He had friends there, and the casinos were friendlier than those in Vegas. He didn't know if he could still beat the roulette wheel, but he was itching to try.

ROB REITZEN

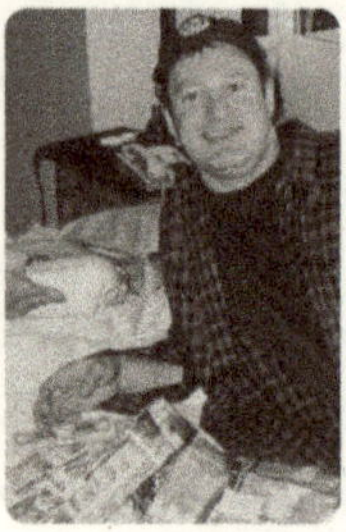

The ad in the newspaper called for a junior programmer. That was about all Fritz Cliver knew when he arrived for his interview at the office in Beverly Hills. A computer science graduate fresh out of college, Cliver was eager to get his career started anywhere he could pull a salary and get some experience.

Things quickly took a surreal turn. There was a modeling agency next door to his potential employer. Angular women in fashionable clothes tottered into and out of the building. Inside, the space was unfurnished, empty apart from a few young guys sitting in front of computers. They were wearing sneakers, Cliver noticed as he walked past in his best church suit. In the fall of 1995, the company, Core Capital Management, was a few months old. But even after having spoken a little with its founder, Rob Reitzen, Cliver wasn't sure what Core actually did.

When the interview formally got started, Reitzen didn't ask about Cliver's qualifications or employment history; instead, he challenged him to solve a series of Mensa-style puzzles. One of them had to do with water displacement: what would happen when rocks that had previously been underwater were placed into a boat. After about twenty minutes of that, Reitzen stuck out his hand and offered Cliver a job on the spot. "You can take off that necktie," he said. "You'll never need it again while you work for me."

Reitzen, Darrell Miers, and a third, silent partner had created Core as a legal home for an increasingly diverse range of gambling activities. The prudent son of a church minister, Miers liked the idea of having an organized structure for payroll and betting funds. Reitzen called it a "think tank." In reality, Core was an advantage gambling corporation. In went a conveyor belt of madcap betting schemes; out came profitable business ventures. At least, that was the idea.

Cliver's first task was to codify the teachings in a book on pai gow poker, by the card counter Stanford Wong, into a computer training program. It would be used to teach Core's players, who were handed bundles of cash, sent from casino to casino, and expected to come back with more. They deployed the full range of Reitzen-approved techniques, from card counting and using wearable computers to tracking the dealer's shuffle. Core also had mathematicians working on financial markets and a horse-racing prediction model. (Unlike Bill Benter's, it barely broke even and was eventually abandoned.)

All of that activity revolved around Reitzen and his unusual brain. "We're in the business of applied mathematics," he told the young scientists he hired to work at Core. His attitude toward risk had been shaped at Vegas blackjack tables and in California poker rooms. What seemed like good luck, he understood, came from putting yourself in enough situations where you had the opportunity to get lucky. Core was intended to maximize those opportunities.

And Reitzen's fortunes had changed, thanks to a torrent of cash from an unexpected quarter. A few years earlier, a friend had contacted him just as Reitzen had been struggling to make a living from poker. Miers was bedridden at the time, recovering from back surgery. The friend had just returned from one of the so-called Indian casinos springing up on California's tribal lands. The casinos had a problem: State regulations prevented them from taking bets from customers. Legally, they could only host games where players bet against one another.

That was an obstacle for games where the house was traditionally the opponent, such as blackjack and pai gow. Reitzen's friend had the solution: With the casino's permission, he adopted the role of banker, taking the other side of wagers himself. In return, he benefited from the advantage normally reserved for the house. By acting last in blackjack, for example, the dealer/banker could expect to win a little over half of all hands played.

The casino, meanwhile, charged a $1 fee for every $100 bet and benefited from having busy gaming tables and happy customers willing to spend their money elsewhere on the premises. After learning of the arrangement, Reitzen signed up to bank a few blackjack games at the Morongo Band of Mission Indians' casino in the hills near Palm Springs. Playing the other side of the game felt strange at first, but it was easier than counting cards and more lucrative. Miers worked out that a single banker's seat was worth as much as $750,000 a year. Best of all, the casinos *wanted* the outside bankers to be there.

One Christmas, a tribal boss called Reitzen to ask if he could send someone over; the tables had lots of customers and no bankers. "We need you," he said. "We'll pay." Miers hashed out a contract between the two parties, and, just like that, he and Reitzen were, indirectly, in the casino business. By the midnineties, such arrangements were Core's biggest source of revenue. The company was getting at least 750 checks in the mail every month from thirteen different casinos. Reitzen recruited friends, friends of friends, and people he met in bars to take banker shifts in return for $200 out of whatever they could win.

Under Miers's careful stewardship, Core Capital established a pension plan and a human resources department and hired accountants. Reitzen, meanwhile, was free to indulge his true passion: obsessing over poker. He set his young employees to work writing software and mathematical models to get him closer to poker nirvana, what game theorists called "Nash equilibrium." This could occur only when a particular strategy was so good that it could never be improved and playing any other way would just mean losing faster. Reitzen bought his team white lab coats because he thought they would look funny. He showed them that the boss was smart, too, by finding errors in the academic papers they read.

In 1995, Reitzen posted on an online poker chat room about a technical problem he'd been working on. "Is anyone else thinking about this?" he asked. To his surprise, someone was. Hein Hundal, then teaching math at Pennsylvania State University, replied with twelve equations proposing the optimal strategy for the final round in Texas Hold'em, the most complicated of all poker games, which was widely believed to be unsolvable. Reitzen suggested a phone call. The two men talked excitedly about John von Neumann, Norman Zadeh's book, the unequal contest, and assumed hand distributions.

"You've got to come out here," Reitzen said. Hundal already had a job lined up at Raytheon, a major defense contractor. For him, poker had never been anything more than an enjoyable challenge. But Reitzen's excitement was contagious. This overgrown teenager with a high school education was grappling with matters that were beyond most of the PhD students Hundal taught. He and his wife flew to LA, where Reitzen met them at the airport. They talked for hours over dinner. When Reitzen first proposed hiring Hundal, the visitor from Pennsylvania laughed. Then Reitzen offered to double his salary.

In the beginning, Hundal thought he was joining a small hedge fund. Core had just been profiled in a glossy magazine about stocks and commodities trading. He discovered the truth on his first day, walking past the entrance of Elite Model Management to find a dozen young men running blackjack and poker simulations on their monitors. His second big surprise came when he played his new colleagues at chess, the breakroom game of choice. Hundal had spent his entire life being the smartest guy in any room he walked into. In high school, he'd never lost a game. At Core, he was the fifth-best competitor. Just ahead of him were a programmer who'd been on the MIT college chess team and Miers, who was a ranked player in his native Nebraska. At the top of the tree were the self-proclaimed "chess champion and arm-wrestling champion" John "The Duke" Wayne and Reitzen himself.

Hundal quickly proved that he was more than just a theorist. He wrote a report showing how Core could exploit the slot machines at the Morongo Casino. Slots were known for having the worst odds around. A slot junkie would typically lose roughly \$5 for every \$100 they spent. But there were still ways to win.

The Morongo slot in question had a huge progressive jackpot, meaning that the top prize got bigger with every spin until someone won. At a certain level, the jackpot got so big that it became profitable to play until you hit it. Hundal computed that there was a 95 percent chance of getting a half-million-dollar payday before their bankroll ran out. All a player had to do was park themselves in front of the machine and pump in money, hour after hour, until the jackpot bell sounded.

It being a Rob Reitzen company, Miers faced an uphill struggle to impose corporate discipline. Reitzen and Wayne ribbed each other constantly. Nothing was off-limits, including the Duke's race and Reitzen's Jewish heritage, until a junior employee told Reitzen that the jokes made him uncomfortable and he agreed to stop. Reitzen made a sport of making dumb wagers: Who invented boysenberry jelly? Can someone tell the difference between tap, mineral, and filtered water? Was Captain Kirk stranded on a moon or an asteroid in a particular episode of *Star Trek*? "Wanna bet?" he'd ask, beaming. His colleagues couldn't resist, even though they knew he was fishing for a sucker.

Cash management was a particular challenge. Reitzen lost $10,000 at the office one day, only to discover that he'd carelessly tossed a wad of bills into the Duke's gym bag. On another occasion, a Core employee accidentally left a fanny pack containing $20,000 in a casino restroom. It was never seen again. The employee was certain that he'd be fired, but Reitzen shrugged it off.

Core was making so much money from sending player-bankers to tribal casinos that Reitzen could finally afford the rock star life he'd always wanted. In 1995, the company grossed $7 million. Reitzen awarded himself a $10,000 monthly salary and a $400,000 bonus. He moved into a house up in Crestwood Hills. Relaxing by the terrace pool, he could see the glittering grid of the LA basin laid out below, planes lining up to land at Los Angeles International Airport, and the dark mass of ocean in the distance.

Reitzen was now so far above the sweat and grind of the city that he looked down on the Getty Center, a newly opened tourist attraction that would become famous for its lofty perch. "I own a mountain," he exaggerated. "That's pretty cool, isn't it?" He hired a private chef to cater his parties and bought a ludicrously expensive pet, a wild African cat called a serval that he had to give away because it kept scratching his daughter.

Not everyone bought into Reitzen's vision. His manic energy

sometimes made him seem fragile, a Walter Mitty figure selling fantasies too implausible to be real. The wives of some of his employees, in particular, viewed him with suspicion. Divorced from Kathryn after just a year of marriage, Reitzen dated a parade of LA beauties, his days of flipping burgers and being ignored by girls a distant memory.

For all his charm, Reitzen remained an oddball with deep insecurities, especially about his appearance. He was never seen in public without a hat, a few wispy tresses escaping from the sides. Whatever was going on under there, he didn't share the details with his employees. There were various rumors: Scars from a car crash? A hair job gone wrong? (Reitzen says that neither is true.) People joked about it behind his back, but to Reitzen it was no laughing matter. When a gust of wind removed his cap, they watched him scramble after it in panic, his hair flapping in the breeze.

Having worked alongside Reitzen for more than a decade, Miers tolerated those quirks, frustrating as they were. Once he visited his partner at the hilltop mansion to find a group of young Core employees goofing around in lab coats. They were testing their latest poker software against a program posted online by University of Alberta researchers, who were leading the academic race to conquer Texas Hold'em. With Hein Hundal's help, Core's system was winning, although there was no real cash at stake. Miers shook his head. "How are you going to monetize this?" he asked.

Reitzen was too busy living to listen. He signed up as a member of the Grand Havana Room, paying $2,000 to join the private club where Arnold Schwarzenegger and Robert De Niro went to puff on Cuban cigars. Michael Keaton and Charlie Sheen went to his parties in the hilltop house and listened to him play his new grand piano. He befriended Emilio Estevez, best known for *Young Guns* and *The Breakfast Club*, and took the actor on gambling trips to Vegas to show him the secrets of advantage play. He met producers who told him that his life should be a movie. Naturally, he agreed.

Darrell Miers first realized how badly Reitzen craved fame in 1997 when a Core employee showed him a copy of a magazine called *New Times Los Angeles*. Staring him in the face was a profile of his partner, chronicling his rise from behind the counter at Hamburger Henry's to the upper echelons of financial success. The article was full of familiar Reitzen escapades, many of which Miers had been involved in and none that he had agreed could be made public. Reitzen had told the author things they *never* talked openly about: the wearable computers, the poker software, being arrested by the Las Vegas Police Department.

Miers was shocked that his partner had lifted the advantage gambler's veil of secrecy. More than that, he was furious that Reitzen had done so without telling him first. Miers was working sixteen-hour days making deals with the casinos. The article made their biggest customers out to be fools. The author, in turn, decided that Reitzen was "a genius but not so smart."

Miers confronted Reitzen at Core headquarters. "We have thirteen casinos mailing us checks," he said. "You are going out and saying they are not as smart as they think they are?" A few weeks later, another article appeared, this time in *Esquire*. Once again, Reitzen was the star. He'd taken a journalist on a card-counting trip to Vegas with his new buddy Emilio Estevez. The story claimed that they had made a million dollars in one night with the help of several other Core employees, including John Wayne, using a technique called "The Hammer," which Miers had never heard of.

Under the title "Fleecing Las Vegas," Reitzen was shown using fake names, cursing a pit boss ("Fuck them"), detailing the weak points in casino shuffling techniques, and calling women bimbos. "A big part of any winning strategy is concealment," he told the writer, who then revealed those same strategies to anyone with a few dollars to buy a magazine. This time Miers had known about the article beforehand but was shocked by the content. Reitzen swore that he'd been promised anonymity, but Miers had finally had enough.

He went to see the silent third partner who owned a minority stake in Core and bought his share for cash. It was enough to give him control of the company. Ready for a fight, he lawyered up. Reitzen moved first, filing a lawsuit in July 1997 that accused his partner of trying to squeeze him out. Miers countersued alleging that Reitzen had "seen fit to glorify himself by unmanaged and reckless self promotion" at the expense of their business. He accused Reitzen of drunkenly breaking into Core's offices at 4:00 a.m. to rifle through files. Reitzen denied it and accused Miers of padlocking the cabinets to keep him out. Miers filed a statement with the court complaining about the damage caused by "Rob's misguided and pitiful quest for media recognition."

Core's fifty-odd employees were stuck in the middle, forced to pick sides like the children of parents going through a divorce. They could hear loud arguments from behind closed doors. Miers and Reitzen separately approached staff members to ask which side they would take after the inevitable split.

Eventually, their attorneys negotiated a clean break. Miers got the player-banker operation, the most profitable part of the business. Reitzen got the rest. His first corporate venture had been smashed into pieces. So had his friendship with Miers. The burly Nebraskan had been a steadfast presence at Reitzen's side for fifteen years. They'd lived together, gone on vacation together, bailed each other out when times were tough. They'd been as close as brothers. They parted ways at the stroke of a lawyer's pen as enemies.

Core's employees had to choose which founder to follow. Among the dozen or so in Reitzen's camp was Hein Hundal, the company's in-house mathematician and leading Texas Hold'em expert. Reitzen's yearning to solve poker was as strong as ever. He'd climbed to impossible heights, achieved the kind of lifestyle—the status, romance, wealth—he could hardly have imagined when he had first thumbed through a copy of *Playing Blackjack as a Business.* Nevertheless, he still felt sure that he, more than anyone else, had the right stuff to scale poker's Olympian summit and steal its sacred flame. He remembered Steve McQueen's unblinking blue eyes in *The Cincinnati Kid,* staring down his opponents across the table.

Darrell Miers could go back to chasing deals with casinos if he wanted to. Reitzen didn't need him.

BILL BENTER

The agreement that put Hong Kong into British hands was signed at cannon point. The Royal Navy, anxious to protect the profitable trade in opium, blasted away Chinese resistance, took the island by force, then secured the surrounding territory with a ninety-nine-year lease beginning in 1898. As the decades rolled by, Hong Kong grew from a fishing village to a trading post to a futuristic metropolis. The British Empire crumbled. China under Communism transformed itself into an industrial powerhouse, lifting hundreds of millions of people out of poverty. The two nations agreed that British rule would end at midnight on July 1, 1997.

The effect on Hong Kong was similar to that of a giant doomsday clock looming over the city, seconds ticking away toward—what? No one was sure. Something unfamiliar, certainly. Residents awaited their fate with a combination of resignation, trepidation, and nervous excitement. Some fled to the United Kingdom or Canada as China's leaders tried to reassure the world that the colony's distinctive culture and economy would be in safe hands.

"Dances will continue to be danced and horses will continue to race," said Deng Xiaoping, who led the country's negotiations with the United Kingdom through the 1980s. But Deng was a comparative liberal in the Chinese Communist Party, a wily, chain-smoking pragmatist among stern authoritarians. And by the time British rule was due to end, he was dead, having passed away in February 1997, leaving less tolerant officials in charge.

Anxiety about Communist rule veered into paranoia. There were rumors of tanks massing on the border. Pager companies were reported to be censoring messages containing insults about Chinese people lest they offend the new regime. Messages calling Chinese premier Li Peng "a turtle's egg" (a grave insult) were blocked by carriers.

Bill Benter, however, was relaxed. He was no fan of the old system, dominated by British military types who got misty eyed reminiscing about the glory days of the empire. He listened to his expat friends debate the merits of leaving but never seriously considered it himself. He had few assets in Hong Kong. He rented his apartment. If everything ended on July 1, he could walk away happy.

Besides, he was in the middle of his best-ever season. His algorithm now included more than seventy variables tied to a horse's performance, factors the rest of the betting market didn't even know how to look for, let alone quantify. His syndicate was up tens of millions of dollars, so much that the figures began to lose meaning. Benter's staff lost US $6 million one month because they didn't get around to cashing the winning tickets within the Jockey Club's sixty-day deadline. Benter wasn't even mad. It was like a surreal joke. In any case, the unclaimed funds were donated to charity, as dictated by club policy.

As the handover approached, news about China was pushed off the front pages by a story from the racetrack: No one had won the Triple Trio for several weeks. The long-shot prize was reserved for a bettor who could pick the top three finishers in three selected races out of more than 10 million combinations. When it went unclaimed, the Triple Trio pool rolled over like a lottery jackpot. In June 1997, it had ballooned to HK $450 million and was expected to reach HK $700 million (around US $90 million). It was said to be the biggest prize in the history of horse racing.

Perhaps residents of the race-mad city saw the last meeting of the season as a final flourish to mark the end of the wild excesses of the colonial era. A few probably suspected that the Communists would break their word and ban gambling as they had done on the mainland. Whatever the reason, Benter had his eye on the winner's pot, which would go to charity if left unclaimed. It would represent not only a massive windfall but a validation of all that he and his team had achieved.

But in the run-up to the season finale, the Hong Kong Jockey Club unexpectedly disconnected his customer input terminals, the machines that allowed him to bet directly from his office. Officials gave no explanation beyond a curt reminder that remote betting was a privilege, bestowed at their discretion. It was an ominous move, Benter thought. He wondered if his winning run was testing the club's tolerance for computer syndicates. His team would have to use the Telebet phone service instead.

Then, on June 14, the day before the last event in the racing calendar, one of Benter's team called the Jockey Club to check their account balances. "Your account has been suspended" was the operator's reply. The news spread swiftly around the computer betting community. A total of nineteen accounts had been closed, all belonging to either Bill Benter or Alan Woods. While the club didn't publicly identify the account holders, it released a statement the next day saying that it had acted to "protect the interests of the general betting public."

Some of the gamblers were furious. Bob Moore, the pill-popping New Zealander, agitated for legal action. Benter, though, could see the logic behind the decision. The Triple Trio jackpot was normally a marketing opportunity. The club could wheel out Mr. Chau the cab-driver for a photo op with his giant check. The betting public would feel the warm glow of success and rush back to the track when they next had the chance, hoping to emulate him. The record-breaking $90 million Triple Trio of June 15, 1997, was likely to make headlines around the world. How would it look if the winner was an American, or an Australian, who'd used computers to secretly skim millions of dollars from the pools? How would Hong Kong's citizens react if they found out that their betting dollars had ended up as prizes for Benter and Woods, not just once or twice but over and over, hundreds of times each week, thousands of times each year?

In the end, no one managed to pull off the Triple Trio and the jackpot was shared among hundreds of punters who correctly picked the top finishers in two of the three races. Benter could only hope that another such opportunity would arise.

The United Kingdom's dominion over Hong Kong ended as it had begun, with a fusillade of deafening explosions; not cannon this time but fireworks, twenty tons of them, detonated over Victoria Harbor as soldiers paraded past Prince Charles, who saluted their departure. "We said we'd go, and go on time," said the ITN anchor in the clipped accent distinctive to British newsreaders. "But we never said we'd go quietly."

The next morning, Chinese troops arrived, riding armored personnel carriers and waving gloved hands in perfect unison. They were greeted by dancing dragon puppets and people brandishing five-star red flags. There were scattered pro-democracy protests, but no one stopped them. It was a day much like any other in the melting pot city. If Benter hadn't been watching television, he wouldn't have noticed the change of government.

Something had shifted, though. Benter could feel it. He returned, as usual, to Las Vegas to spend the summer break plotting his next move. He'd sent a letter to the Hong Kong Jockey Club expressing his shock and dismay over his treatment but had never received a response. All officials would say over the phone was that the accounts were closed "by order of the stewards." Benter carefully reviewed the language in the club's public statements. Nowhere did they say that he and his computers were prohibited from betting.

That summer in Nevada, he came up with a solution. It would require a lot of planning, additional manpower, and some extra risk, but it would allow him to stay in business. The answer lay in the offtrack betting shops located in every Hong Kong neighborhood. Anyone could walk in and put a bet down with some cash or a voucher—no account required and no way to trace winning slips back to Benter.

In September, he was back in Hong Kong. He brought over friends from Vegas and hired some Filipinos to boost the team's numbers. The night before the first race of the new season, some of them checked into a hotel close to a betting outlet in North Point.

Benter's employees arrived lugging a fifty-pound printer. It had taken him weeks of testing to find the right model; most ran too hot and wrecked the thermal paper of the betting slips.

On the morning of the race, the team connected their laptops to Benter's office using the hotel modem, testing the dial-up until they heard the grinding, rattling beeps that indicated a successful connection. More employees arrived with stacks of unmarked betting tickets. They hung a DO NOT DISTURB sign on the hotel room door. Fifteen minutes before the starting pistol, Benter's office transmitted the first rounds of bets to the laptops, up to a hundred at a time. The team in the hotel loaded betting slips into the printing tray, ready to be marked automatically in the boxes representing the algorithm's choices.

As the printer began churning out completed tickets, they grabbed them by the fistful and hustled over to the betting shop. There, under the blue logo of the Jockey Club, locals squatted outside, smoking, chatting, and reading the racing papers. Benter's employees hurried past them and the tellers behind glass barriers, heading straight for the electronic betting machines lined up against the wall. After inserting a voucher with cash credit, they fed in betting tickets as fast as they were physically able to, making sure to pocket the dozens of receipts that emerged. Then it was back to the hotel room to sort out which tickets were winners and dump the rest into the trash.

Benter had teams doing the same thing simultaneously in two additional locations. *God, this is hard work*, he thought to himself at the end of the first day. It took dozens of people to move the printers and computers around the city, then hit the betting shops in sufficient volume for the computer's statistical advantage to pay off.

Benter was particularly worried about criminal gangs tailing his workers and stealing the cash vouchers, some of which were worth as much as US $1 million. So he switched locations every week and took to joining his employees in the hotels whenever he could. Over time, he found that the computer's advantage was still there. He could still make money.

A cloud settled over the small community of computer bettors, cast out from their sacred places—Happy Valley and Sha Tin—into the wilderness of urban Hong Kong. Even the Wan Chai bar scene seemed subdued. Bob Moore, always erratic, spiraled into depression and rage, telling friends that he couldn't leave home without taking MDMA. He attempted suicide, taking thirty pills and texting his girlfriend to say goodbye, surviving only after being taken to the hospital, raving, tied to a stretcher.

Then, on October 17, he was found dead at his house from an apparent overdose. The man the press had once called "the God of Horses" had died penniless. Ostracized by the computer teams, he'd wasted millions on gut-feeling wagers, the exact opposite of the strategy he'd worked on with Benter and Woods. "It just proves that you can't win off horse racing," a friend told the *South China Morning Post.*

The gambler's hex—publicity—seemed to have struck again. Next, Hong Kong's tax authority began an investigation into the Alan Woods syndicate. Racetrack winnings had always been exempt from taxation under British law, but the territory had new rulers now. The syndicates looked more like corporations than individuals betting for fun, and the government was reviewing whether to treat them as such.

Faced with a potential bill for years of racing profits, Woods fled to Manila in the Philippines. Benter stayed, with yet another potential crisis to worry about. By the year 2000, the threat of a tax probe had passed, but he was drained and restless. He'd done nothing but bet on horses for the past sixteen years. Did he really want to spend the rest of his days doing the same thing?

Now in his forties, he started to think about his purpose in life. He'd spent his career searching for an advantage, eventually finding one that had made him rich beyond the wildest dreams of his twenty-two-year-old self, selling Slurpees at a Vegas 7-Eleven for three bucks an hour. He should have been satisfied. But he wasn't.

If things didn't change, he decided, he would cash in his chips and move back to the States.

PART 7

PLAYING GOD

I am convinced that *He* [God] does not play dice.
—Albert Einstein

PART

—Albert Einstein

ROB REITZEN

Reitzen's time in the spotlight was both calamitous and brief. He'd imagined the magazine profiles propelling him to fame as a gambler extraordinaire. He was talking to Hollywood contacts about a movie deal for his life story, to be called *Card Counters*. Perhaps he would make a TV informercial about how to beat casinos at their own game. Instead, the articles had only succeeded in ending his fifteen-year partnership with Darrell Miers. He retreated to his hilltop redoubt, wishing he'd heeded the words of Ed Thorp, the father of card counting. Whether in business or gambling, if you have something special, Thorp had written, "you might want to keep it secret."

The debacle did bring one lasting benefit, though: Reitzen's half brother, Bill Arnold, saw the "Fleecing Las Vegas" piece in *Esquire*. The two had never properly met, although they knew of each other's existence. Reitzen was away in San Francisco when he got a call from the LA house saying that there was a man at the gate claiming to be his brother. "Let him in," Reitzen said and instructed his private chef to cater to Arnold's needs until his return.

Reitzen was always quick to welcome people into his life, despite Thorp's warning and the advantage gambler's ingrained suspicion of outsiders. "Rob's the biggest sucker in the world," his pal John Wayne said. "He'll do anything for people." Whether it was the keys to his Bentley or thousands of dollars in cash to risk at the blackjack table, Reitzen gave readily, and friends worried about him being ripped off.

As it turned out, he had plenty in common with his long-lost sibling. They both liked girls and guns (friends say that Reitzen was known to get his pistol out at parties; Reitzen insists that would have happened only unloaded, with the safety on). Arnold had served in the navy and was at that moment working for their biological father, William Arnold Sr., the rocket scientist who'd walked out on Reitzen when he was small. The brothers bonded over fine wine, gourmet cooking, and the blockbuster view from Reitzen's living room.

Arnold knew next to nothing about gambling, but he was looking for a career change, so Reitzen offered him a job. After the breakup with Miers in 1997, the two decided to go into business together. Arnold, with his military discipline, could become the pragmatic counterpart that Reitzen had always needed. And Reitzen was more convinced than ever that he knew where his future lay.

In 1998, Matt Damon starred in the hit film *Rounders*, which was steeped in the subculture of professional poker, specifically Texas Hold'em, "the Cadillac of poker," as Damon's character put it. "The only pure game left." The movie spurred a surge of interest in a variant that had overtaken all others as the discerning gambler's choice. Relatively simple to learn, Texas Hold'em offers unbeatable drama by breaking the action down into stages, increasing the stakes until a climactic showdown.

First, players are dealt two "hole" cards, which they show to no one, followed by a first round of bets, calls, or folds, based on the strength of those cards. Next, three cards are dealt face up for anyone to use in combination with their hole cards. This stage, "the flop," can change everything, requiring another round of bets. Someone with a strong pair at the start can suddenly find themselves in trouble at the flop if a higher-ranked hand appears.

A fourth face-up card, "the turn," precedes another opportunity to bet before the final face-up card, "the river," and a final round of wagers. Players make the best five-card hand they can from any combination of community cards and their own. At each stage, they need to recalculate the shifting odds and scrutinize how their opponents respond to the flop, the turn, and the river.

Part of the game's appeal comes from the way it seems to distill the Darwinian essence of human interaction into a simple contest.

Rich players often get richer. They can use their pile of chips to bully the rest—unless they take too many risks; then they can lose it all. A player can play the right way, make all the right moves, and still go bust if bad luck comes along to bite them in the ass.

Matt Damon himself was caught out by Texas Hold'em's habit of delivering shocks. While promoting *Rounders*, he entered a poker tournament in Las Vegas. With a pair of kings in the hole, he confidently pushed $6,000 into the pot. The deal, though, handed a pair of aces to his opponent, two-time World Series of Poker winner Doyle Brunson, and Damon was out. "That was one of the biggest thrills of my life," he gushed afterward.

A whole genre of books and countless consulting businesses emerged to mine the lessons of Texas Hold'em. As in real life, success required assertive communication, evidence-based deduction, flexibility, guile, and calmness under pressure. Those same qualities made the game exceptionally hard to analyze, even with the benefit of a computer.

But by the mid- to late 1990s, researchers were finally building software models capable of strategic thinking in games against people. In 1994, the University of Alberta's Chinook checkers program surpassed the world champion, a deeply religious man. At one point, a journalist from a Christian newspaper approached its programmer to ask, "Are you the devil?" IBM's ominous-looking black cabinet, known to the world as Deep Blue, conquered chess grand master Garry Kasparov in 1997.

Poker, the most human of games, remained the ultimate test of machine intelligence. In 1998, Alberta academics complained that their most advanced poker robot, Loki, struggled with the unpredictability of real opponents and was vulnerable to bluffing. "Developing Loki seems to be a cumulative process. We improve one component of the program until it becomes apparent that another aspect is the performance bottleneck."

Loki could barely compete in a low-stakes casino game, and it was a long way from being a match for the likes of Doyle Brunson. It would be another seven years before university researchers could replicate a winning strategy in two-player (heads-up) Texas Hold'em and another eleven years in a multiplayer contest.

Reitzen, however, was confident that he was closer to a solution than the eggheads at IBM and Alberta. He'd proven he could make money from poker tech a decade before with the buzzing, wearable lowball computer. He could remember going on card-counting trips with Darrell Miers in the days before Core, lying on a hotel bed somewhere in Canada, bugging his roommate at one in the morning to listen to his latest musings on the unequal contest. It was, Reitzen believed, only a matter of time before his efforts would pay off.

Soon after he reunited with his half brother, Reitzen's doorbell rang. He opened it to find a petite Chinese woman standing on his doorstep wearing white jeans, spray-on tight. She was so slight, with a cascade of salon-styled hair, it looked as if a strong wind might blow her off the hillside down into Bel-Air. Her name was Lisa. A friend had told her about Reitzen's gambling business, she explained in uncertain English, and she was looking for work.

Arnold, who was single, pushed past him to invite her inside. Soon they were dating, and Lisa was learning the skills needed to join Reitzen's gambling team. His mathematicians had already calculated the optimal opening strategy for two-player poker and were working on game theory solutions for the later stages of the game. Lisa memorized the openings and logged hours on Reitzen's training software, which could tell her when she made mistakes and suggest a more statistically sound approach. She went to sleep dreaming about busted flushes and bottom pairs, then went back the next day for more.

Lisa emerged from her schooling a ruthless poker machine. The daughter of a government scientist, she'd been an engineer in China. Game theory poker worked best in a two-player heads-up game (more than two players tended to snarl the math). In card rooms and casinos, her opponents, mostly men, would see a minuscule Asian woman opposite them and try to bully her with aggressive bluffs and calls. She would grind them into dust under her four-inch heels. In no time, she became the most profitable player on Reitzen's team. Arnold was smitten.

Meanwhile, Reitzen's scientists continued their assault on Texas Hold'em. Hein Hundal, the Pennsylvania academic, filed patents with

Reitzen for the tools they used to cut through the game's Gordian knot of complexity. They developed a "multidimensional model" and an engine that could simulate intelligent play by opponents. Hundal spent his days on "stochastic gradient descent techniques" and "no-man's-land approximate solutions." It was the kind of arcana that few people on the planet could comprehend. It amounted to probably the most advanced and best funded poker research happening anywhere, led by a dyslexic prankster with a high school education who wouldn't be seen in public without a baseball cap on.

Reitzen's singular innovation was to take John von Neumann's dense algorithms and translate them into actions that virtually anyone could follow. Imagine a heads-up game, for example. You have an ace and a 4. The three table cards are a king, a 10, and a 4. You have a weak pair at the flop. Your opponent raises. What should you do? Reitzen's training software knew the answer.

He called one of his programs "The Noodler" because of the way countless strands of probability tangled together in it. All that was required of users was hard work and a willingness to absorb lessons. Experience could be, if anything, a hindrance, since players had to unlearn their suboptimal habits.

One morning in 2001, Reitzen approached Hundal with an idea. "How many turn situations are there?" he asked, referring to the different combinations of cards, moves, and scenarios in the middle stages of Texas Hold'em. There were an awful lot of them. It took Hundal about two hours of computer time to churn through all the possible futures stemming from just one such situation. "Why don't we just solve them all? How long would that take?" asked Reitzen.

Hundal thought for a moment. "That would take roughly a thousand years for a single computer," he estimated.

"Well, then," Reitzen said. "We'd better get started."

Like Reitzen, Hundal believed they had a head start on the competition. He'd written his first poker program in the late 1980s on a Commodore 64. Now he decided they would need at least thirty computers, the fastest models available in 2001. And they would have to run simulations 24/7. Arnold set them up in a house in Florida, filling an entire room with thrumming machines. His electricity bill was so large that local cops came out to check that he wasn't running a cannabis farm.

Reitzen's poker project might have gone the way of Klaatu, the talking robot investor, had it happened at any other moment. By pure blind luck, his timing was perfect.

In 2003, Chris Moneymaker, an unheralded accountant from Atlanta, Georgia, won the World Series of Poker and changed the course of poker history. The man with the too-perfect name entered the tournament by paying $40 to join a satellite qualifier hosted by PokerStars, one of the new internet card rooms. He walked away from the final table at Binion's Horseshoe in Las Vegas with $2.5 million in his pocket.

Moneymaker, who was working part-time at a restaurant at the time, had been playing online poker for only three years. "If I can win it, anybody can," he said. His victory captured the imagination of millions of people who would never have considered going to the Bicycle Club or playing a cash game in a Vegas casino. Online poker was faster, simpler, and just as exciting. There were no choking clouds of cigarette smoke, no muggers waiting in the parking lot. Enthusiasts could play after work, while their kids were asleep.

The following year, three times as many competitors entered the World Series of Poker through the online portal. Digital poker had existed in rudimentary form for at least a decade. Suddenly it was big business. The world's largest online gaming company bought ParadisePoker.com for $298 million in 2004. The company behind PartyPoker.com was listed on the London Stock Exchange, giving the business a market value of $8.5 billion.

Those profiting from the boom were only too happy to propagate the myth that anyone could make a fortune by playing online poker. "It's the last American gold rush," said Norman Chad, a sportswriter who provided commentary for ESPN's live poker coverage. And no one seemed particularly concerned that online poker was still technically illegal in the United States, thanks to the same federal laws that had landed Bill Nelson and the Computer Group in a Las Vegas courtroom. Legal experts advised that the Justice Department was more interested in terrorism and drugs than people playing cards.

Happily for Reitzen, online tables were ideal for testing game theory. Without seeing an opponent's face, the only clues came from bets, or the lack of them, which was all Reitzen and other von Neumann disciples cared about. Mathematical poker, like online poker, was about numbers, not sweaty brows or twitching eyes.

Before the digital era, Lisa, the strongest player in the Reitzen stable, could manage twenty-five or thirty hands per hour in a bricks-and-mortar casino or card room. Online, without chips to handle or a dealer shuffling and distributing cards, she could burn through two hundred hands an hour, sometimes playing as many as ten tables at once. She once endured a hundred straight days in front of the computer, crushing all challengers in ten-hour shifts. When she had first moved to the United States from China, she'd had $300 to her name. Working for Reitzen, she could gross a million dollars a year.

Lisa was a prodigy, but the whole point of Reitzen's system was that virtually anyone could use it. When testing new players, he would reach out and hold their fingertips. If they felt too cool, that suggested constricted blood flow, a sign of stress. Stress might make a person abandon their training and go "on tilt," in poker jargon, making reckless, emotional decisions.

Reitzen briefly dated the barmaid from his local Morton's Steakhouse, a blond Texan named Lary Kennedy. He gave her printouts of the proper opening moves and set her up on the training software. To help her randomize bluffs, in line with von Neumann's teaching, Reitzen made a little wheel of connected disks marked with different strategies. No opponent could predict her next move if she didn't know it herself before spinning the wheel.

Kennedy played on the Full Tilt website as pokergirl_z and quickly built her bankroll. When other users realized how good she was and started avoiding her, she used greggo777, an account set up by her new boyfriend. She also played as SillySal and Mad Haddie. Lisa was redgard1, redgar3, or beatme1. None of their opponents knew who they were losing to, and in the brave new world of online poker, it didn't seem to matter.

Reitzen, recognizing that the game was changing, decided that he needed his own website to host games. With nearly 2 million people logging on every night to buy virtual chips with real dollars, running a platform was a lucrative proposition. The sites charged a small fee known as a rake, generally between 2 and 10 percent of each winning pot. Reitzen and Arnold acquired the digital architecture, programmers, and an office in Costa Rica, where many gambling businesses set up shop to avoid US legal restrictions. They called their site Pokertropolis, giving it a 1920s futurism theme, airships hovering over a grainy New York. "Welcome to Pokertropolis," the home page announced. ". . . Our players enjoy the luxury of sleek performance and easy to use online poker game software . . . all without the long drives, waiting lists and tipping."

The site was functional, if a little clunky compared to more slickly marketed competitors. It struggled to attract enough customers to keep the tables busy. Having live games available at all hours was essential to stop players logging off in frustration. Reitzen solved the problem by deploying the simulated opponents he'd used in his game theory research. With a few tweaks to integrate the software into the platform, those algorithmic stand-ins could review their own and table cards, monitor an adversary's actions, and calculate whether to bet, call, raise, or fold. They were fully automated poker robots, or "bots."

At first, the people using Pokertropolis had no idea they were playing against machines. All they could see was a pixelated table and empty chairs with "Bill123" or "CactusKid" written inside. The main challenge for Reitzen was dialing down the bot skill level so as not to drive away customers. The bots were already too good for all but the most capable players.

In 2004, after three years of nonstop computation in Florida, Hein Hundal finally solved all the moves for the turn in two-player Texas Hold'em. He stored them in a 60-gigabyte database. Thousands of lines of C++ code were absorbed into Reitzen's poker model. His software could now compute a nearly optimal strategy for the majority of situations in a heads-up game. He was curious about what it would be like to play against such a powerful engine.

"How good is it?" he asked Hundal.

"It could probably be beaten," the mathematician replied. "But only by God."

Playing against poker bots was a different kind of game. They would make huge, aggressive bets before the flop, based only on the information contained in the two hole cards. Real players preferred to wait until the community cards appeared to weigh their chances. Bots tended to bluff more. Their actions were confoundingly hard to make sense of. That, of course, was the point.

Once, Lisa was on Pokertropolis when she encountered an anonymous player who was winning more than anyone else on the site. Reitzen could tell it was a professional with an elite skill set. He decided to turn the Pokertropolis bots up to the maximum setting to see what would happen. Man and machine jousted back and forth. Both sides scooped big pots and had a few losses alongside hundreds of seemingly inconsequential skirmishes.

As the hours wore on, it became clear that the professional was bleeding chips. After a few days, the player gave up and logged off. Reitzen and his team noted the significance of the moment with some satisfaction. Their poker robots didn't just think like the beings that had created them; they could *outthink* them, too.

It was the brass ring Reitzen had been reaching toward since the 1980s, when Nevada lawmakers had killed the blackjack computer with the antidevice law. A dazzling future opened up in front of his eyes. All he had to do was walk into it with his brother and his best friend at his side.

Reitzen first sensed that something was wrong with John Wayne when he noticed that the Duke had lost weight. He'd always been wiry and athletic, with a military posture and a megawatt smile. But in 2004, he looked drawn and exhausted. His coffee-colored skin took on a yellow tinge. Reitzen dragged him to a hospital for tests. When he pestered him for the results, Wayne argued that he must have been fine or the hospital would have contacted him already. "You gotta call, man," Reitzen urged.

"You were right," Wayne said, after getting through. "I have liver cancer."

The prognosis was grim. The oncologist told Wayne to get his affairs into order, as he probably had only months to live. Reitzen wouldn't accept that. He couldn't. He found the top liver surgeon in LA and chased him down in the medical center parking lot, begging for a consultation. The surgeon was struck by two things. First, Wayne was obviously close to death. The Duke was so weak that Reitzen had to help him through the door of the clinic. Second, the patient's friend was doing most of the talking, which was unusual. Reitzen had obviously done his own research into various experimental treatments; he fired out questions and data points. The Duke seemed bemused by all the fuss.

As it happened, the doctor agreed that Wayne was a good candidate for a risky surgery to remove the tumorous section of his liver. He was young, otherwise healthy, and not an alcoholic. They had little to lose and plenty to gain by taking a chance. That was exactly what Reitzen, a gambler to his core, wanted to hear.

The Duke began treatment. While it was under way, Reitzen and his brother formed a new company, Momentum Investment Services, to monetize their poker bots. Arnold was responsible for the day-to-day management. At his house in Encino, California, he set up a room with thirty computers, thirty poker machines competing against real opponents twenty-four hours a day, seven days a week. They didn't need food, rest, or wages to win.

To stop them from being identified as robots, a couple of human operators went from screen to screen to type into a chat sidebar if someone tried to talk to them or deal with site administrators if there was a problem. Momentum's technicians wrote code that could automatically move the mouse pointer, click the icon for "raise," and enter a dollar amount, just as a person would.

That gave the bot room a surreal atmosphere. A ring of monitors lit up the gloom in green and brown, the screens showing virtual replicas of felt and wood. Pixelated playing cards appeared and disappeared at a rapid clip as tiny chip stacks rose and shrank and rose again. Amid the frenetic motion, mouse cursors floated around independently, guided by an invisible hand.

This time around, Reitzen was determined to keep his innovation a secret. Software could be copied and stolen, so Arnold banned operators from taking electronic devices into the bot room. A staff member was fired on the spot after he was discovered with a portable hard drive. Employee access to the room was strictly limited.

Just how good were Reitzen's bots? Certainly better than experts in the field thought possible. An NBC News article in 2004 called the commercially available software "woefully inadequate" and "no match for humans." The University of Alberta's lead researcher claimed that a system to read an opponent's cards and respond in real time, as Reitzen's did, was years away. So much for the experts.

Did Momentum's bots play perfectly, in the mathematical sense, as defined by John von Neumann? No—and that continued to bug Reitzen, who was fixated on the holy grail of the Nash equilibrium. The truth was, they didn't need to be perfect. In the post-Moneymaker era, there was so much dumb money flooding into online poker that they didn't need elite performance to win. They just needed to be better than Jim, an attorney from Chicago fooling around after work; criminology student Evan in Maryland, trying to win enough to take his girlfriend to Disneyland; John, a London stockbroker logging on during his lunch break; and millions of others around the world taking their chances in what they thought was the only pure game left.

Wayne responded well to a regimen of anticancer drugs. Reitzen put Momentum's data scientists to work researching the efficacy of alternative treatments, such as naturally occurring antioxidants. When insurers refused to cover surgery, Reitzen threw himself into a fundraising campaign: "The Friends of the Duke." He poured in his own money and tapped his gambling contacts for more. Wally Simmons, the man who'd first spotted Reitzen's potential as a card counter, chipped in $30,000. In the end, they raised the half-million dollars they needed, and the surgery was a resounding success.

With Wayne recovering, Reitzen decided that they needed a change of scenery. On a whim, he and the Duke moved to London to open a new poker bot hub there and oversee another in Spain. For three months, they lived in a suite at the Savoy, the city's most famous hotel, where guests were treated like royalty. Some of the guests actually were. Afterward, they moved into a rental house in upscale Knightsbridge, the fairy-tale London of a Hugh Grant romantic comedy (the star owned a property nearby).

Reitzen and the Duke lived on the upper floors. In the basement, they installed sixteen computers, hiring a dozen operators to work rolling shifts watching the bots day and night. It was draining work, monitoring eight screens each for twelve hours at a time, but Reitzen paid well. He could have halved costs by housing the computers almost anywhere else. They chose London's priciest neighborhood, as Reitzen put it, "for shits and giggles."

He anointed his best friend "the Duke of Knightsbridge." They did their daily shopping together at Harrods, the luxury department store popular with tourists and blue bloods. Reitzen's favorite game was to go to the counter and bellow, in his best American redneck voice, "WHERE CAN I BUY GUNS?"

His daughter, now in her twenties, came over from California to work for him. He paid for her to stay in a flat opposite Harrods. They dined on steak and sushi and clinked cocktails with celebrities in fashionable bars. When it came to money, Reitzen was inclined to spend it while he had it. He knew that winning streaks don't last forever.

Exactly how well Momentum was doing in that period wasn't clear to most of its employees. Only a select few—Reitzen, Arnold, and Wayne—had oversight of all the different elements of the business. They had the Pokertropolis website; the bots; and the trained human professionals, including Lisa and Lary. There were other sidelines, too: an offshore bookmaker for American horse racing and a unit selling gambling tech to casinos. Low-level staff understood not to ask questions about areas outside their purview.

When he wasn't in gregarious party mode, Reitzen could be withdrawn and secretive. For his part, Arnold went around with armed bodyguards for a time. But for all their eccentricities, the brothers were almost absurdly loyal. Their top coders and statisticians made six-figure salaries and received VIP tickets to Disneyland and loans for mortgage down payments. When one of them ran out of things to do, Arnold told him to take some time off and "learn something," on full pay.

Later, Reitzen would say that Momentum had won more than $30 million between 2004 and 2006, the most lucrative period of his career. He could afford to spend thousands of dollars every month on medication for the Duke's cancer, which went into remission. Many of their friends believed that Reitzen's stubborn refusal to accept fate had saved Wayne's life. The Duke believed it, too.

The first signs of a backlash against poker bots came as early as 2004. Users noticed evidence of automation on Reitzen's Pokertropolis website. Robotic opponents sometimes ignored attempts to chat, for one thing. And there were always the same number of players on the site, whether it was the after-dinner peak or five in the morning.

BonusWhores.com, a comparison website, put Pokertropolis on its blacklist of platforms to avoid:

> *They use poker bots (computerized players run by the house) at their tables. Their management denies this, but anyone who plays there will realize that they are not playing against human opponents.*
>
> *For what it's worth, the bots do not appear to have any unfair advantage over the players. However, the fact that they are used and then lied about is cause for rather large concern.*

Reitzen saw things differently. The online critics had no idea how hard he'd worked to build software that could play like a human. Besides, Pokertropolis had never made him any real money. But the growing public awareness of bots looked likely to become a problem for the rest of his empire. Using poker software wasn't illegal unless you took a wearable computer into a Vegas casino, violating Nevada's antidevice law. It was, however, cheating in the opinion of a clear majority of poker fans. The game was designed to be a battle of wits, not a competition to see who had access to the most computing power. Poker players have always hated losing, especially to someone with a hidden advantage. In the days of the Wild West, card sharps were shot. In the digital age, bullets were replaced by all-caps invective.

Online forums filled up with accusations that this or that account was a bot, and many of them were. The first widely available software assistance tools, or "solvers," cost anywhere from $25 for a basic package to $200 for a year's premium membership. Ray E. Bornert II, the creator of one such program, took a lot of flak. "You are a pathetic immoral piece of shit loser," one chat room post read, "completely devoid of morals and ethics."

"I'd rather be unethical than be a victim," Bornert fired back.

Reitzen and his team had to step up their efforts to avoid being identified and barred by poker websites, which prohibited software tools under pressure from users. Momentum began using screen-scraping technology so it didn't have to run the bots from the same computers accessing the website, thus avoiding detection systems. It also coded the mouse cursor automation to move erratically, more like a human hand.

But the paranoia intensified, with amateur vigilantes joining the hunt. A guy using the name Crazy Mike set up a website called destroythebots.com, accusing the big platforms of not doing enough to combat cheats. Crazy Mike had spent years learning the game, only to encounter rookies making money using off-the-shelf software. And he was furious. "I HATE BOTS," he wrote. "They do not need rest and play mathematically correct all the time . . . Bots will destroy the integrity of the game." He posted a list of accounts he suspected, sent the names to website administrators, and encouraged others to do the same. One of the accounts, BeatMe1, belonged to Lisa, the prodigious heads-up poker specialist who was Arnold's girlfriend.

In 2007, Lisa logged on to Full Tilt, as usual, to find a message from the security team. Her account had been locked and more than $70,000 of her winnings confiscated by the website.

> *We have detected an overwhelming amount of evidence indicating illegal bot use.*
>
> *For the protection of our players we have closed your account. All funds remaining in your Full Tilt Poker accounts have been seized in order to compensate the victims of your bot use.*

It was ironic, really. Reitzen oversaw a global network of poker bots spanning Europe, Central America, and California. The antibot crusaders had singled out an account used by a real person, one who happened to play like a machine.

BILL BENTER

The crowd at the Happy Valley Racecourse erupted into a deafening, throaty roar, rumbling up from the foundations of a city that had been built on the thrill of speculation and risk.

"They're off! Heading to Win ridden for speed, likewise Flying Knight . . . Really Lucky third, and Lucky Lucky's getting close on the outside . . ." The Australian commentator's voice reverberated around the stands. On the upper levels, the expat suits laughed and whooped and gulped beer from pitchers. Trackside, the locals cheered on their favorites with an intensity that anywhere else might have been mistaken for rage. They leaned forward, mouths gaping, knuckles white around the rolled-up pages of racing newspapers.

The thoroughbreds responded, surging down the track with huge, gleaming eyes, their legs a dark blur underneath them. The ground shook as they hammered past the horseshoe arch framing the finishing post.

It was November 6, 2001. "Triple Trio fever is back in town," the press declared in the buildup to race night. The whole city was abuzz with news of another massive rollover jackpot. For the last six meetings, no one had picked the top three finishers in the selected races. The Triple Trio pool had swollen to more than HK $100 million, equivalent to around US $13 million.

"If the winner wins the jackpot with a $10 bet, it will certainly be another world record," predicted Wilson Cheng Kwok-ming, a spokesman for the Hong Kong Jockey Club. In the excitement, gamblers lined up around the block at offtrack betting shops and thronged the counters at Happy Valley. A million people, one in seven of the city's population, took a punt on the Triple Trio. The racetrack heaved under the weight of a human wave that rushed in to watch the action.

Bill Benter monitored the first leg of the Triple Trio from his new office on the twenty-seventh floor of the Chinachem Century Tower, a couple of blocks away. The floodlights of Happy Valley were visible through the double glazing. But from his air-conditioned summit, he couldn't hear the crowd thunder as Heavenly Wind crossed the finish line first.

The only sounds in the office were the hum of a dozen computers and the clicking of keyboards and mouse buttons. Live footage was playing on a television mounted in the corner, with the volume turned down, but Benter's attention was elsewhere. His eyes were fixed on a monitor showing a matrix of all the bets his syndicate had placed on the Triple Trio, some 51,381 different combinations in all, costing HK $1.6 million (about US $200,000). Heavenly Wind's triumph was, as the Australian pundit noted, a "tough result" for Triple Trio hunters. Few had picked the unfancied horse in their top three.

Benter watched his system filter out the losing wagers. Down at the track, patrons ripped up their betting slips, made anguished faces, or retreated to the bar to find their evening's entertainment elsewhere. The lucky few still in the game clutched their tickets all the more tightly. There were two legs to go, both to be held later that night.

Benter almost hadn't bet on the Triple Trio. He'd debated doing so with colleagues as the jackpot soared. The computer syndicates were still excluded from online and telephone betting systems, as they'd been since 1997. That meant they were still wagering over the counter, sending runners out with cash vouchers and stacks of preprinted betting slips. Benter wasn't eager to provoke another confrontation with the Hong Kong Jockey Club.

In the end, though, he couldn't resist. The Triple Trio was the ultimate test of his software's predictive power. He'd been crafting it for seventeen long years, most of his adult life. The algorithm now included more than 120 factors. He had a statistics professor at the Chinese University of Hong Kong on payroll as a consultant, running simulations to fine-tune the modeling, as well as former racing journalists watching video footage for anything that might be missed in the data, such as a slow start or being blocked in.

On a whim, Benter sent one of his Filipino operators down to Happy Valley with a voucher and a sheaf of betting slips with the computer's top picks for the Triple Trio, each piece of paper containing thousands of combinations. "If we win, we won't collect it," he told his staff. The money could go to charity in line with the club's policy on unclaimed jackpots. His team would gain bragging rights in the computer betting community but little else. In any case, he didn't expect it to be an issue. There were more than 10 million possible permutations of placed finishers.

After the second leg, though, Benter was still in the hunt. The monitor told him that he had three live tickets, each one marked with dozens of potentially winning combinations. He rarely watched the horses in action. To him, they were numbers on a screen. This time, however, he walked over to the office television and turned up the sound to watch the final leg.

"They lock the gate. They're set. Last leg of the Triple Trio, and away they go." Twelve thoroughbreds exploded out of the stalls. One stumbled immediately and fell behind the pack. The rest hit their stride and flew past the crowd to begin a full lap of the track. Bobo Duck, the favorite, trained by a member of Hong Kong's most illustrious racing family, hugged the inside rail behind the leader, Sincere and Faith, ridden by a jockey in luminous yellow.

The horses were now on the far side of the track, away from the glare of the stands. The cheering dropped to a low hubbub before swelling into a pounding crescendo as the runners turned the corner and bolted for the final straight. The commentator's voice rose above the din: "Bobo Duck sweeps to the front, from Mascot Treasure, Frat Rat, and Top Light . . . Bobo Duck in front. Mascot's fighting back!"

Benter inched forward in his seat. The two leading horses bucked and strained against the reins, flank to flank, neither animal willing to yield. The crowd rose a final time and roared them across the line.

"Bobo Duck beat Mascot Treasure. Frat Rat in third. A popular result in the last leg of tonight's Triple Trio!"

A hush descended on Benter's office. He turned from the TV screen to the monitor showing the active Triple Trio bets in columns. His team called the display function the "sweat program," since you had to wait for it to process the result, discarding the losing wagers to display the winners. There were thirty-six lines left on the monitor. Thirty-five of their bets had correctly called the finishers in two of the races, qualifying for a consolation prize. One had correctly predicted all nine horses. "Fuck," Benter said. "We hit it." In the background, he could hear a voice emanating from the television: "Oh my goodness! The Triple Trio has gone off, and the dividend is $118 million!"

"Wait a minute, is this right?" Benter asked a colleague. They found an old betting slip and began scribbling out sums to calculate the prize. As well as HK $118 million for the jackpot, they had hit dozens of consolation prizes by calling two out of three races correctly. Moments later, the computer confirmed the figures: They'd won the equivalent of US $16 million by spending around $200,000 on wagers, an 8,000 percent return on their investment.

Benter tracked down the winning tickets from a nearby stack and put them onto the table: three little scraps, dog-eared at the edges. He stared at them for a while. His syndicate had pulled off multimillion-dollar wins before, but nothing close to this. "We can't claim this—can we?" he asked, although he knew the answer already. "It would be unsporting. We'd feel bad," he mused.

Instead, he sent an employee to fetch some champagne and posed for pictures, laughing, holding the pieces of paper representing the biggest prize of his career, one that he would never claim. Then he locked the tickets away in the office safe.

Benter's windfall was the largest from a single bet in the history of the Hong Kong Jockey Club. When no one came forward to claim the jackpot, the media worked itself into a frenzy of speculation. The existence of a winning ticket meant that someone, willingly or not, had given up a fortune.

"The ghost of the unclaimed $118 million Triple Trio ticket is still banging around like an unwanted poltergeist," the *South China Morning Post* reported. Benter heard that Alan Woods, managing his syndicate from exile in Manila, suspected some sort of conspiracy at the Jockey Club to keep hold of the money. He tried to get the word out through mutual friends to stop his former partner stirring up trouble. But the Australian refused to believe it. He loved the Triple Trio too much to cede it to his rival. It was the only type of wager he could still get excited about.

One group of bettors was said to be considering bringing a lawsuit to force the club into revealing more information. There was a rumor circulating that the ticket holder had watched the final leg and died of shock. Ultimately, Benter decided it would be safest to send an anonymous letter to the Jockey Club containing the ticket's serial number for verification. "We are a betting group," he wrote. "We are happy to have the funds donated, as is club policy, to the Hong Kong Jockey Club Charitable Trust."

The letter was never released to the public. Henry Chan, the club's head of betting, told the *South China Morning Post* that there was no way of knowing who the ticket holder was. "Although this is bad luck for one winner," he said, "it means there will be a lot of winners through the charities."

When the dust settled, Benter decided that things had worked out just the way they were meant to. His syndicate was making tens of millions of dollars every season, even with the restrictions of over-the-counter betting. He could afford to be generous. In fact, he liked it. He had never felt guilty about his chosen career, but the taint of vice hung heavier in middle age.

Lately, he'd taken to wearing a blazer and tie. A friend invited him to join the Rotary Club of Hong Kong, a charitable organization with the motto "service above self." Its members were good corporate citizens—doctors, lawyers, and bankers—eager to use their wealth to help others. Benter was thrilled to be accepted into their ranks.

The Wan Chai bar crawls of his youth were relegated to memory. At Rotary Club meetings, members didn't talk endlessly about card-counting systems or casino villainy; they were interested in the wider world. When people came to him for money, he didn't have to pick and choose his causes. He found he could just say yes. Combined, all of his donations amounted to less than a week's income betting on horses.

Then, midway through the 2001–2002 season, the Hong Kong Jockey Club unexpectedly lifted its ban on computer syndicates using the telephone and online betting services. The Board of Stewards never explained the reversal. Perhaps Benter's Triple Trio gift had appeased the gambling gods. More likely, the club recognized that its monopoly was under threat from new offshore betting websites and was under pressure to embrace the digital era. That would be impossible without inviting its biggest, most technically minded customers back into the fold.

Benter was back online. So was Alan Woods. While most of Woods's employees were based in Hong Kong, the Australian ran his syndicate remotely from his flat in Manila, waited on by a rotating crew of young Filipinas. Disconnected from his business and his old friends in Wan Chai, he plunged deep into libertarian manias. He rarely left home except to pick up new companions from go-go bars in the red-light district. He would be unreachable for days, bingeing on drugs, only to reappear more paranoid than ever.

Working for the Woods team became an ordeal. He started calling himself "MOMU," short for "Master of My Own Universe," and insisted that his employees take IQ tests so he could show them how much smarter he was. Still, as the multimillionaire founder of the world's second most successful horse-betting syndicate, few people in his life were prepared to challenge him.

One day in December 2007, he sent a letter to *Business Review Weekly*, an Australian magazine, asking that the publication recognize his achievements by putting his name on its rich list. "I had planned to delay my hope for inclusion until I could make it into the top 10," he wrote. "However, as of today, it does not appear I will live long enough."

Woods had late-stage colon cancer, a diagnosis that he didn't share with his colleagues or girlfriends until it was terminal. He met the news with the same flinty stoicism he'd shown when confronting past setbacks, such as being blacklisted in the *Griffin Book* and his conflict with Benter. Now in his sixth decade, he had few regrets. He'd lived the life he'd wanted.

Woods returned to Hong Kong for treatment at a hospital overlooking Happy Valley. He spent his days bedbound, adrift on an analgesic sea, playing card games with friends. Benter heard that Woods was back, but he wasn't tempted to visit him. The two men had barely spoken in decades. It wasn't so much that Benter was still angry; he was busy living the life he wanted, too.

Guided by the Rotary Club, Benter made large contributions to a medical center in Haiti and a new school in rural China, which named a dormitory after him. On Rotary Club expeditions to Ghana and India, he had the chance to see real poverty up close. His money could go a long way in places where the students sat on dirt floors and teachers went barefoot. He found it particularly satisfying to donate computers, the machines that had made such a difference to his own destiny.

And he fell in love, to the astonishment of colleagues who thought he'd never settle down. She was Vivian Fung, a fellow Rotarian. Benter was at a summit meeting of the forty or so Hong Kong chapters when he spotted her. She looked so poised, with a smile that radiated kindness. The old Bill would have been too nervous to approach her, but with his best jacket and tie as protective armor, he walked over to introduce himself.

Alan Woods's funeral was held at a sanatorium near Happy Valley in early 2008. His two favorite songs, Frank Sinatra's "My Way" and "The Best" by Tina Turner, played over the sound system. Woods was in an open casket with a packet of Benson & Hedges, his chosen brand of cigarette, resting in one hand and a lighter in the other. A rogue's gallery of punters, misfits, and ex-girlfriends filed past to pay their respects. Benter was notably absent.

Later, the crowd went to a wake at the racecourse, which was conducted in a spirit that the deceased would have approved of. "After the speeches saying how wonderful he was, everybody got drunk and said what a bastard he was," a friend recalled.

The sixty-two-year-old left behind a web of offshore trusts holding his AUS $900 million fortune and a single-page will. He didn't like dealing with tax agencies, so he didn't officially live anywhere. Legally speaking, he was "without domicile," which made settling his financial affairs complicated. After court hearings, his two Australian children received the biggest share, with the remainder divided among various exes and racing buddies. The Filipino mother of his third child got $1 million. Another less fortunate acquaintance was bequeathed $100.

Toward the end, friends noticed, Woods had mellowed in his attitude toward Benter. He could finally say out loud what everyone knew: that Benter's model was superior to his own. And he accepted that Benter was behind the unclaimed Triple Trio, although he couldn't comprehend why anyone would turn down a $16 million prize.

Whatever had divided them no longer mattered so much. The man the *Racing Post* had dubbed "the world's greatest gambler" was ready to admit that he owed much of his success to the real holder of that title. "Benter was the author of Alan's racing system and thus the probable generator of Alan's wealth," one mutual friend said after Woods's death. "I suspect that without Bill, Alan would have been one of many struggling card counters."

BILL NELSON

The wheel of Bill Nelson's life turned again. His years with the Computer Group slid into history, and he was happy to see them go.

Tony Spilotro and his ilk were ghosts, enduring only as characters in gangster movies. Billy Walters got rich all over again and bought a couple of golf courses. Doc Mindlin absconded to Europe. Mike Kent, the Computer Group's mercurial founder, retreated to the Pennsylvania backwoods, where he was later killed in a quad biking accident.

Nelson's wife, Liliana, tried to persuade him to quit gambling and get a regular job. But he thought back to his campus encounter with the Goldman Sachs recruiter, the miasma of self-regard as thick as overpriced cologne. No, he still couldn't face the corporate treadmill, even with a family to provide for. He was back where he'd started. He decided to take another look at roulette.

It wasn't an easy decision. In the decades since graduating from UCLA, his distaste for casinos had developed into outright disgust. Early in his career, he'd lost an entire bankroll at the blackjack tables in Reno. He couldn't work out what had gone wrong until a friend spotted it. The dealers were cheating, using basic sleight of hand. Yet, after being arrested in Northampton for doing little more than using his brain, the casino industry had spread the word that *he* was a cheater, to be thrown out on sight. Thinking about that made his piss boil.

Nelson was still barred from playing roulette in most of Las Vegas. He had a recurring nightmare about going back into the casinos. In it, he'd be at a roulette table trying out some improbable system, such as smearing his fingers with jelly to make the ball sticky. His friends and family would be there, willing him on. He would be distracted, looking over his shoulder for security, waiting for the inevitable. Then rough hands around his arms, dragging him away toward some unfurnished room to be humiliated or worse. He'd wake up gasping for air.

Even so, he needed money. The regular business world was full of cheats and liars, too, he reminded himself. He sought out an old friend, a veteran poker hustler, who assured him that it was still possible to beat roulette. In fact, the man had been doing it quietly for decades. His method was nearly as old as the game itself and didn't require Nelson to be anywhere near a casino when it went down.

Roulette wheels are designed to be random number generators: chaos, elegantly rendered in circular motion. But their creators are imperfect beings, and the things they make are just as imperfect. The flaws might be barely perceptible: a pocket glued a little less tightly than the rest or a metal divider a nanometer higher than it should be.

Over time, roulette wheels become even less perfect due to wear and tear. It can happen surprisingly quickly on an apparatus that never stops moving. Dust particles accumulate. Wooden panels warp. One corner of the table sinks a few filaments deeper into the casino carpet, tilting the playing surface by a fraction of a degree. These imperfections lead to bias, which means that the ball will drop into some pockets more than others.

One of the first to notice was an enterprising nineteenth-century Englishman named Joseph Jagger. Jagger was a machinist in a cotton mill who knew a thing or two about spinning machines and their quirks. In the late 1800s, he traveled to Monte Carlo, hiring six clerks to record the result of every spin for a week. Sure enough, one of the wheels, identifiable by a tiny scratch on the rim, had a definite bias toward a few of its pockets. Over several days he won a pile of francs that would be worth millions today before returning home. It was said that he never gambled again.

Nelson's friend made it sound deceptively simple: Just bet the favored numbers over and over again. But he knew from experience that there was a reason so few gamblers could pull it off. A player needed thousands of spins to separate true bias from the normal fluctuations of chance. One couldn't just stand in front of the table with a notepad writing down numbers without attracting suspicion, especially in the card-counting era. The only viable strategy was to play the game for low stakes for days on end to identify a vulnerable wheel, all the while hemorrhaging money.

In the 1980s, when Nelson had been predicting roulette, he'd laughed at the biased wheel teams he encountered on his travels. As far as he could tell, all they did was sit there recording numbers, hour after hour, to eke out tiny sums—before the casino noticed and took away the faulty wheel. Back then, he could walk up and start winning almost immediately. Twenty years later, though, he was prepared to reevaluate his view.

In the 1990s, digital displays appeared next to roulette tables, showing the winning numbers and colors from the last dozen or so spins. Casinos put them up to exploit the mistaken belief that five consecutive blacks made a red more likely or that it was worth betting on the twenties if they hadn't appeared in a while.

The displays made it much easier to collect data. So Nelson began recording the wheels at the MGM Grand, one of the new generation of Las Vegas megaresorts. The MGM was the perfect place to go unnoticed. A 16,000-seat arena hosted events—Mike Tyson and Oscar De La Hoya fights, comedy by Carrot Top, Britney Spears concerts—that filled the vast casino floor with rowdy, big-spending patrons. Nelson could stroll around unbothered, reading numbers into a voice recorder.

The results were encouraging. Nelson could hardly believe that there might be biased wheels in a billion-dollar Vegas casino, one of the most tightly controlled gambling spaces on Earth. But the truth was in the numbers. Data from several thousand spins showed undeniable spikes of certain numbers and sections. Nelson hired a team of "writers," paying them $12 an hour to monitor wheels across the Strip and beyond. They found defective wheels all over Vegas, just waiting to be beaten.

Next, Nelson posted on an online message board for advantage gamblers to see if anyone had the skills to help him get a team going. A man named Todd, who ran a lawn-mowing business in Missouri, responded. When they exchanged messages, he sounded as though he had a good grasp of statistics. In his free time, Todd chased gigantic Midwest thunderstorms, looking for tornados. They arranged to meet next time he was in Vegas.

Soon afterward, Nelson took Todd on a tour of the MGM Grand casino floor. The Missourian clearly had a deep knowledge of roulette probabilities. He also had an apparent ability to spot a machine's flaws on sight, something Nelson couldn't do. "Look at that," he said, gesturing at a wheel Nelson already knew to be biased. "Look at the way the lights reflect off the cone."

Todd explained that a slight ridge, which Nelson couldn't see, would knock the ball into a specific section. That night, they hashed out a deal to become partners in a new team to target the oldest advantage of all, predating Ed Thorp, legalized gambling, and even the existence of Las Vegas as anything more than a staging post for mule caravans.

Nelson found a couple of backers in the card-counting community to put up betting money, and they were ready to go. The final element was to hire players, which proved to be the most challenging by far. Not just anyone could sit at a roulette table for hours, choosing the same numbers, and get away with it. Casinos had a habit of throwing out anyone they deemed suspicious. The best players looked and acted like big shots, charming the pit bosses and tipping dealers, winning in a style that made it look as though they could lose it all at any moment and not care.

At first Nelson tried using minor sports professionals, but they didn't have the patience. Then he met Bart, a wealthy oilman from Alabama. Bart was a proven loser, which in some ways made him perfect for the job. Convinced that he could manipulate dice, he spent hours trying to throw lucky number seven on a craps table he'd installed at home. The evidence suggested that his conviction was misplaced. He'd lost so much money playing craps that casinos gave him cash rebates to soften the blow.

Nelson took his time training Bart how to play the roulette system correctly. His writers found a suitable wheel at Caesars Palace, a luxury casino where the wonders of ancient Rome merged seamlessly with swim-up blackjack tables and live performances by Céline

Dion. Bart took the team's bankroll and disappeared among the mock marble statues and designer clothing outlets.

They met up later in a shopping mall restaurant. "Well, I won over a million dollars," Bart told Nelson. "The bad news is, I lost it all on craps." He had played the biased wheel perfectly, betting the correct numbers in the proper amounts. Casino staff, recognizing a regular, never challenged him. Immediately after finishing, he had hauled his chips over to a craps table. Why not make a little more while he was there? Caesars had given Bart a $200,000 rebate, which meant that the team walked away with a small profit, but Nelson was livid. "This is a fucking disaster," he told Bart. The oilman wasn't invited to play again.

Eventually, Nelson found a group of players with the right mix of charisma, feigned stupidity, and self-discipline. There was Chuck, an older guy who rolled in on a mobility scooter, and Derek, whose British accent seemed to be enough to pass for a high roller. Randy looked like a retired Californian surfer dude and convinced dealers that the pockets he bet on over and over were the numbers he had worn as a college football star. They learned to recognize the biased wheels on sight, even when the casino moved them around. "Scratch 16" was identifiable by the mark near pocket 16. "Dark nine" had an odd-colored patch.

The team found its rhythm and began to inch into the black—not enough to satisfy the card counters who bankrolled the operation, since wins had to be shared among writers, players, and investors, but enough to suggest that, with the right conditions, the system had the potential to deliver the kind of golden night that could change the course of Nelson's life.

In early 2010, Todd found what looked like a promising target in Caesars. The casino had just cemented its place in popular culture as a byword for bacchanalian excess with the release of *The Hangover*, starring Bradley Cooper. Filmed mostly on location, the movie revolved around a disastrous bachelor party in a high-roller suite. Caesars, burnished with Hollywood stardust, was on a roll and announced a billion-dollar expansion. It also had the highest-stakes roulette in Vegas. Gamblers could risk up to $3,000 a number, while a winning number would pay out $105,000.

Todd took Nelson to see what he'd found. The wheel was on a bustling thoroughfare in the middle of the Caesars gaming floor. Todd pointed out the machine's central cone. Though Nelson couldn't see anything wrong with it, Todd assured him that it was misshapen enough to push a bouncing ball into a specific section containing six to eight pockets. When Nelson sent writers to log the numbers, Todd was proven right. After a couple of thousand spins, their spreadsheet showed a spike in one segment.

Then, suddenly, the wheel was gone. Nelson's writers searched for days and eventually located it again, tucked away in the corner of the Caesars entertainment zone. A few roulette tables had been deposited there, seemingly to fill a narrow space between the theaters and the rest of the casino. The female dealers were dressed like showgirls, in skimpy outfits, in place of the stern, waistcoated croupiers of the main casino floor. The nearest pit boss was out of sight, his vision obscured by a dancer's ramp. In other words, it was the perfect wheel in the perfect spot.

Normally, Nelson would have preferred to accumulate data from a week's worth of spins before risking the team's capital. The team had just lost six figures on a wheel that hadn't been as predictable as they'd hoped. His backers were pushing him to get results. This time, Nelson decided, he couldn't afford to wait. He summoned their most effective player.

Serge was a diamond dealer from Flanders—or said he was. He wore expensive suits and a yarmulke, a sign of his Jewish faith. What made Serge so successful wasn't his flamboyance or charm; he was a quiet presence at the table, rarely celebrating or showing emotion. It was the fact that he conformed to a stereotype of the kind of customer all casinos coveted: the whale.

Whales were the biggest losers of all, rare and exotic beasts who could afford to blow a million dollars in a sitting. Casinos went to extraordinary lengths to win their custom—laying on private jets, front-row seats, even, in the old days, call girls—whatever it took to get them through the door, safe in the knowledge that they would spend vastly more than they received in gifts. The biggest whales often hailed from overseas: Asian tech billionaires and oligarchs from Eastern Europe. They always seemed to come back for more, unlike regular addicts, who had a frustrating habit of dropping dead or joining the parade of homeless panhandlers on Las Vegas Boulevard.

So when Serge showed up at Caesars in March 2010 and put half a million dollars on the counter, staff were eager to give him whatever he wanted. He chose a table in a quiet corner of the entertainment district, close to a dancer's ramp—for privacy, he explained. Moni, one of Nelson's female writers, joined Serge to act as his date and to record the numbers on roulette cards supplied by Caesars. The team needed to be sure that the wheel was as good as they thought it was.

Serge began at around 6:00 p.m. with hundred-dollar chips, pushing them onto the six preferred numbers among three columns laid out on the felt. Moni ordered coffee and mineral water; she scribbled the results onto the card and patted Serge's arm in encouragement when they won or in sympathy if they lost. Soon, Serge upgraded to five-hundred-dollar chips, risking $3,000 each time. The dealer, a young woman in a sparkly outfit, seemed not to notice that he was winning once in every three or four spins. She chatted with other casino workers and smiled politely when Serge tossed her the occasional chip.

"I can't believe it," Moni thought. "They're not paying attention."

Their chip pile grew steadily. All was quiet. Easy listening music drifted across the casino floor. Tourists ambled past on their way to a show or dinner. After a couple of hours, Moni went up to the hotel room they'd booked to call Todd or Bill with the numbers. She was instructed to keep going. Serge asked for the table to be reserved just for him and for the distracted dealer to extend her shift. He got what he wanted. Whales always did.

His pile of chips grew into a mountain. He stuffed the bigger denominations into his pockets to keep them from overflowing and causing a scene. He kept betting the same six numbers, robotically, hour after hour. A uniformed guard came out, pushing a plexiglass trolley full of colored tokens to replenish the dealer's dwindling supply. Serge switched to thousand-dollar chips. Still, no one asked any questions.

Midnight came and went. Nelson was at home, drinking to calm his nerves, primed to hear at any moment that Serge had been thrown out. He and Todd had a debate over the phone about whether to take what they had already won and call it quits. Until that moment, the team had always limited their profit from a biased wheel to avoid attracting attention. Not this time. Nelson was worried about getting caught, of course, but there was one thing that scared him more: the idea of being stuck and having to grind out a living in casinos for the rest of his life. "Let's crush it," he said.

By 2:00 a.m., Moni was exhausted. She called Nelson from Caesars and asked if she could go home to sleep. She had to work the next day. Nelson said that was fine. Serge was up around a million dollars and showing no signs of flagging.

Moni walked out of Caesars as quickly as she could, forcing herself not to look back. She hurried away from the indoor fountain where animatronic statues reenacted the myth of Atlantis, stepping around out-of-work models dressed as Roman gladiators, past the Temple of Gucci, a Cheesecake Factory, and billboards for yet another Céline Dion show. At any moment, she expected to feel the weight of a hand on her shoulder. But it never came.

Nelson resolved to get some rest, too. There was nothing to be gained by staying up all night next to the phone. It would be late the next morning before he discovered what had happened to Serge.

Remarkably, the Belgian played on for another eight hours, an unbroken sixteen-hour stint at the roulette table. What finally stopped him wasn't exhaustion or casino security; it was speed. Serge had outlasted several dealers, who had worked their shifts at his table and accepted his tips without complaint. Then, around 10:00 a.m., a new dealer arrived who spun the rotor so fast that Serge's edge seemed to disappear.

Later, Nelson would speculate that the increased velocity had made the ball skip over the warped section, rather than bouncing back down. In any case, Serge lost $200,000 in a few spins and decided to quit while he was ahead. He stumbled, bleary eyed, back to the hotel room to get some rest, leaving his winnings in the casino account in his name. The total was $2.2 million, by far the biggest roulette windfall of Nelson's life. Serge managed to get a few moments of sleep before he was awakened by hammering at the door. Five heavies from casino security were outside, demanding to search his room. "Look anywhere you want," Serge said. They turned the place upside down. There was nothing to find.

Next, a casino manager arrived to explain that Caesars was going to freeze the account containing the $2.2 million and refer the matter to the Nevada Gaming Control Board. The man never said the word "cheating," but it was clear to Serge what he was implying. Hearing that over the phone, Nelson spat out a stream of curses: against the casino, its lackeys, the gaming regulator, and his own stinking bad luck for coming so close to a career-defining haul only to have it snatched away at the last. "We've got to fight," he said.

His partners agreed. Since most of the Vegas legal community worked for casinos, there was only one lawyer they could turn to. Bob Nersesian ran a little practice with his wife in a house downtown. Once upon a time, he'd been a casino attorney with a poker habit. One day, he'd heard about a gambler who'd been assaulted by casino staff. His lawyer friends had felt that there was no chance of winning damages in a company town. "This here's Nevada," they'd joked. Nersesian had felt differently; he'd taken on the victim as a client and won. Since then, he'd carved out a niche representing people who were swindled, beaten, detained unlawfully, or denied jackpots by the casinos. Stout and scrappy, he looked and sounded less like an attorney and more like the card counters he often represented. His Twitter handle was @casinonemesis.

Nelson met him and explained the play. "This can't be illegal," Nelson said. "It's a well-known system."

Nersesian got to work, exchanging letters with Caesars and the Gaming Control Board. He was a fighter, but Nelson didn't think much of his chances. It wasn't just that the casinos had more expensive lawyers or that the Gaming Control Board seemed more pro-business than pro-consumer, although both of those things were undoubtedly true from Nelson's perspective. It was just the way things worked. "They're going to fuck us," he told his partners. "They always do."

Except this time, they couldn't. Maybe it was Nersesian's track record that convinced Caesars to fold. Possibly the casino was persuaded when Nersesian cited a state regulation mandating that it was the proprietor's responsibility to repair defective gambling equipment, meaning that Caesars was the party at fault in the eyes of the law. Or perhaps casino executives simply wanted to avoid the embarrassment of a trial that would reveal to their investors and customers, in excruciating detail, just how easy it had been for a team of advantage players to take them for more than $2 million.

Whatever the reason, Nelson and his partners got their money. All of it.

In the old days, Nelson used to relish the thrill of victory, fleeting as it was. It felt good to win after so much toil. To dream up an idea, test it, model it, hold trial runs, execute it under pressure, and then see it proven by reality—that was the reward. It provided a rush of cerebral gratification that kept him and other advantage players coming back. But after Caesars paid up, he didn't know what he felt. Pride? More like relief.

The card counters who had provided the betting money got the largest share of the $2.2 million. Serge got the next biggest chunk, followed by Todd, who had spotted the bias in the first place. There were salaries to pay to all the writers who'd scouted the wheel. Nelson ended up with a little over $100,000, a handsome sum but not enough to vault him into the ranks of Las Vegas high society alongside Billy Walters and his golf courses.

Normally, after a big win, Nelson would take six months off to decompress. He'd read for hours on the couch, hang out with his family, and mooch around with gambling friends. The break would help clear his mind so he could think about where to find the next advantage. And he'd always found it. It was what he was known for. His old roulette partners used to call him "Wiz," short for "Wizard," because of his supernatural ability to conjure up an edge. Others knew him as "Bottom-line Bill," a guy who could be relied on to deliver a winning strategy. Whether it was card counting, roulette, sports betting, or roulette again, he'd always been able to dust himself off and start over. By the middle of 2010, though, and approaching retirement age, Nelson was no longer sure he wanted to.

PART 8

TIME ENOUGH FOR COUNTING

There'll be time enough for counting / When the dealing's done.
—Kenny Rogers, "The Gambler"

I am forced to wager, and am not free.
—Blaise Pascal, Pascal's Wager

ROB REITZEN

It wasn't just Reitzen's protégée Lisa who got swept up in the backlash against poker robots; Lary Kennedy, the former barmaid whom Reitzen had briefly dated and who was another top player in his stable, also found her accounts at Full Tilt Poker closed and her winnings seized, around $80,000 in all.

Both women responded with righteous fury. Lisa offered to play in person at the Bicycle Club in LA in front of representatives from the website. Kennedy tried sending in copies of her passport and bank statements to prove she wasn't a piece of software, then ranted on the Two Plus Two poker forum about Full Tilt's "thievery," writing, "I can hardly wait until they are exposed as the scum they truly are."

When that didn't work, Kennedy sued Full Tilt and its founders for fraud, slander, and unjust enrichment with the backing of Reitzen, who by then was no stranger to lawsuits. They accused the website's owners of secretly populating tables with their own bots while holding up a "zero-tolerance" policy to mollify Web vigilantes such as Crazy Mike. (Kennedy's complaint neglected to mention her affiliation with Reitzen, a prolific bot maker, or the fact that his Pokertropolis platform was populated with bots.)

Kennedy also alleged that Full Tilt had profited from the antibot crusade (her lawyers compared it to a jihad) by keeping confiscated funds for its own benefit. Afterward, she posted details of the case on Two Plus Two Forums, where other users demonstrated why it's a bad idea to look for sympathy on the internet. "I lolled so hard," one wrote. "Meh, good luck to you," said another.

In the legal melee that followed, Full Tilt denied everything and accused Kennedy of harassment. Kennedy's lawyers, meanwhile, pointed to media reports about a potential grand jury investigation into Full Tilt's activities. They asked the judge to speed up proceedings because of the "risk that the United States may confiscate all of the cash and assets of the defendants, leaving nothing for the plaintiffs," or that the company might collapse, leaving nothing for anyone. Full Tilt claimed ignorance of any probe.

On April 15, 2011, a day that would come to be known in the online poker community as "Black Friday," Full Tilt users logged on to find an FBI logo instead of the usual images of colored chips and felt. The websites of the other two most popular platforms, Absolute Poker and PokerStars, were also seized by the federal government, which posted a takedown notice: "This domain name has been seized by the F.B.I. pursuant to an Arrest Warrant."

Full Tilt's founders were among eleven executives charged with committing bank fraud, money laundering, and violating gambling laws. Prosecutors said the sites had skirted regulations by disguising customer deposits as payments to fictional online merchants for nonexistent pieces of jewelry or golf balls. Several million outraged users were left unable to access the sites even to withdraw their own funds. "Online poker is not a crime," said Senator Alfonse D'Amato of New York, a spokesman for the advocacy group the Poker Players Alliance.

"I TOLD YOU SO," Lary Kennedy wrote on Two Plus Two Forums.

Eventually, all three companies paid fines to settle the charges without admitting wrongdoing. Full Tilt Poker founder Raymond Bitar pleaded guilty to, among other things, plundering customer accounts when the company needed capital. He avoided prison time because of a heart condition. Kennedy's lawsuit rumbled on for a few years before petering out, with Full Tilt under new management and the entire industry in turmoil. The accusation that Full Tilt had used in-house bots remained unproven and unsupported by evidence. Kennedy never got her money back. Nor did Lisa.

While Black Friday was a setback for them, it was catastrophic for Reitzen's poker bot business. Online traffic plummeted. No one was sure whether the government's next move would be full legalization or more indictments. Most Americans were understandably reluctant to pay into a system associated with money laundering.

Even before Black Friday, the dumb money that made early online poker so lucrative was disappearing. Amateurs such as Jim the Chicago attorney and Evan the criminology student got no enjoyment out of losing their chips night after night, and they gradually stopped playing. Starved of prey, the professionals turned on one another in a brutal struggle for shrinking resources.

The bots kept multiplying. A group of Swedish students called theirs Maggie. It played 8 million hands before being discovered by the state-owned gaming provider. In the frozen north of Russia, enterprising Siberian computer scientists put together an operation so large and well organized that it became known as the "Bot Farm Corporation." These bots could scrape the online records of opponents to review previous hands and exploit specific weaknesses.

In the new world Reitzen had helped create, online poker was fought over by an army of unstoppable machines and a dwindling pool of pissed-off humans. Reitzen's bot rooms, no longer the world's most advanced, stopped being profitable, so he shut them down one by one. Hein Hundal, the academic who had helped Reitzen develop and patent his game theory system, went back to Pennsylvania State University, where he worked on torpedo guidance technology for the navy. Another senior programmer quit, saying that Reitzen had defaulted on a $20,000 debt. (Reitzen denies this.)

Only a few years after living in the luxury suite of the Savoy in London, Reitzen was back in California and running out of cash. He'd sunk much of his fortune into the dream house overlooking Los Angeles. In 2011, he filed for bankruptcy protection while he settled his debts. His creditors included his ex-wife Kathryn, a Brazilian jiu-jitsu coach, and the medical facilities providing cancer care for John Wayne. He sold his car, at that point a humble Chevy. He withdrew the bankruptcy filing in 2013.

Reitzen kept on hustling, working for Wally Simmons, his old card-counting partner and Benter's onetime horse-racing affiliate in Hong Kong, and trading on the financial markets, never his most reliable source of income. He settled down with a long-term partner, Larissa, a beautiful Ukrainian immigrant who was formidable enough to keep him in check. She learned card counting to get his attention. He helped her start her own business in fashion technology. They got a tiny dog and fussed over it together.

In 2016, though, Reitzen had to sell the hillside house, another blow to the self-image he'd constructed of himself as the gambling genius with a rock star lifestyle. Those who knew him well weren't surprised to see his fortunes change. "He never saw limits," one former colleague observed. It was both a gift and a weakness. Reitzen had always played big. He didn't know any other way. But his losses had been oversized, too. "I've never known anyone who made and lost more fortunes," the colleague said.

For most of January 2017, a team of top poker professionals set up camp in the Rivers Casino in Pittsburgh. They sat separately, facing computer monitors for twelve hours at a time, until they had completed their daily target of 1,500 hands. Their opponent was Libratus, the latest machine challenger to human supremacy in no-limit Texas Hold'em. After twenty days, Libratus was declared victorious. The software hadn't just beaten its opponents; it had obliterated them. It was up by $1.8 million worth of chips. Its opponents were all in the red, with the top performer down $86,000.

Carnegie Mellon academics had built the system from the same game theory foundation that Reitzen had taught himself thirty years earlier. But Libratus was several evolutionary leaps ahead of anything at Core or Momentum. It could simulate millions of hands, identify mistakes, and then *teach itself* how to avoid them in the future. Researchers called this feature "regret minimization," a synthetic version of what happens when a baby puts a shoe in its mouth and bursts into tears because it doesn't like the taste.

Initially, the pros playing against Libratus spotted a few strategic weaknesses in its game. "We attacked them and attacked them, and now they're gone," said one of them. At night, while the mortals slept, Libratus used a supercomputer as powerful as 3,330 high-end laptops running simultaneously to identify and patch errors. It was learning from its opponents.

Libratus's triumph was hailed as a milestone in the development of true artificial intelligence—another Deep Blue moment for thinking machines. "Imagine that your smartphone will someday be able to negotiate the best price on a new car for you," said Carnegie's Frank Pfenning. "That's just the beginning."

Another academic acknowledged that such a powerful bot might spell doom for the online poker industry, which was still recovering from Black Friday. "That could happen, but that's not really my concern," he said.

It was no longer so important to Reitzen, either. Watching the Libratus coverage, he felt a momentary longing for what might have been. But in truth, his attention was elsewhere. He had had his own cancer scare a few years earlier when doctors had discovered a large tumor on his kidney. He'd attacked the disease with the same zeal he'd shown when faced with John Wayne's diagnosis. He'd used keyword detection software to scrape the internet for suitably aggressive clinicians and probability theory to calculate his life expectancy, adjusted for quality, with or without chemotherapy. The resulting treatment regimen had worked, and he had recovered. His best friend, though, was getting sicker and sicker.

The Duke moved in with Reitzen and Larissa in Brentwood, back down on ground level in West Los Angeles. He was in constant pain. Reitzen wanted him to fight on, persuading a specialist to authorize experimental therapy. Sitting in the doctor's office, though, Wayne demurred. "What if I grow horns?" he joked. Wayne said he wanted to wait a while, but Reitzen could see what was really going on. His friend was ready to die, and he didn't want Reitzen to interfere any longer. Some odds can't be overcome.

Reitzen set Wayne up in a guest room with end-of-life care and anesthesia to manage his pain. The Duke died over Christmas. At the end, he was too frail even to say goodbye.

A few months later, Reitzen heard that he'd been nominated for the Blackjack Hall of Fame, a kind of Who's Who run by and for advantage gamblers. The induction ceremony, known as the Blackjack Ball, was held every year at a top secret Vegas location. Even getting an invite was tricky. New attendees had to be nominated by an existing member and approved by a committee of veteran card counters. Ed Thorp, the man who had started it all, was a Hall of Famer and regular at the ball. Within Reitzen's community, being inducted conferred instant recognition and respect. He'd struggled his whole life to be taken seriously by the big-brained high achievers around him, people such as his biological father, the rocket scientist who had run out on him as a child. Being recognized by Thorp and the rest gave him something he hadn't been able to find in casino high-roller suites or celebrity parties.

The 23rd Annual Blackjack Ball was held during the spring of 2019. Security guards were stationed at the gate to keep out casino industry spies and other enemies of profitable betting. A hundred or so guests milled around, drinking champagne. Bill Benter was there to cheer on his old friend. Other guests included hedge fund managers, CEOs, college professors, and, word had it, at least one genuine billionaire. All of them had shared the experience of having the course of their lives altered at the blackjack table.

When the time came for Reitzen to be inducted, the emcee noted his achievements in blackjack, slot machines, and poker: "Rob's done it all." Reitzen stood up to give a rambling speech. He paid tribute to the founding fathers of advantage play, Thorp and his partner, Claude Shannon, the "inventor of modern information theory." He thanked Wally Simmons, the leader of his first card-counting team, who was sitting in the audience. "Most of all," Reitzen said, "I miss John Wayne. He was a great blackjack player and a great friend. This is for the Duke."

His status assured, Reitzen found other outlets for his energy. He bought a motor home, painted it jet black, and took to driving across the American West. Grilling steaks in the forests around Mount Shasta, he felt free, perhaps even more than in his youth. He finally made up with Darrell Miers, his former partner at Core and once his closest confidant. The two men agreed to forgive and forget, then embraced as friends.

Reitzen still gambled, but only when he wanted to. Friends noticed a change in him, too. He seemed lighter. Everything was Jake.

One of the perks bestowed upon members of the Blackjack Hall of Fame is a lifetime of free room and board at the Barona Resort & Casino, a tribal casino in the hills outside San Diego. The sole condition: that they agree never to use their skills on the property. Members also get a spot on Barona's Wall of Fame, a display tucked away at the top of some escalators, dedicated to framed photographs of the world's greatest gamblers. Most of the images show older men in suits, posing as if for an employee-of-the-month award.

Reitzen supplied his own headshot for the wall, where it hangs to this day—a little boy, no older than five, staring at the lens with a mischievous expression, his head covered by an LA Dodgers baseball cap.

BILL BENTER

In 2010, Bill Benter got married twice, a wedding in each of the cities he'd called home. The first ceremony was at the InterContinental Hotel in Kowloon, across the bay from Happy Valley. Through the ballroom windows, the Hong Kong skyline burned through the evening haze, painting the water's surface with fiery brushstrokes.

Vivian, the young woman from the Rotary Club, was a Buddhist, so Benter flew in a posse of Tibetan monks to bless their union. Members of the city's computer betting syndicates came out in force as well. Most of them had learned their craft from Benter or Woods before setting out on their own.

Benter was confident enough in the superiority of his own model to be supportive of them. He'd given talks at universities and published an academic paper on the mathematical basics of handicapping that was used as a blueprint by his competitors. The Hong Kong betting pools were growing increasingly crowded with computer syndicates; getting an edge was harder than ever. But the community put aside its rivalries to pay homage to the master on the occasion of his wedding, dancing and drinking through the night.

The second ceremony was in Pittsburgh, Benter's birthplace and the scene of a lucrative second act in his career. He'd been betting on American racetracks since the late 1990s, but the business had really taken off in the mid-2000s. From a statistical point of view, it was the same principle as in Hong Kong, with one key difference: The Jockey Club was a monopoly, whereas the United States had more than a dozen major racecourses. Like Vegas casinos jostling for attention, they had to compete for customers, offering cash rebates to the biggest spenders, typically around 10 percent of the money wagered.

This, alongside the lack of competition from rival computer syndicates, had ensured another golden period for Benter. His American venture tapped into the virgin betting pools at Churchill Downs, Santa Anita, Belmont Park, and elsewhere. He kept the Hong Kong business going, too, but soon after winning (and not claiming) the Triple Trio, he moved back to Pittsburgh with Vivian to manage what was now a global operation from his hometown.

Their American nuptials reflected Benter's newfound status as a respected local businessman. He booked the Carnegie Music Hall, named for its patron, Andrew Carnegie, the Gilded Age steel tycoon who had believed that the wealthy had a responsibility to give away their fortunes. Amid the marble columns, local politicians and newspapermen mingled with Benter's charitable contacts, entertained by Chinese dragon dancers. The *Pittsburgh Post-Gazette* wrote up the event, quoting the Buddhist master who had overseen the ceremony: "May all beings attain supreme wisdom."

Benter and Vivian settled into their roles as wealthy philanthropists in a city with a long history of philanthropy. The benefactors of the past had left their names on parks, museums, and street corners: Carnegie, Mellon, Frick, and Schenley. Benter, as uncomfortable in the spotlight as ever, preferred a quieter kind of giving. He didn't ask for publicity or plaques when making a donation. Once, at a black-tie ball, the host mentioned his generosity and invited attendees to give him a round of applause. Benter was too embarrassed to stand in acknowledgment. The Benter Foundation, a charitable trust he established in 2007, bears his name, but otherwise you'd be hard pressed to find any mention of the man who funds its work. Most of the people he met at jazz galas or opera fundraisers had no idea what he did for a living. Those he did tell assumed that he was joking. The press referred to him simply as a business leader and philanthropist.

Benter put his betting profits into Alzheimer's disease research, theater groups, homeless shelters, libraries, women's refuges, academic grants for the study of mathematics, a Jewish community center, and financial education for kids from low-income neighborhoods. In meetings at his foundation, he sat quietly, listening to the volunteers talk about their work, trying to absorb as much information as possible. He also started a medical tech company but found the business world to be more unforgiving than gambling. "I'm kind of a one-trick pony," he joked afterward. He and Vivian had a son, Henry, in 2015. She resolved that he would learn Cantonese alongside English. Benter joined the Duquesne Club, a members-only Pittsburgh institution where the waiters speak with European accents and the lounges are redolent of old money.

As happy as he was with the life he'd built, he sometimes got tired of being the boss. He'd reminisce about his days as a card counter, cruising around in Reitzen's rust bucket of a car or soldering gadgets with Wally Simmons—back when he was just Bill, not Mr. Benter, the esteemed philanthropist. Around 2018, he saw a television ad calling for Uber drivers and signed up on a whim. Periodically, when his wife and son were out of town, he'd switch on the app and take fares in his Land Rover.

He found that he liked listening to his passengers talk. One ride, it might be a die-hard hockey fan on the way to a Penguins game, the next a woman with a suitcase leaving her boyfriend. Each journey was an adventure in miniature. Benter was comforted by the fact that no one really knew who he was or what he'd done.

Nonetheless, he kept on gambling. As the years wore on, he assumed that one day his system would stop working. It never did. All told, he guessed that he'd made close to a billion dollars in his three decades of betting on horses, although he wasn't a billionaire, since those profits had been shared with investors and partners. Nonetheless, it was such a manifestly absurd sum for a gambler to win that it fueled his desire to give as much away as he could.

One of his few indulgences was a plush top-floor office in downtown Pittsburgh. There he could see the Monongahela River roll by and hear the rumble of freight trains from his desk while fiddling with a stack of decommissioned casino chips, a memento from his youth. His coffee table was made from an old roulette wheel, still functioning. A marble bust of a horse adorned the mantelpiece, splashed with lurid paint in an avant-garde flourish, handpicked by his personal art director.

In another room, a group of young employees sat at computer terminals working intently on his betting model. Graduates from the top math and computer science programs, they were continuing the work Benter had started in the eighties. The horse-racing pools were more efficient now but not perfect. There were new revelations waiting to be discovered in the data, fresh mathematical insights to be found in the interplay of factors that determined the difference between winning and losing. The latest: What was the effect on performance when a horse switched trainers in midseason?

Benter's impact on the sport as a whole could be felt by anyone making a bet at any racetrack, anywhere in the world, if they knew where to look. In Hong Kong, the Jockey Club belatedly embraced the new era of data-driven wagers, publishing reams of technical data on its website. The odds boards at Happy Valley and Sha Tin were color coded to show late swings in the volume of betting on each runner. When the odds shifted dramatically in the seconds before the starting gun, that was the computer syndicates making their move. In 2024, officials estimated that Benter and his rivals accounted for around 15 percent of all the money put into the Hong Kong betting pools and an unknown (though certainly higher) percentage of all the money taken out.

In the United States, computer syndicates were thought to be responsible for roughly 20 percent of all the dollars wagered at racetracks, rising to 40 percent in some states. The biggest players could trace a lineage directly to the Benter-Woods axis. The Australian Zeljko Ranogajec, for example, has been described as the world's biggest horse-racing punter, wagering upward of a billion Australian dollars each year. He started his career counting cards with Benter and Woods in Vegas, followed them to Hong Kong, then went global. "A substantial portion of our success is attributable to the pioneering work done by Benter," he said in a rare interview.

Phoenix, a sports data firm headquartered in Malta, won a

multimillion-dollar investment from a trust chaired by Lord Jacob Rothschild, of the global banking dynasty, on the strength of its racetrack betting. That company was founded by former employees of Woods, including his protégé Paul Longmuir.

For some, the rise of computer betting syndicates has been an unwelcome development. The money they take out of pari-mutuel pools would otherwise be going to the regular gamblers whose enthusiasm keeps racetracks in business. The effect is similar to that caused by algorithmic high-frequency traders in financial markets, skimming a little from the flow of capital, working like a tax on participation. In either case, retail investors are generally the losers.

From another perspective, though, Benter and his disciples have rescued the sport of kings from fading to insignificance. The halcyon days of 78,000 fans cheering on Seabiscuit at Santa Anita are long gone. Many racing venues today are shabby, faded places. In the last two decades, the amount bet at American racetracks by regular, non-professional customers has fallen by 63 percent, adjusting for inflation, even as other forms of gambling have exploded. *The New York Times* described horse racing as a "battered old sport" with an aging fan base, beset by concerns about animal welfare and competition from the NFL and others.

In an era in which digital betting is the sport's most important source of income, computer syndicates can be seen as a lifeline. The Hong Kong Jockey Club seems to think so. So does Scotty McKeever, an aspiring Bill Benter with a handicapping algorithm and a subscription service. "They're putting so much money into the pools," he told the *Financial Times*. "If it wasn't for that, horseracing would be done."

BILL NELSON

In the spring of 2004, a tall, thin Croatian wearing rimless glasses walked into the Ritz Club casino in London. The man signed in using the name Niko Tosa—an alias, as security staff would later discover. He and his companions sought out a roulette table in one of the club's *salles privées*, semiprivate rooms set apart from the main gaming area, bought £100,000 worth of chips, and sat down to play.

When they left in the early hours of the next morning, the group had won more than a million pounds. Casino staff were mystified. Betting fifteen pockets at a time, Tosa's team's win rate defied logic. At one point, they had hit the right number on thirteen consecutive spins. When he returned the next night, a Ritz manager called the police and had him arrested. But he was never charged, and eventually the casino was forced to give the Croatian the spoils.

Afterward, someone leaked the story to the British press, causing a minor sensation. Reporters speculated, inaccurately, that he might have used a laser connected to a microcomputer to track the ball's progress. One of Tosa's companions told police that they'd used only their skill and experience to predict the outcome. Publicly, the Ritz Club declined to comment. But in private, casino executives were worried. Few of them had had any inkling that roulette could be so vulnerable.

The Ritz flew in a security consultant from Australia, a former advantage gambler himself, who demonstrated how it was possible to beat the wheel by timing the ball and rotor. The Gambling Commission, the

British regulator, ordered a government laboratory to run tests, which only confirmed the consultant's thesis. It *was* possible to predict roulette under certain conditions, investigators found, as with equipment that was degraded or had a slight tilt.

The agency's report, which was circulated widely within the casino industry, also recommended countermeasures. Roulette wheels would have to be redesigned to make them less predictable.

Bill Nelson first noticed the changes while scouting for biased wheels around Vegas, where his eye was drawn to a shiny new piece of equipment. The Starburst model, made by the British manufacturer TCSJOHNHUXLEY, didn't have traditional pockets at all. Instead, the ball dropped into triangular metal grooves. The patented system was "statistically proven" to be more random than any other type of wheel, the manufacturer boasted.

Other exotic designs soon appeared. One had smooth, scallop-shaped grooves for pockets. They increased the amount of time the ball spent in the final, most chaotic phase of its orbit, bouncing and skidding around the rotor. When Nelson recorded the numbers, he could find no discernible bias. As far as he could see, the new wheels were unbeatable.

By 2010, when Serge the Belgian diamond dealer pulled off his big win for Nelson and his team at Caesars, the old-style models were getting harder to find. One by one they were being replaced by machines containing inclinometers that could detect a hair's breadth of tilt and built-in computers to record data and flag irregular patterns.

Nelson's team had a couple of costly failures, losing six figures on wheels that weren't quite biased enough. Friends noticed that Nelson was drinking too much. Sitting around recording numbers was boring. There was little else to do but drink. His investors began pressuring him for action. "What are you going to do next?" they asked. Nelson wondered if they'd forgotten how much money he'd made for them in the past.

"Let's give it a rest," he said. He told the wheel scouts to stand down. He tried a few things, then lost interest in them. He stopped looking for games to exploit. He'd always hated casinos, with their constant noise, their crappy carpets, the heady mix of greed and despair. Now in his midsixties, he believed he'd be content never to set foot inside one again.

For a while, he worked on a computer program to trade on inefficiencies in international currency markets, buying and selling dollars, yen, and euros as the algorithm commanded. He even got in touch with his old friend Bill Benter to pitch him on the idea. But Benter was pessimistic. He warned that Nelson wouldn't be competing with other gamblers. He'd be in a race against hedge funds with proprietary software years in the making, in an environment where a few millionths of a second could make all the difference. "I'm thankful we don't have to be that good in horse racing," Benter wrote back, declining to invest. Nelson eventually dropped the project.

His wife, Liliana, took the initiative without him. Throughout their marriage, Nelson had given her half his gambling income. A friend persuaded her to invest in property in her native Poland, no longer a Soviet satellite but one of the fastest-growing economies in the European Union. Warsaw was a forest of cranes erecting new shopping malls and modern apartment blocks. Google had opened a tech campus in an old vodka factory.

Nelson flew out to inspect the apartment Liliana had chosen in a leafy suburb outside Warsaw and liked it so much that he stayed. His retirement income went twice as far in Poland as it did in Vegas. Polish Paul, his friend and partner from the days of the roulette computer, lived nearby. Life seemed less complicated.

"Games are wonderful," the British mathematician Marcus du Sautoy once wrote. "But you cannot lose yourself forever in a game. It is important to leave the game and rejoin the real world." Advantage gambling had been Nelson's way of making sense of the chaos around him. Predictive roulette and card counting had a comforting clarity. Either the bankroll grew, or it didn't. Now he felt he no longer understood what roulette had become. The numbers didn't add up. Not anymore.

One evening, Paul persuaded him to take a trip to a casino in Warsaw to check out the roulette tables. Sure enough, Nelson observed, the next-generation wheels had spread to Europe, too. He could see the metal grooves where the pockets used to be. Paul had always believed that Nelson's gift for prediction was like magic. He was the Wiz, after all. "Come on, let's play," Paul urged.

Nelson watched as a technician arrived to do some maintenance. The man pulled out the revolving disk, revealing the guts of the machine. Inside, clearly visible against the polished steel and plastic, Nelson could see a single red beam. A laser. What was it for? He could only guess. He shook his head. "It's no good," he told Paul. Then he walked out of the casino into the cold.

INTERLUDE

WHAT A FOOL BELIEVES

In June 2000, a new online gambling platform called Betfair paraded a coffin around the streets of London. Inside, supposedly, was the metaphorical corpse of the traditional bookmaker, who "emptied punters' pockets" and "took the shirts off their backs," according to leaflets distributed during the stunt. Betfair was heralded, by its own publicists, as the dawn of a new era, one in which gamblers could compete against one another in an open market, enabled by the internet. It was to be a fairer, more inclusive system. No longer would the house be the only winner.

Alan Woods invested some of his fortune in Betfair a few years before his death. It proved to be one of his better decisions. Online gambling's meteoric rise had only just begun.

The big British bookmakers piled into digital betting first, then American casino brands, alongside a flood of digital start-ups. Evolution Gaming grew from its origins in a Latvian warehouse to become one of the world's biggest gambling companies by live-streaming casino games, with real dealers and equipment, into people's homes. The release of Apple's iPhone in 2007 put a gambling platform into people's pockets. Making a bet was never easier.

The corporate world found digital betting more agreeable, too. Companies could get around irksome regulations and shrink their tax bills by establishing themselves in friendly offshore jurisdictions such as Costa Rica and Malta. America's legal framework remained a thorny problem—until for-profit fantasy sports arrived on the scene.

FanDuel and DraftKings began with an old idea: Fans picked a "fantasy" team of their favorite baseball, football, or hockey professionals, putting them together in a league with friends. The professionals were awarded points based on their real-life performance in games.

At the end of the season or weekend, the creator of the top fantasy team got bragging rights or received a few bucks from the pool.

Just like online poker platforms, FanDuel and DraftKings took a fee for hosting the contest. Although customers played for real money, the two companies hoped that the business model was far enough removed from the traditional idea of gambling to prevent the FBI shutting them down. What followed was a headlong scramble into a new market expected to be worth billions of dollars.

By 2015, FanDuel and DraftKings were the biggest television advertisers in the United States, showering networks and sports teams with hundreds of millions of dollars for airtime and brand placement. "If you looked closely, there was actually some football being played between those endless hours of FanDuel and DraftKings commercials," one journalist quipped.

The two companies then went from state to state in a bare-knuckle lobbying campaign to persuade lawmakers to kill local prohibitions on sports betting, using gifts, donations, and exaggerated promises of potential tax revenues. Finally, in 2018, the US Supreme Court struck down a federal law against single-game betting. The floodgates opened. Once permitted only in Nevada, as of January 2025, sports betting had spread to thirty-eight states plus Washington, DC.

"Every moment in life is a bet," a FanDuel commercial declared, only slightly overstating reality. Today, prediction markets allow anyone who feels the urge to wager on the highest daily temperature in Austin, Texas, the top-rated weekly show on Netflix, or whether President Donald Trump will buy Greenland. Americans are probably making more than $1 trillion worth of bets annually, including on lotteries and the black market. Gambling isn't just mainstream; it's universal.

"The scent of vice," as Vegas casino owner Bob Stupak once described it, has all but disappeared, buried by an avalanche of corporate dollars. In the most important ways, however, the game hasn't changed. Advantage players understand this better than anyone.

The house still profits by targeting the minority of players who seem unable to control their habit. If anything, online gambling has made this easier and more lucrative. In 2023, a British customer sued the FanDuel group, accusing it of illegally harvesting his data. The man, a self-confessed gambling addict, had lost everything playing online slots. He had tried setting spending limits and excluding himself from various websites, but his phone had kept pinging with promotions whenever he felt tempted. The platform's algorithm had identified him as a high-value customer and learned his habits. "The more he responded—trying new things, accepting bonuses, going up a level—the more the marketing models responded with more, and more tailored or directed, marketing," a judge found.

And the gambling industry still excludes winners for the crime of winning. Imagine if Warren Buffett were banned from the New York Stock Exchange for being too good at his job. That's how advantage players feel whenever their accounts are restricted or closed because of their success.

When Dave Holmes, an online sports bettor in Chicago, started using a math-based strategy, his bets were rejected or limited to under a dollar by companies including BetMGM, ESPN BET, and Caesars. "I would love to actually be given an answer to why it's happening, and they refuse to do that," Holmes told *The Wall Street Journal.*

Nate Silver, the statistician and poker professional, had his bets limited to as low as $10 a game by BetMGM, PointsBet, and DraftKings after he started winning. "If a sportsbook known to aggressively limit winning players *is* taking your action, you should ask yourself why," he said. "They are basically telling you they think you're a loser."

Like many other marketing ploys, Betfair's coffin stunt was an alluring fantasy. The platform was eventually swallowed up by exactly the type of entity whose demise it had predicted, becoming part of Flutter Entertainment, a supersized bookmaking corporation that includes FanDuel and PokerStars. In other words, the house didn't die, and it probably never will. It evolved instead into a many-headed hydra, hiding its true nature inside a glossy corporate wrapper. Love it or hate it, there's no escape. The industry has more money, power, and influence now than at any other point in history.

Some observers were left feeling nostalgic for the old outlaw days of Las Vegas. Back then, gambling's impact was limited by criminals' incompetence and their desire to avoid prison. In his book *Temple of Chance*, the journalist David Cay Johnston argued that the Mafia would never have extended credit to many of the people who have been allowed to bankrupt themselves in the decades since. "Bad as the mob is, having corporate America dominate the casino business is worse."

EPILOGUE

The Lou Ruvo Center for Brain Health looks as though it's been left out too long in the desert sun. Its stainless-steel shell, an architectural flourish, twists and warps in on itself as if superheated. The windows glow in radioactive hues. The effect is strikingly weird, especially in the gloaming light of Las Vegas at dusk.

I'm here in my well-worn tuxedo for the 26th Annual Blackjack Ball. This gathering of elite gamblers used to be closed to all but a privileged few. Hall of Fame members had veto powers to keep out anyone who might conceivably cause a problem. A prominent player once got himself uninvited after he took a job at a casino trying to thwart advantage gamblers. These days, it seems, they let almost anyone in, even nosy writers.

I scan the crowd. There's an older guy in a cream-colored cowboy hat and buckskin jacket. He has a handlebar mustache and is wearing sunglasses indoors. When I ask around, no one seems to know who he is. There are more women than I had expected, given how male dominated professional gambling has always been. More young people, too. Maybe the ball is a sign that times are changing.

I find Rob Reitzen talking to a friend about Brazilian jiujitsu, acting out moves against an imaginary opponent. Someone comes up to him and says, "Man, I've *never* seen you not in a hat." Tonight he's sporting a smart black cap, turned backward. Speaking a language I think he'll understand, I offer all the cash in my wallet—$17—if he will take it off. He laughs but doesn't take the bait.

At that point, I had known Reitzen only a few months. He took some persuading to share details of his gambling life. I'd had to drive all the way from Vegas to his brother's ranch in Oregon, a fifteen-hour straight shot through the desert, mountains, and forest, after he had changed our meeting point at the last minute. Afterward, I'd learn that Reitzen often tests people like this, for reasons that have to do with his idea of loyalty. He needs to know that you take him seriously.

On that first encounter, I told him about a conversation I'd had with one of his former partners about how they used to dismantle dildos to retrieve the vibrating mechanisms for their blackjack computers. Reitzen guffawed. "Did he tell you about the time it got *stuck in his ass*?" I found myself thinking, This *is the guy? The genius who was solving poker twenty years before the first AI models?*

"That's Rob," one of his friends told me. "Still twelve years old in many ways."

Champagne in hand, I go out in search of conversations to blunder into. It isn't the friendliest crowd. People are polite but guarded, looking me up and down, trying to work out who I am. Most of them don't offer their names—not real ones, anyway. There's a guy who calls himself the Candyman, another who goes by Night Train.

I can hardly blame them for their caution. Every time the general public notices that advantage gambling exists, bad things seem to happen. Reitzen's magazine profiles blew up his first business. After Bob Moore was hailed as Hong Kong's "God of Horses," the Jockey Club cracked down on computer syndicates. Bill Nelson's arrest in Northampton and the attendant media coverage were enough to end his career in predictive roulette, though not his career as an advantage player.

Nelson isn't at the Blackjack Ball. Instead, he's at home in Poland with Liliana and Jade, his cat. He told me he couldn't think of anything worse than spending an evening in the company of gamblers talking about gambling. Since walking away from roulette, he's watched the industry's expansion with growing horror. Initially, he was reluctant to help me with this book, for reasons different from those of Reitzen. He said he wouldn't want to participate in any project that might glamorize his former career. Occasionally, he'll send me links to articles about predatory behavior by betting firms. "The dark side to gambling is getting darker," he warned me once. "But who wants to hear about that?"

There's a familiar awkwardness to the drinks mixer portion of the Blackjack Ball as people congregate in little groups, glancing around for familiar faces. I meet a young college graduate who has a system for Keno, the quick-fire lottery game played in casinos. Another gambler shows me a picture on his phone of what he says is necessary to succeed in the era of online betting. It shows an industrial shelving unit holding dozens of laptops, each one automatically running betting software.

Everyone I talk to at the ball says that old-school card counting is more difficult than ever. Casinos now use shuffling machines that can scramble six decks of cards into perfect disorder in a few seconds.

I doubt that it's impossible, though. One thing I've learned while writing this book is that gamblers will explore every conceivable edge whenever there is money at stake. If you can imagine it, it's probably happening somewhere in the world. Advantages are as reliable as the tides: They appear and crest into a peak before disappearing, crashing like waves on the shore. But there's always another one on the horizon waiting to be caught. The game has no end.

Bill Nelson may have given up on roulette, but his successors haven't. Evolution, the biggest provider of live-streaming casino games, employs several hundred "game integrity" specialists to constantly monitor its equipment for any signs of predictability. These days, advantage gamblers use software to track the roulette wheels' ball and rotor automatically or scrape video feeds to collect data on hundreds of tables, singling out the vulnerable ones.

There are even systems to engineer lottery wins. It works when rollover prizes get so large that it becomes profitable to buy a majority of the available tickets. In 2023, a betting syndicate won a $95 million Texas jackpot by buying virtually all of the 25.8 million possible number combinations, causing a good deal of controversy in the Lone Star State. The syndicate is run by Zeljko Ranogajec, the Benter/Woods protégé who used to employ Bill Nelson and who is good friends with

Rob Reitzen. The advantage play methods pioneered four decades ago remain effective.

"The reason it still works is that we care more," a Blackjack Ball attendee told me. The house can rely on human nature to deliver profits. "*They* don't have to work hard to make money," the gambler added. "*We* work harder." I've heard stories of advantage players so desperate for an edge that they were willing to have computer chips implanted in their skulls.

After dinner, Maria "The Greek" is inducted into the Hall of Fame. A blackjack veteran, she's only the second woman to be honored in the history of the ball. Looking down the list, I'm reminded how small the world of advantage gambling is. Other Hall of Famers include Wally Simmons and his former partners Rob Reitzen and Bill Benter. The honor has also gone to Keith Taft, the devout Baptist who invented the wearable blackjack computer, and Bob Nersesian, the attorney who helped Bill Nelson's roulette team recover their record payout from Caesars.

Late in the evening, there's a quiz so indulgently niche that I have to blindly guess every answer. I scrawl down one of the questions in my notepad to laugh at later:

> *You're getting a 25% loss rebate: Pennsylvania rules.*
> *The maximum bet is $100,000—aka "a Johnson" on one spot.*
> *When you're winning, within a quarter million dollars, what is your win/stop playing one hand on this trip?*

Clearly, I'm never going to be a candidate for the Blackjack Hall of Fame. That doesn't mean I've learned nothing on the way here. I've realized that there's no trick to gambling success, no hack or secret formula. It takes a combination of talent, luck, resilience, and extraordinarily hard work. Advantage gamblers do share certain traits, such as a passion for rigorous scientific analysis and the creative application of new technology. But you could say the same about successful people in almost any field.

I suspect that my time with advantage gamblers *has* influenced the way I make decisions. I've learned something about taking intelligent risks, lots of them, to increase my chances of hitting the jackpot. But any inclination I might have harbored to try my luck more seriously has evaporated. Why would I play online poker when there's a significant chance that I'll be up against a machine that can process a billion possibilities in the time it takes to blink? Why would I bet on horse racing when I'll be competing against Bill Benter's algorithm or one like it? It seems futile and not particularly fun.

The latest battleground of advantage gambling is artificial intelligence. Benter himself is in the middle of a late-career renaissance thanks to the development of neural networks. His early success was achieved meticulously, assembling the pieces by hand, relying on trial and error to find out which factors worked. Now all he needs to do is feed blocks of data and race results into an AI system. It can teach itself how to interpret the numbers. "It's made it exciting again because we had kind of hit a wall with our improvement," he says. His top rivals in the field are benefiting, too.

I find it fascinating to think about people like Benter dedicating their entire careers to getting a marginal advantage in a game. With their extraordinary talent and willpower, Benter, Reitzen, and Nelson could probably have earned more doing something else. The appeal lies in the challenge itself.

Gambling is one of the most ancient obsessions, older than money. The remains of clay dice have been uncovered in archaeological sites from the third millennium BC, the Bronze Age, in what is now Iraq. Knucklebones, carved into cubes and inscribed, probably go back even further. Some philosophers have argued that games of risk are a key part of what separates us from animals.

Yet we are reminded every day that gambling is a losing game. Regular folks, myself included, hear the adage "The house always wins," shrug, and accept it. A minority of people hear the same and think *Wanna bet?* An even smaller minority are actually capable of overturning the odds. Understanding what drives them and the extraordinary lengths they will go to is why I'm still here, nearly a decade after first hearing about Bill Benter and his billion-dollar betting syndicate.

Benter is sitting at one of the Blackjack Ball's top tables, a privilege reserved for Hall of Famers. I approach to ask if I can take a picture of him with Rob Reitzen. It requires ten minutes of negotiation to get permission from the ball's organizers, who seem keen to retain some of the event's mystique. Afterward, Benter and I talk about the situation in the United Kingdom, where I live. It happens to be the world's most developed betting market, especially when it comes to online products.

Benter and I agree that Great Britain might hold clues to America's future. Under heavy lobbying by the gambling industry, the UK authorities have largely outsourced the burden of ensuring responsible gaming to the addicts themselves, who are expected to self-exclude and freeze their own accounts if they are betting too much. The system is comparable to putting drunks in charge of a bar, and about as effective. Around 8 percent of suicides in the United Kingdom are estimated to be linked to gambling debts.

Benter says that the proceeds from the ball will be donated to the National Council on Problem Gambling, a US nonprofit. The organization's executive director, Keith Whyte, is here to give a keynote speech. It strikes me as ironic for this particular community to be concerned about the negative consequences of betting. Benter elaborates that having gained so much from the business of gambling, he feels some responsibility to mitigate the damage it causes.

"You are outcasts and pirates and proud of it," Whyte tells the audience after he takes the stage. The people in this room are the 1 percent who know how to win, he goes on. There's another 98 percent, casual gamblers who lose only what they can afford. And then there's the 1 percent for whom gambling is destructive, according to Whyte. Because of the gambling boom, their numbers are swelling daily.

What Whyte calls "gambling literacy"—basically, understanding how probability functions—is generally poor, even among the well educated. He points out that college graduates are more likely to become addicted to sports betting, perhaps because they believe, wrongly, that their knowledge will protect them against losses. The main sources of information and education about how gambling works are the same entities that profit from people's ignorance. "You make informed decisions about gambling," Whyte tells his audience. "The problem is: All the rest of us, all the normies, don't."

The Blackjack Ball wraps up around midnight. Outside, another Las Vegas night is in full swing. Whatever your feelings about gambling, there is a strange magic to this place. Casino tycoon Steve Wynn saw it the first time he set foot on the Strip—a potent cocktail of danger and opportunity. "It was like stepping back into the frontier," he recalled years later.

Tonight the place is swarming with tourists, ready to feed their dollars into Sin City's money-eating machine. On Fremont Street there's mayhem. People are dancing to the din of competing sound systems outside an Irish-themed pub identifiable by the giant luminous beer glass on its roof. A man wearing a nightmarish clown mask and no shirt stands nearby, rock still. No one stops to ask why.

For most of these revelers, losing a few bets is the price they have to pay to get a taste of a glamorous world that seems at once close enough to touch and just out of reach. It's right there—behind the ropes in the VIP section and in the high-roller suites with private hot tubs and killer views of the Strip. There it is again, behind the bars of the cashier's cage, a pile of plastic tokens worth a lifetime's honest wages.

There's no shortage of people in Las Vegas who are willing to pay that price. In return, they get a glimpse of a better life and—who knows—maybe even a shot at winning enough to buy one.

Not the legendary gamblers of the Blackjack Ball, though. They want no part of it. Reitzen makes an early exit for the suburbs to stay with his old friend Wally Simmons. Later, I see Benter outside with his wife, waiting for a cab. It was he who first introduced me to Reitzen and Nelson all those years ago, after realizing that he couldn't talk me out of writing about his career. He's been my guide ever since. It's getting late. I decide not to bother them now and hurry past, leaving Benter and Vivian standing quietly in the darkness, arm in arm.

ACKNOWLEDGMENTS

It's been seven years now since I stumbled into the world of advantage gamblers. Learning about their lives has been a surreal, unforgettable experience. I've driven hundreds of miles across the American West, spent more time in casinos than I care to admit, and met some fascinating, odd, singular people. I owe a good many of them thanks for their help with this book.

First and foremost, Bill Benter, for responding graciously to my relentless hounding and for subsequently becoming my guide around the gambling universe. Without his kindness, *Lucky Devils* would not exist. I'm also grateful to Rob Reitzen and Bill Nelson for dealing patiently with many, many dumb questions and for hosting me in Oregon and Poland, respectively.

Ethan Bassoff is the kind of agent every writer should have, with a keen critical eye and a kind word when required. And a special mention for another superb agent, Toby Mundy, who gave me a nudge in the right direction some years ago and shaped the direction of this project.

My publisher Yaniv Soha's enthusiasm was infectious, and his careful shepherding made the book possible. Thanks also to Jake Lingwood in London.

I'm damn lucky to have access to advice from friends who have achieved great things in journalism and publishing and also some who have nothing to do with those careers, which makes their feedback all the more valuable. My former coauthor Matt Campbell deserves special thanks, alongside Liam Vaughan, Zeke Faux, Jonathan Browning (for Hong Kong doorstepping), Kaye Wiggins (for Hong Kong color), and FOI wizard Jason Leopold (for doing what he does).

For draft-reading services rendered, I'm indebted to Sue Macmillan, Bill Marquino, and Lisen Runsten, a light in the darkness.

From the outset, my employer, Bloomberg, has offered unhesitating support for this book and the articles that led to it. I owe particular thanks to Reto Gregori, Kristin Powers, Jeremy Keehn, Joel Weber, Brian Bremner, and the late, great Richard Vines.

When it came to pulling records, the good folks at the University of Nevada library's Special Collections in Reno and Las Vegas went the extra mile, as did the staff of the Riverside Federal Archive and John Hartmann of Chess Life. Adam Kucharski's math prowess and John Marlow's filing system came through when I was most in need. Thanks to Larissa and Liliana for help wrangling their partners.

Blackjack Ball organizers Max Rubin and Richard Munchkin did me a great service by allowing me to attend the event, despite my profound ignorance of the Pennsylvania rules on loss rebate. I'm grateful to each and every one of the gamblers, family members, industry professionals, and other sources who took a chance by sharing their stories with me. There are far too many to mention here, and in any case, I'm confident that most of them would rather I didn't.

Thanks to Lindsey, Jim, and Bee for looking after the kids so I could work and to Greg for the throwaway remark that made it all happen. And finally: Callum. Yes, I did steal your idea for the title of this book. Happy now?

NOTES

INTRODUCTION

7 *The "father of information theory"*: James Gleick, *Chaos: Making a New Science* (Open Road, 2011), Kindle, location 377.

7 *tinkered with roulette computers*: "Wearable Roulette Computer," MIT Museum, https://mitmuseum.mit.edu/collections/object/2007.030.014.

7 *His theories underpinned*: Annie Duke, *Thinking in Bets: Making Smarter Decisions When You Don't Have All the Facts* (Portfolio, 2018), 18.

7 *He also developed*: Allan Schaffer, "Jess Marcum, Mathematical Genius, and the History of Card Counting," *Blackjack Forum* 24, no. 3 (2005).

8 *The owners of two Premier*: Andy Naylor and Jay Harris, "'A Cold War': The Rivalry Between Brighton's Tony Bloom and Matthew Benham at Brentford," *New York Times*, March 29, 2023.

8 *Von Neumann was once asked*: Duke, *Thinking in Bets*, 20.

PART 1: EPIGRAPH

11 *When a lamb goes*: Edward O. Thorp, *Beat the Dealer: A Winning Strategy for the Game of Twenty-one* (Vintage Books, 1966), 74.

11 *The day of the lamb*: Thorp, *Beat the Dealer*, 74.

PART 1: BILL NELSON

15 *One day he sent*: Jonathan R. Laing, "Computer Formulas are One Man's Secret to Success in Markets," *Wall Street Journal*, September 23, 1974.

15 *"In the modern casino"*: Thorp, *Beat the Dealer*, 4.

15 *His real innovation was*: Thorp, *Beat the Dealer*, 3.

16 *At the time it*: Montse Garze, "A Brief Journey Inside the IBM 704," MIT Computation Archives, https://comphist.dhlab.mit.edu/archives/story/IBM_mechanics.

16 *American casino operators were still*: Ray Hennedy, "The Odds Couple," *Sports Illustrated*, April 16, 1979, https://vault.si.com /vault /1979 /04/16 /the-odds-couple-keith-taft-a-devout-baptist-and-ken-uston-a-high-living-ex-stockbroker-blackjacked-vegas-casinos-for-a-small-fortune-with-the-help-of-a-computer.

16 *"The one thing about system players"*: Hennedy, "The Odds Couple."

PART 1: BILL BENTER

19 *There were reports of customers*: David Johnston, *Temples of Chance: How*

America Inc. Bought Out Murder Inc. to Win Control of the Casino Business (Doubleday, 1992), 45.

20 *an international arms dealer*: Johnston, *Temples of Chance*, 7.

20 *a money launderer for the Medellín*: Johnston, *Temples of Chance*, 2.

PART 1: ROB REITZEN

23 *"I got Fs in every subject"*: Steve Lowery, "Game Boys," *New Times Los Angeles*, January 1997.

24 *ask to borrow ten bucks*: Lowery, "Game Boys."

25 *However, Revere claimed*: Lawrence Revere, *Playing Blackjack as a Business* (Ishi Press, 2011 updated edition), 2.

25 *"If winning is your goal"*: Revere, *Playing Blackjack as a Business*, 9.

25 *"You will not be gambling"*: Revere, *Playing Blackjack as a Business*, 12.

25 *"a bear to learn"*: Mark Billings, *The Ultimate Edge* (Booksurge Publishing, 2009), 78.

26 *"there are many points"*: Revere, *Playing Blackjack as a Business*, 8.

26 *"I am cold blooded"*: Revere, *Playing Blackjack as a Business*, 11.

26 *"You can practice your skills"*: *Orange Coast*, August 1980.

INTERLUDE: AMERICAN GOMORRAH

27 *"It is the child of Avarice"*: George Washington, letter to Bushrod Washington, January 15, 1783, Center for Digital History, Washington Library, https://www.mountvernon.org/library/digitalhistory/past-projects/quotes?search=it+is+the+child+of+avarice&topic=Allotes.

27 *from the Founding Fathers, who*: Philip G. Smucker, "The Founding Fathers Would Literally Bet on Anything," The Daily Beast, July 4, 2017.

27 *Casinos first appeared in*: Marcus du Sautoy, *Around the World in 80 Games: From Tarot to Tic-Tac-Toe, Catan to Chutes and Ladders, a Mathematician Unlocks the Secrets of the World's Greatest Games* (4th Estate, 2023), 264.

28 *"The man whose tools"*: Larry Gragg, *Bright Light City: Las Vegas in Popular Culture* (University Press of Kansas, 2013), chap. 2.

28 *Gambling took place in full public view*: John M. Findlay, *People of Chance: Gambling in American Society from Jamestown to Las Vegas* (Oxford University Press, 1986), 83.

28 *For $75 per month*: Johnston, *Temples of Chance*, 27.

29 *"Come as you are to"*: Findlay, *People of Chance*, 163.

29 *One had been self-defense*: Johnston, *Temples of Chance*, 31.

29 *"hoodlums from the east"*: Gragg, *Bright Light City*, 68.

29 *"What this town needs"*: Johnston, *Temples of Chance*, 15.

29 *When the military tested nuclear*: "Nevada Test Site," Atomic Heritage Foundation, https://ahf.nuclearmuseum.org/ahf/location/nevada-test-site.

30 *The famous evangelist and firebrand*: Gragg, *Bright Light City*, 100.

30 *That year, 10 million tourists*: "Visitor Statistics," Las Vegas Convention and Visitors Authority, https://www.lvcva.com/research/visitor-statistics.

30 *Throughout the 1970s, a diminutive*: Nicholas Pileggi, *Casino: Love and Honor in Las Vegas* (Open Road International Media, 2016), 122.

30 *The author James Ellroy called*: Gragg, *Bright Light City*, 230.

30 *The social critic James Howard Kunstler*: "Historian: Vegas 'Where American Spirit Crawls to Die,'" *Las Vegas Sun*, April 14, 1998, https://lasvegassun.com/news/1998/apr/14/historian-vegas-where-american-spirit-crawls-to-di/.

PART 2: BILL NELSON

33 *"electro-graphic car fantasy"*: Tom Wolfe, "The New Life Out There: Electro-graphic Architecture," *New York*, December 9, 1968, https://nymag.com/article/tom-wolfe-electro-graphic-architecture-neon-as-art.html.

35 *One card counter was punched*: Hennedy, "The Odds Couple."

35 *Another had his arm twisted*: David Layton, director, *The Hot Shoe: A Documentary About Card Counting in the Casino Game of 21*, 2004.

35 *So was the Aladdin*: "Chronology of the Aladdin Hotel-Casino," *Las Vegas Sun*, August 18, 2000, https://lasvegassun.com/news/2000/aug/18/chronology-of-the-aladdin-hotel-casino.

35 *Gambling lore said that the*: Robert A. Nersesian, *The Law for Gamblers: A Legal Guide to the Casino Environment* (Huntington Press, 2016), 67.

38 *Thorp had predicted that winning*: Thorp, *Beat the Dealer*, 180.

38 *Resembling the bastard offspring*: "Kilobytes Megabytes Gigabytes Terabytes," Stanford University Introduction to Computing Principles, https://web.stanford.edu/class/cs101/bits-gigabytes.html.

38 *The earliest software could just*: Laine Nooney, *The Apple II Age: How the Computer Became Personal* (University of Chicago Press, 2023), 14.

38 *Thorp claimed that the method*: Thorp, *Beat the Dealer*, 181.

PART 2: BILL BENTER

40 *Gas prices were sky high*: "Too Lame a Horse for 1980?," *Economist*, March 10, 1979.

40 *"A convention city like Las Vegas"*: "Names in the News," Associated Press, May 11, 1979.

41 *They lived in cardboard condominiums*: Marc Fisher, "The View from Vegas: Casino Mecca Basks in Sun Belt Boom," *Miami Herald*, May 11, 1986.

41 *Later, researchers found that*: "National Gambling Impact Study Commission Final Report," https://govinfo.library.unt.edu/ngisc/reports/fullrpt.html, 7-1.

43 *Woods had been born in Murwillumbah*: Michael Atherton, *Gambling* (Hodder & Stoughton, 2006), Kindle, location 576.

PART 2: ROB REITZEN

48 *"If casinos wanted to put an end"*: Peter Griffin, Luncheon Speaker Session, Fifth National Conference on Gambling and Risk Taking, October 22–25, 1981 (audio file), University of Nevada, Reno, Special Collections Department.

48 *John Gwynn, a computer science professor*: Hennedy, "The Odds Couple."

48 *"We have a feeling that throughout"*: Peter Griffin, paper, Session 1, Fifth National Conference on Gambling and Risk Taking, October 22–25, 1981.

49 *the fund had earned an additional*: Edward Thorp, "A Blackjack Player on Wall Street: How We Made 41 Million Dollars," Luncheon Speaker Session, Fifth National Conference on Gambling and Risk Taking, October 22–25, 1981.

49 *Next, the card counter Ken Uston*: Ken Uston, "Does the Gambling Industry Have a Conscience?," Session 3, Fifth National Conference on Gambling and Risk Taking, October 22–25, 1981.

49 *A Walter Funkenbusch from Michigan*: Walter Funkenbusch, paper, Session 17, Fifth National Conference on Gambling and Risk Taking, October 22–25, 1981.

PART 3: BILL NELSON

55 *Consumers began seeing computers*: Randolph E. Schmid, "Coping with Computers," Associated Press, April 19, 1979.

55 *In 1979, a group of students at UCLA*: "Are Colleges Training Computer Criminals?," *U.S. News & World Report*, January 8, 1979.

55 *"Our basic idea was to determine"*: Edward O. Thorp, "Optimal Gambling Systems for Favorable Games," *Review of the International Statistical Institute* 37, no. 3 (1969), http://www.edwardothorp.com/wp-content/uploads/2016/11/OptimalGamblingSystemsForFavorableGames.pdf.

56 *The program had four thousand*: Thomas A. Bass, *The Eudaemonic Pie* (Random House, 1986), 102.

56 *The quote was likely made up*: "Quote Origin: No One Can Win at Roulette Unless He Steals Money from the Table While the Croupier Isn't Looking," Quote Investigator, September 9, 2012, https://quoteinvestigator.com/2012/09/09/einstein-roulette.

59 *A casino guard had eventually*: Johnston, *Temples of Chance*, 32.

61 *Blaise Pascal, the seventeenth-century*: du Sautoy, *Around the World in 80 Games*, 265.

61 *Fyodor Dostoyevsky, the Russian literary great*: Idrees Kahloon, "The Power of Thinking Like a Poker Player," *New Yorker*, September 2, 2024.

62 *The first Dutch venue had opened*: "Going Dutch at the Casino," *Economist*, February 19, 1977.

62 *The casino at Scheveningen required men*: Marylin Bender, "Scheveningen, North Sea Spa for All Seasons," *New York Times*, February 20, 1983.

63 *Going back even further*: Miranda J. Green, *Dictionary of Celtic Myth and Legend* (Thames and Hudson, 1992).

66 *Anyway, most of the Italian officers*: "Vincevano alla roulette col computer," *La Stampa*, December 24, 1982.

69 *None of the team members was identified*: Terry Morris, "Gamblers Used High Technology to Win £20,000," *Northampton Chronicle & Echo*, 1982.

PART 3: ROB REITZEN

72 *"You must give in to that"*: CasinoExaminer, "Blackjack Forum: Arnold Snyder's Card Counting Sermon," YouTube, November 29, 2010, https://www.youtube.com/watch?v=R8lW6vVbpXU.

72 *Snyder told anyone who would listen*: Layton, *The Hot Shoe.*

72 *One MIT team member argued*: Layton, *The Hot Shoe.*

73 *an East Vegas joint called Alias*: Jack Sheehan, "Good Riddance to Vegas' Mobster Past," *Las Vegas Review-Journal*, March 17, 2013, https://www.reviewjournal.com/opinion/good-riddance-to-vegas-mobster-past.

75 *a Zilog Z80 microprocessor containing*: Simon Sharwood, "Zilog to End Standalone Sales of the Legendary Z80 CPU," The Register, April 22, 2024, https://www.theregister.com/2024/04/22/z80_cpu_end_of_sales.

78 *An aspiring casino tycoon spent years*: "Table Game Employing Two Sets of Cards," US4362303A, Google Patents, https://patents.google.com/patent/US4362303A/en.

78 *"In the last part of the twentieth"*: Thorp, *Beat the Dealer*, 183.

PART 3: BILL BENTER

79 *Some of the costumes Benter saw*: Hennedy, "The Odds Couple."

80 *One gambler was taken out*: Nersesian, *The Law for Gamblers*, 67.

81 *The agency tried to distance itself*: Layton, *The Hot Shoe.*

83 *Billed as a "traveling computer"*: "Traveling Computer for Home or Office," United Press International, November 17, 1982.

83 *Hong Kong's 5 million citizens bet*: Kit Chellel, "The Gambler Who Cracked the Horse-Racing Code," Bloomberg Businessweek, May 3, 2018, https://www.bloomberg.com/news/features/2018-05-03/the-gambler-who-cracked-the-horse-racing-code.

85 *"Searching for Positive Returns at"*: Ruth N. Bolton and Randall G. Chapman, "Searching for Positive Returns at the Track: A Multinomial Logit Model for Handicapping Horse Races," *Management Science* 32, no. 8 (1986): 1040–60.

INTERLUDE: THE ELEPHANT AT THE TABLE

87 *an advantage system dissected*: *Phillip Ivey v. Genting Casinos UK Ltd*, Mr Justice Mitting, High Court of Justice, Queen's Bench Division, EWHC 3394 (QB), 2014, https://www.bailii.org/cgi-bin/format.cgi?doc=/ew/cases/EWHC/QB/2014/3394.html&query=(ivey)+AND+(crockfords).

88 *infuriating enough two centuries ago*: Thomas Barker and Marjie Britz, *Jokers Wild: Legalized Gambling in the Twenty-first Century* (Praeger, 2000), 21-26.
88 *A poker sharp called Gentleman Jack*: Basil Newton, *Gentleman Jack Newton: Confessions of a Crossroad Gambler* (Top Hat Publishing, 2008), 48.
88 *courts have upheld their right*: Robert A. Nersesian, *The Law for Gamblers: A Legal Guide to the Casino Environment* (Huntington Press, 2016), Kindle, location 853.
89 *"Is it fair for Tom over here"*: Layton, *The Hot Shoe*.
89 *"law says that the casinos"*: Hennedy, "The Odds Couple."
89 *"Players on each side of this"*: Nersesian, *The Law for Gamblers*, Kindle, location 744.
89 *The control board is viewed as*: Nersesian, *The Law for Gamblers*, Kindle, location 1384.
89 *"The law is fickle"*: Nersesian, *The Law for Gamblers*, Kindle, location 1504.
90 *A Crockfords attorney called*: "Poker Player Loses Court Battle over £7.7m Winnings from London Casino," *Guardian*, October 25, 2017, https://www.theguardian.com/law/2017/oct/25/poker-player-phil-ivey-loses-court-battle-over-77m-winnings-from-london-casino.
90 *initially booked under "bunco steering"*: Hennedy, "The Odds Couple."

PART 4: BILL NELSON

93 *the quickie wedding, that age-old*: Norm Clarke, "Las Vegas Sets Marriage Record," Associated Press, February 14, 1981.
93 *Inside, trapeze artists dangled from*: Kristen DeSilva, "Check Out What Circus Circus Looked Like Back in the Day," *Las Vegas Review-Journal*, October 23, 2015, https://www.reviewjournal.com/uncategorized/check-out-what-circus-circus-looked-like-back-in-the-day-photos.
95 *Mike Kent had once been*: *United States of America v. Ivan Mindlin et al.*, United States District Court, District of Nevada, Judge Clarence C. Newcomer, CR-S-90-2-CNN(RJJ), reporter's transcript, January 7, 1992.
96 *By 1979, he was spending*: *United States of America v. Ivan Mindlin et al.*, 80.
96 *sensitive enough to require security clearance*: *United States of America v. Ivan Mindlin et al.*, 201.
96 *"the odd, slightly uncouth child"*: Albert Chen, *Billion Dollar Fantasy: The High-Stakes Game Between FanDuel and DraftKings That Upended Sports in America* (Houghton Mifflin Harcourt, 2019), xii.
96 *the TV hanging on the wall*: Chen, *Billion Dollar Fantasy*, 189.
97 *wagering on sports since he was*: Billy Walters, *Gambler: Secrets from a Life at Risk* (Avid Reader Press, 2023), 29.
97 *Chicago Gary ran a crew of thirty*: Walters, *Gambler*, 118.
97 *A real estate agent in Baltimore*: *United States of America v. Ivan Mindlin et al.*

98 *"There was no shortage of"*: Walters, *Gambler*, 118.
98 *In 1984, the team bet*: *United States of America v. Ivan Mindlin et al.*
99 *There was a runner known*: *United States of America v. Ivan Mindlin et al.*
100 *An Oklahoma Sooners coach reportedly*: John Underwood, "The Biggest Game in Town," *Sports Illustrated*, March 10, 1986, https://vault.si.com/vault/1986/03/10/the-biggest-game-in-town.
100 *a market worth anywhere from*: Underwood, "The Biggest Game in Town."
100 *gambling was second only to drugs*: Underwood, "The Biggest Game in Town."
101 *There were eighteen crime families*: "Report Says Las Vegas Filled with Organized Crime Families," Associated Press, December 15, 1984.
101 *Raids on suspects as far*: Robert Stewart, "12 of 20 Seized in Alleged Mafia Move Face Bookie Charges," *Los Angeles Times*, January 16, 1985.
101 *The Stardust, where Nelson*: Wallace Turner, "Bugging by U.S. Produces Big Cases Against Las Vegas Crime," *New York Times*, November 8, 1983.
101 *He ran an off-Strip jewelry*: Christopher Lawrence, "Monkeys, Skee-Ball and Nudity: Recalling the Strip's Wildest Casino," *Las Vegas Review-Journal*, September 11, 2022, https://www.reviewjournal.com/business/casinos-gaming/monkeys-skee-ball-and-nudity-recalling-the-strips-wildest-casino-2638605.
101 *According to the FBI, he*: Pileggi, *Casino*, 9.
101 *The FBI believed that Doc*: Affidavit of Thomas B. Noble, *United States of America v. Ivan Mindlin et al.*
102 *On a call intercepted by*: Affidavit of Thomas B. Noble, *United States of America v. Ivan Mindlin et al.*

PART 4: BILL BENTER

103 *The Cathay Pacific jet dropped through*: Maggie Hiufu Wong, "25 Years On: Remembering the Glory Days of Hong Kong's Old Kai Tak Airport," CNN, June 29, 2023, https://www.cnn.com/travel/article/hong-kong-kai-tak-airport.
103 *more than five hundred microscopic dwellings*: Annette Chiu, "'Hectic Centre Has Its Charm; Despite Its Negatives, Causeway Bay Still Manages to Please the Area's Inhabitants—with Convenience and Shopping," *South China Morning Post*, September 22, 2002.
105 *The British started racing horses*: Yiu-Wai Chu, *Hong Kong Pop Culture in the 1980s: A Decade of Splendour* (Amsterdam University Press, 2023).
105 *The top jockeys of the 1980s*: Michael Cox, "Fame Game: Hong Kong Jockeys and Trainers Reveal Their Celebrity Status in Racing-Mad Culture," HK Racing, April 18, 2016, https://www.scmp.com/sport/racing/article/1936979/fame-game-hong-kong-jockeys-and-trainers-reveal-their-celebrity-status.
105 *The territory's residents wagered*: Bert Okuley, "Hong Kong Racing Season Opens Amid Hangover of Major Fixing Scandal," UPI, September 20,

1986, https://www.upi.com/Archives/1986/09/20/Hong-Kong-Racing-NEWLNHong-Kong-Racing-Season-Opens-Amid-Hangover-of-Major-Fixing-Scandal/4257527572800.

105 *provided a sizable chunk of*: Bert Okuley, "Hong Kong Racegoers Eye the Track Not the Calendar," UPI, January 27, 1985.

PART 4: ROB REITZEN

110 *The lens was no more than*: Mark Billings, *The Ultimate Edge* (Booksurge Publishing, 2009), 277.

110 *They hadn't even told their wives*: Bob Dancer and Richard Munchkin, "Gambling with an Edge—Robert Reitzen," *Gambling with an Edge* (podcast), June 1, 2019, https://www.youtube.com/watch?v=l3q1a4I-4EI.

111 *A security guard stumbled across*: James Coates, "Dumb Luck Shorts Out Hi Tech Scam," *Miami Herald*, April 12, 1984.

111 *the Duke only just made it*: Dancer and Munchkin, "Gambling with an Edge—Robert Reitzen."

112 *"A computerized device is strapped"*: Minutes of Senate Committee on Judiciary, Senate History, 63rd Session, May 10, 1985, Nevada Legislature Research Library.

112 *"It is unlawful for any person"*: Nevada Revised Statutes Chapter 465, Crimes and Liabilities Concerning Gaming, 465.075, Nevada Legislature Law Library.

112 *using a pen and paper to scrawl out sums*: Minutes of Senate Committee on Judiciary, Senate History, 63rd Session, May 10, 1985, 17, Nevada Legislature Research Library.

112 *Some attorneys claimed that*: Layton, *The Hot Shoe.*

113 *Harry Truman, Dwight D. Eisenhower*: Oliver Roeder, *Seven Games: A Human History* (W. W. Norton, 2022), 184.

114 *Earlier efforts by math professors*: Darse Billings, "Computer Poker," Department of Computing Science, University of Alberta, August 30, 1995, https://poker.cs.ualberta.ca/publications/billings.msc.pdf.

115 *There had been chess computers*: Roeder, *Seven Games*, 69.

115 *For that reason, serious academic*: Billings, "Computer Poker."

116 *a neighborhood better known*: James Gomez, "Police Find Children Are Turning to Gang Membership, Life of Crime," *Los Angeles Times*, September 11, 1988.

117 *Competitive poker is "hours of boredom"*: "From Boredom to 'Sheer Terror' in a Matter of Moments," *Baltimore Sun*, November 13, 2020.

PART 5: BILL NELSON

121 *It took them two hours to count*: *United States of America v. Ivan Mindlin et al.*, 13.

121 *In the six-week period around Christmas*: *Michael and John Kent v. Ivan*

Mindlin, United States District Court, District of Nevada, CV-S-88-864 RDF (JJ), complaint, November 2, 1988.

121 *"drain you dry before you"*: Walters, *Gambler*, 17.

122 *Nelson wasn't sure that Doc*: Deposition of William Nelson, *United States of America v. Ivan Mindlin et al.*, April 12, 1989.

122 *There were maybe sixty games*: Ian Thomsen, "The Gang That Beat Las Vegas: The Saga of the High-Tech Gambling Syndicate that Revolutionized Sports Betting," *National Sports Daily*, June 6, 1990.

122 *getting the line from bookmakers on*: "College Basketball Roundup," UPI, January 19, 1985.

122 *"You won't get away"*: Deposition of William Nelson, *United States of America v. Ivan Mindlin et al.*, April 12, 1989.

123 *"What are you doing?"*: Thomsen, "The Gang That Beat Las Vegas."

123 *Kent's only brush with the law*: Thomsen, "The Gang That Beat Las Vegas."

123 *They took betting sheets from*: Thomsen, "The Gang That Beat Las Vegas."

123 *Afterward, Doc rushed back to Vegas*: Witness testimony of Candice Rainey, *United States of America v. Ivan Mindlin et al.*, Janaury 9, 1992.

124 *Billy Walters blew his top*: Affidavit of Special Agent Thomas B. Noble, *United States of America v. Ivan Mindlin et al.*, July 25, 1991.

124 *Goodman was well known as*: Walters, *Gambler*, 124.

125 *Walters would later recall looking*: Walters, *Gambler*, 128.

125 *The agent had thereafter referred*: Nicholas Pileggi, *Casino: Love and Honor in Las Vegas* (Open Road International Media, 2016), Kindle, location 1326.

125 *The few murders that occurred*: Pileggi, *Casino*, Kindle, location 1778.

125 *in the gossip pages for having an affair*: Pileggi, *Casino*, Kindle, location 354.

125 *"He dared you to murder him"*: Pileggi, *Casino*, Kindle, location 1326.

126 *Spilotro's final resting place, a few*: Pileggi, *Casino*, Kindle, location 1326.

126 *told him that his lawyer*: Thomsen, "The Gang That Beat Las Vegas."

126 *Kent filed a lawsuit against*: Affidavit of Ivan Mindlin, *Michael and John Kent v. Ivan Mindlin.*

PART 5: BILL BENTER

129 *Patrons could buy books written*: Steve Schatt, "Atlantic City Weekend Is a Mixed Blessing," *Newsday*, September 18, 1988.

129 *His wife Ivana flew*: Michael Shnayerson, "Inside Ivana's Role in Donald Trump's Empire," *Vanity Fair*, January 2, 1988, https://www.vanityfair.com/news/1988/01/ivana-trump-business-empire?srsltid=AfmBOoq54vPwlrdggRqUKb6Yw8mN2ewxPihHVr5frWV9ehRKj-4TV_7C.

130 *"Be our next president"*: Johnston, *Temples of Chance*, 136.

130 *a stage show, where the performers*: Frank Tanner, "Donald Trump Is the Greatest Political Entrepreneur of All Time," *Maxim*, November 2, 2024,

https://www.maxim.com/news/donald-trump-is-the-greatest-political-entrepreneur-of-all-time.

130 *The Claridge was promoting*: Joyce Venezia, "More Atlantic City Casinos Means Shift in Gaming Tactics," Associated Press, April 11, 1987.

131 *The 1988 horse-racing season*: The Royal Hong Kong Jockey Club, Hong Kong Racing Record for the Racing Season 1988/89, 1989.

131 *The animals spent their off months*: Mike Bingham, *Sunday Tasmanian*, October 9, 1988.

133 *The symbolism had such power*: Mabel Lui, "Lucky Phone Numbers and Wedding Dates to Dining Don'ts, Chinese Numerology Superstitions," *South China Morning Post*, July 25, 2024, https://www.scmp.com/lifestyle/arts-culture/article/3271721/lucky-phone-numbers-and-wedding-dates-dining-donts-chinese-numerology-superstitions.

135 *The chief executive, Major General Guy Watkins*: "Officials First Past the Post in Cricket Match," *South China Morning Post*, November 26, 1992.

135 *and went to the ballet*: Peter Woolrich, "Wraight to Quit His Position at HK Ballet," *South China Morning Post*, December 6, 1992.

137 *He boasted about the betting power*: Stephen Vines, "Obituary: Robert Moore," *Independent*, October 22, 1997.

137 *he faxed death threats to his colleagues*: Alison Smith, "All Bets Off," *South China Morning Post*, November 2, 1997.

PART 5: ROB REITZEN

141 *"primordial soup phase"*: Nate Silver, *On the Edge: The Art of Risking Everything* (Penguin Random House, 2024), 45.

141 *Even the most talented players*: Silver, *On the Edge*, 108.

141 *In 1991, state legislators finally*: James P. Sweeney, "Whatever 'Stud-Horse Poker' Is, It's Legal Now," *San Diego Union-Tribune*, June 25, 1991.

141 *Lowball fell out of favor and*: Jamie Beckett, "New Games Help Poker Parlors Draw Full Houses," *San Francisco Chronicle*, November 6, 1990.

142 *his father had introduced*: Norman Zadeh, *The Rise and Fall of Perfect 10* (independently published, 2021), 1.

142 *He'd developed a rating system*: Zadeh, *The Rise and Fall of Perfect 10*, 15.

142 *Economic models treated people*: John von Neumann and Oskar Morgenstern, *Theory of Games and Economic Behavior* (Princeton University Press, 1944), 9.

143 *"Real life consists of bluffing"*: Duke, *Thinking in Bets*, 20.

144 *it was greater than the number*: Keith Romer, "How A.I. Conquered Poker," *New York Times*, June 15, 2023, https://www.nytimes.com/2022/01/18/magazine/ai-technology-poker.html.

145 *the fastest processors remained*: Reuters, "What Computers Need Is Not More Intelligence but a Little Common Sense," *Toronto Star*, September 29, 1991.

146 *In 1991, it took a supercomputer*: "Computer Unravels Chess Knot," *Miami Herald*, October 29, 1991.

146 *"I was puzzled, because there"*: Harold C. Schonberg, "Kasparov Beats Chess Computer (for Now)," *New York Times*, October 23, 1989, https://www.nytimes.com/1989/10/23/nyregion/kasparov-beats-chess-computer-for-now.html.

148 *"I was sure I was playing"*: John Watson, "Yermolinsky Wins World Open . . . but von Neumann Steals the Show," *Inside Chess*, August 9, 1993.

148 *"No clock. Three minutes"*: Watson, "Yermolinsky Wins World Open."

149 *"The Von Neumann Affair"*: Watson, "Yermolinsky Wins World Open."

INTERLUDE: THE AMERICAN WAY TO PLAY

151 *Using a gilded pan to sweep*: Johnston, *Temples of Chance*, 140.

151 *In the 1980s, casinos sold*: Johnston, *Temples of Chance*, 14.

151 *The FBI finally broke the*: Micheal Wright and Caroline Rand Herron, "Alleged Mafia Chiefs Convicted," *New York Times*, January 26, 1986.

151 *"successfully repackaged the popular view"*: Johnston, *Temples of Chance*, 11.

152 *Jay Leno made a cameo*: The TV Madman, "Las Vegas—The American Way to Play (1989)," YouTube, November 6, 2020, https://www.youtube.com/watch?v=ec0Ln68jRn0.

152 *Residents of Deadwood, South Dakota*: "Deadwood, S.D., Votes to Bring Back Gambling," *Chicago Tribune*, April 13, 1989.

152 *Legislators in Colorado, Illinois*: Johnston, *Temples of Chance*, 16.

152 *"it is difficult to quantify the emotional"*: *National Gambling Impact Study Commission Final Report*, U.S. Department of Justice, June 1999, NCJRS Virtual Library, https://govinfo.library.unt.edu/ngisc/reports/7.pdf, 7-2, 7-29.

152 *"Instead, they have transformed it"*: Johnston, *Temples of Chance*, 53.

153 *"Too many guns, too many drugs"*: "Gary, Indiana, Victim of Violent Crime," ABC News, January 3, 1994.

153 *"Gary has had some rough times"*: "Trump Breaks Ground in Gary," *South Bend* [Indiana] *Tribune*, September 6, 1995.

153 *His lawyers argued that his*: Sophia Tareen and Michael Biesecker, "As Trump Appeals to Black Voters, Gary Recalls Casino Deal," Associated Press, September 21, 2016.

153 *The complex boasted a fifty-foot-tall*: Tom Furlong, "Gambling on a Mirage," *Los Angeles Times*, November 21, 1989.

153 *An obsidian-black pyramid shot*: Jessica Seigel, "A Bit of Egypt Rises from Desert to Dazzle Las Vegas," *Chicago Tribune*, October 17, 1993.

153 *While investors in his enterprises*: Russ Buettner and Charles V. Bagli, "How Donald Trump Bankrupted His Atlantic City Casinos, but Still Earned Millions," *New York Times*, June 11, 2016, https://www.nytimes.com/2016/06/12/nyregion/donald-trump-atlantic-city.html.

PART 6: BILL NELSON

157 *The morning was unusually cold*: "Gray Skies over Midwest; Rockies Storm Moves into Upper Plains," Associated Press, January 7, 1992.

157 *Anthony "The Ant" Spilotro had once*: Jane Ann Morrison, "Oscar Goodman, Ex–FBI Agent Tangle over Real-Life 'Casino' Story," *Las Vegas Review-Journal*, November 12, 2015, https://www.reviewjournal.com/news/news-columns/jane-ann-morrison/oscar-goodman-ex-fbi-agent-tangle-over-real-life-casino-story.

157 *So, too, had the German-born*: "German-Born Illusionists Siegfried & Roy Become Citizens," United Press International, October 4, 1988.

157 *As had Reuben Sturman*: "Trials: The Porn King Gets Off," *Time*, November 4, 1991.

157 *"Oh, come on," he'd said*: Deposition of William Nelson, *United States v. Mindlin et al.*, April 12, 1989.

159 *"The sole purpose of this venture"*: *United States of America v. Ivan Mindlin et al.*, January 7, 1992, 16.

159 *"great American story"*: *United States of America v. Ivan Mindlin et al.*, 40.

160 *And one other case that has*: *United States of America v. Ivan Mindlin et al.*, January 8, 1992, vol. A, 49.

160 *"I am not a gambling expert"*: *United States of America v. Ivan Mindlin et al.*, January 8, 1992, vol. B, 78.

160 *"I can't hear you, Mr. Noble"*: *United States of America v. Ivan Mindlin et al.*, vol. B, 113.

161 *"large wagering operation"*: *United States of America v. Ivan Mindlin et al.*, January 14, 1992, vol. B, 15.

161 *"Michael Kent after a period"*: *United States of America v. Ivan Mindlin et al.*, January 7, 1992, 41.

161 *Alongside his Mob contacts*: Argument of Irwin Molasky, *United States of America v. Ivan Mindlin et al.*, January 15, 1992, 16.

161 *"one of the most conniving people"*: Walters, *Gambler*, 117.

161 *The Kentuckian would call his own man*: *United States of America v. Ivan Mindlin et al.*, January 14, 1993, 32.

162 *He'd tried, unsuccessfully, to use*: Affidavit of Special Agent Thomas B. Noble, *United States of America v. Ivan Mindlin et al.*, July 25, 1991, 9.

162 *grossing an estimated $2 million*: Thomsen, "The Gang That Beat Las Vegas."

162 *the FBI claimed that the material*: *United States of America v. Ivan Mindlin et al.*, January 15, 1993, 70.

162 *"latch on and they're like"*: Argument of Richard Wright, *United States of America v. Ivan Mindlin et al.*, January 16, 1993, 11.

162 *Another defense attorney went further*: Argument of Kenneth Hense, *United States of America v. Ivan Mindlin et al.*, January 16, 1993, 17.

162 *"Our society cannot allow tyranny"*: Argument of Kenneth Hense, *United States of America v. Ivan Mindlin et al.*, 12.

162 *"This was just a terrible waste"*: Walters, *Gambler*, 163.

PART 6: ROB REITZEN

166 *The company was getting at least*: Declaration of Darrell Miers, *Robert Reitzen v. Darrell Miers*, Superior Court of California, Los Angeles County, BC175005, August 1, 1997.

167 *A slot junkie would typically*: Silver, *On the Edge*, 153.

168 *In 1995, the company grossed*: Lowery, "Game Boys."

168 *Reitzen awarded himself a $10,000*: Declaration of Darrell Miers, *Robert Reitzen v. Darrell Miers.*

168 *"I own a mountain"*: Lowery, "Game Boys."

169 *the private club where Arnold*: "Actor's Career's Smokin'," *Toronto Star*, July 4, 1995.

170 *The story claimed that they*: Michael Angeli, "Fleecing Las Vegas," *Esquire*, May 1997, https://classic.esquire.com/article/1997/5/1/fleecing-las-vegas.

170 *Reitzen moved first, filing*: Complaint, *Robert Reitzen v. Darrell Miers*, July 22, 1997.

171 *Miers filed a statement with*: Declaration of Darrell Miers, *Robert Reitzen v. Darrell Miers.*

PART 6: BILL BENTER

172 *"Dances will continue to be"*: "In Hong Kong, Even the Communists Like a Good Horse Race," Associated Press, September 19, 1987.

172 *And by the time British rule*: Seth Faison, "Deng Xiaoping Is Dead at 92; Architect of Modern China," *New York Times*, February 20, 1997, https://www.nytimes.com/1997/02/20/world/deng-xiaoping-is-dead-at-92-architect-of-modern-china.html.

173 *Messages calling Chinese premier*: "Life in Hong Kong Before the Handover," Agence France Presse, June 5, 1997.

173 *It was said to be the biggest*: "For the Record," Agence France Presse, June 15, 1997.

174 *it released a statement the next day*: Lawrence Wadey and Robin Parke, "Mega-punters in $700m Triple Trio Ban," *South China Morning Post*, June 15, 1997.

174 *In the end, no one managed*: "For the Record (Updates with Winners)," Agence France Presse, June 15, 1997.

175 *"We said we'd go, and go on time"*: ITN Archive, "Hong Kong Handover Ceremony—ITN Special Programme 'Farewell to Hong Kong (1997),'" YouTube, September 26, 2024, https://www.youtube.com/watch?v=S0hQZv4LpvM.

177 *"It just proves that you can't"*: Smith, "All Bets Off."

PART 7: EPIGRAPH

179 *I am convinced that* He: *The Oxford Dictionary of 20th Century Quotations* (Oxford University Press, 1998), 96.

PART 7: ROB REITZEN

181 *He was talking to Hollywood contacts*: Declaration of Darrell Miers, *Robert Reitzen v. Darrell Miers.*

181 *"you might want to keep"*: Edward O. Thorp, *A Man for All Markets: From Las Vegas to Wall Street, How I Beat the Dealer and the Market* (Random House, 2017), 167.

183 *"That was one of the"*: David T. Friendly, "The Ultimate Gamble," *Los Angeles Times*, May 20, 1998.

183 *At one point, a journalist from*: Roeder, *Seven Games*, 44.

183 *"Developing Loki seems to be"*: Denis Richard Papp, "Dealing with Imperfect Information in Poker," master of science thesis, University of Alberta, 1998.

186 *"If I can win it, anybody can"*: "Internet Player Named Moneymaker Wins $2.5 Million at World Series of Poker," Associated Press, May 24, 2003.

186 *The following year, three times*: David Montero, "Put Your Hands Together for World Series of Poker," *Los Angeles Times*, May 28, 2019.

186 *The world's largest online gaming*: Paul Jarvis, "Sportingbet Profit Almost Triples on Poker Purchase," Bloomberg News, June 2, 2005.

186 *The company behind PartyPoker.com*: Paul Jarvis and Christine Harper, "PartyGaming Stock Jumps After 4.6 Billion-Pound Debut," Bloomberg News, June 27, 2005.

186 *"It's the last American gold rush"*: Montero, "Put Your Hands Together for World Series of Poker."

186 *Legal experts advised that*: Brad Stone, "Going All In for Online Poker," *Newsweek*, August 15, 2005.

187 *With nearly 2 million people*: Stone, "Going All In for Online Poker."

191 *An NBC News article*: Mike Brunker, "Are Poker 'Bots' Raking Online Pots?," NBC News, September 20, 2004, https://www.nbcnews.com/id/wbna6002298.

191 *better than Jim, an attorney*: Rob Kaiser, "Players Make Career Out of Online Poker," *Chicago Tribune*, October 10, 2004.

191 *criminology student Evan in Maryland*: Sam Sessa, "Online Poker Gives Gambling a Facelift," *The Diamondback*, December 8, 2004.

191 *John, a London stockbroker*: Robin O'Brien Lynch, "Online Poker Brings New Faces to Challenge the Old Hands," *Irish Times*, December 10, 2004.

192 *the star owned a property nearby*: "Stars Move into New Millionaire's Row," *Liverpool Daily Echo*, May 5, 2004.

192 *Later, Reitzen would say*: "TEAM," Random Order, accessed July 23, 2020, via Wayback Machine.
193 *BonusWhores.com, a comparison website*: "Blacklisted Sites," BonusWhores .com, accessed March 30, 2005, via Wayback Machine.
194 *"You are a pathetic immoral"*: David Kushner, "On the Internet, Nobody Knows You're a Bot," *Wired*, September 1, 2005.
194 *"I HATE BOTS"*: "Welcome," Destroythebots.com, accessed June 16, 2006, via Wayback Machine.
194 *"We have detected an overwhelming"*: "Mr. Gatorade's Lies Cost Me over 70k at Full Tilt," vBulletin, June 2007, https://archives1.twoplustwo.com /forums/showthread.php?t=417328.

PART 7: BILL BENTER

195 *"Triple Trio fever is back"*: Clint Hutchison, "Monza Revved Up for Bumper TT," *South China Morning Post*, October 30, 2001.
195 *The Triple Trio pool had swollen*: Chellel, "The Gambler Who Cracked the Horse-Racing Code."
195 *"If the winner wins the jackpot"*: Cheung Chi-fai, "Punters Line Up in Hope of $200m Triple Trio Payout," *South China Morning Post*, November 6, 2001.
199 *"The ghost of the unclaimed"*: Alan Aitken, "Lost or Given Up for Charity—a $118m Mystery," *South China Morning Post*, January 16, 2002, https://www.scmp.com/article/368740/lost-or-given-charity-118m-mystery.
199 *But the Australian refused to believe it*: Michael Kaplan, "The Hundred and Fifty Million Dollar Man," *Cigar Aficionado*, November–December 2003, https://www.cigaraficionado.com/article/the-hundred-and-fifty-million-dollar-man-8366.
199 *with the motto "service"*: "Rotary's Two Official Mottoes," Rotary, https://www.rotary.org/en/rotary-mottoes.
200 *Then, midway through the 2001–2002*: "HK Law Change Stacks Odds Against Offshore Punters," Agence France Presse, January 31, 2001.
200 *He rarely left home except*: Kaplan, "The Hundred and Fifty Million Dollar Man."
200 *"I had planned to delay"*: Chellel, "The Gambler Who Cracked the Horse-Racing Code."
201 *Alan Woods's funeral was held*: Angus Grigg et al., "The Gambler," *Australian Financial Review*, August 20, 2011.
201 *"After the speeches saying how"*: Grigg et al., "The Gambler."
202 *he was "without domicile"*: Grigg et al., "The Gambler."
202 *He could finally say out loud*: Alan Aitken, "Super-punter Woods Quietly Masterminded a Revolution," *South China Morning Post*, January 30, 2008.
202 *"the world's greatest gambler"*: David Ashforth, "Mister Huge: The World's Greatest Gambler," *Racing Post*, February 14, 2008.

PART 7: BILL NELSON

203 *Billy Walters got rich all over*: Walters, *Gambler*, 177.

204 *It was said that he never*: Michael Kaplan and Ellen Kaplan, *Chances Are . . . : Adventures in Probability* (Viking, 2006), 58.

205 *A 16,000-seat arena hosted events*: Chris Jones, "Restaurants, Theater to Be Part of Las Vegas Hotel MGM Grand's Makeover," *Las Vegas Review-Journal*, March 11, 2004.

206 *a luxury casino where the wonders*: Philippa Jacks, "USA: Caesar the Day in Vegas; Caesars Entertainment," *Travel Trade Gazette UK & Ireland*, February 11, 2011.

207 *announced a billion-dollar expansion*: Oskar Garcia, "Caesars Palace Tops Off Sixth Tower on Vegas Strip," Associated Press, October 21, 2008.

208 *Casinos went to extraordinary lengths*: Johnston, *Temples of Chance*, 42.

210 *the indoor fountain where animatronic statues*: Erica Singleton, "How to Enjoy Las Vegas Without Going Broke," *Charlotte Post*, May 1, 2008.

211 *"This here's Nevada"*: Nersesian, *The Law for Gamblers*, Kindle, location 102.

PART 8: ROB REITZEN

215 *ranted on the Two Plus Two*: "FTP Bans 5 Players Without Giving Reasons. 3 Are Regulars, 2 Are Beginners at Poker (Long Post)," Two Plus Two Forums, August 7, 2009, https://forumserver.twoplustwo.com/28/discussion-poker-sites/ftp-bans-5-players-without-giving-reasons-3-regulars-2-beginners-poker-long-post-542003/index9.html#post12278839.

215 *They accused the website's owners*: *Lary Kennedy et al. v. Full Tilt Poker et al.*, U.S. District Court, Central District of California (Western District—Los Angeles), 2:11-cv-08591-MMM-AGR.

216 *"I lolled so hard"*: "Fulltilt Froze My Account with 47 Grand in It . . . ROUND THREE," Two Plus Two Forums, October 2, 2009, https://forumserver.twoplustwo.com/28/discussion-poker-sites/fulltilt-froze-my-account-47-grand-round-three-598769.

216 *"This domain name has been"*: Nathaniel Popper and Tiffany Hsu, "Feds Call Poker Sites' Bet: Major Online Venues Are Shut Down and Their Founders Charged with Bank Fraud," *Los Angeles Times*, April 16, 2011.

216 *"Online poker is not a crime"*: Matt Richtel, "U.S. Cracks Down on Online Gambling," *New York Times*, April 15, 2011, https://www.nytimes.com/2011/04/16/technology/16poker.html.

216 *"I TOLD YOU SO"*: "Reuters: Full Tilt Poker, Pokerstars and Absolute Poker Charged with Illegal Gambling," Two Plus Two Forums, April 15, 2011, https://forumserver.twoplustwo.com/29/news-views-gossip/reuters-full-tilt-poker-pokerstars-absolute-poker-charged-illegal-gambling-1020606/index67.html#post26059945.

216 *Eventually, all three companies*: Christie Smythe and Chris Dolmetsch, "Poker Websites Agree to Settle U.S. Money-Laundering Probe," Bloomberg, July 31, 2012, https://www.bloomberg.com/news/articles/2012-07-31/online-poker-companies-agree-to-settle-laundering-probe.

216 *Full Tilt Poker founder Raymond Bitar*: Bob Van Voris, "Full Tilt Poker Founder Pleads Guilty in U.S. Gambling Probe," Bloomberg, April 15, 2013, https://www.bloomberg.com/news/articles/2013-04-15/full-tilt-poker-founder-to-plead-guilty-to-two-counts.

217 *It played 8 million hands before*: Judgment of the Court of Appeal, Södertörn District Court, December 19, 2014, case no. B 5929-13.

217 *In the frozen north of Russia*: Kit Chellel, "The Russian Bot Army that Conquered Online Poker," Bloomberg Businessweek, September 20, 2024, https://www.bloomberg.com/features/2024-poker-bots-artificial-intelligence-russia.

218 *For most of January 2017, a team*: Joshua Brustein, "A Computer Just Beat Poker Pros, Achieving a Major AI Milestone," Bloomberg, January 31, 2017, https://www.inkl.com/news/a-computer-just-beat-poker-pros-achieving-a-major-ai-milestone.

219 *"Imagine that your smartphone"*: Byron Spice, "Carnegie Mellon Artificial Intelligence Beats Top Poker Pros," *Carnegie Mellon University News*, January 31, 2017, https://www.cmu.edu/news/stories/archives/2017/january/AI-beats-poker-pros.html.

219 *"That could happen, but"*: Brustein, "A Computer Just Beat Poker Pros."

219 *He'd used keyword detection software*: Michael Kaplan, "How I Used Math to Conquer My Cancer," *New York Post*, February 13, 2017, https://nypost.com/2017/02/13/how-i-used-math-to-conquer-my-cancer.

220 *New attendees had to be*: Nicholas G. Colon, "Inside the Blackjack Ball," *Forbes*, May 17, 2016, https://www.forbes.com/sites/greatspeculations/2016/05/17/inside-the-blackjack-ball-an-exclusive-look-at-the-gathering-of-the-smartest-gamblers-in-the-world.

221 *The sole condition: that they*: Todd Dewey, "Blackjack Ball brings world's greatest gamblers to Las Vegas," *Las Vegas Review-Journal*, February 29, 2020, https://www.reviewjournal.com/sports/betting/blackjack-ball-brings-worlds-greatest-gamblers-to-las-vegas-1969539.

PART 8: BILL BENTER

223 *offering cash rebates to the biggest*: Oliver Roeder, "I Used AI to Bet on Horse-Racing. Here's What Happened," *Financial Times Magazine*, March 29, 2023, https://www.ft.com/content/402955aa-21fa-42d5-b1d7-f79e7f19a617.

223 *"May all beings attain supreme wisdom"*: Dan Simpson, "Twisting China's Tail," *Pittsburgh Post-Gazette*, February 24, 2010, https://www.post-gazette.com/dan-simpson/2010/02/24/Twisting-China-s-tail/stories/201002240205.

223 *Benter put his betting profits into*: "Grant Recipients," The Benter Foundation, https://benterfoundation.org/grant-recipients.
224 *"I'm kind of a one-trick pony"*: Chellel, "The Gambler Who Cracked the Horse-Racing Code."
224 *She resolved that he would learn*: Natalie Bencivenga and Sara Bauknecht, "Motherly Wisdom from Pittsburgh Moms," *Pittsburgh Post-Gazette*, May 8, 2016, https://www.post-gazette.com/life/lifestyle/2016/05/06/motherly-wisdom-from-new-pittsburgh-moms/stories/201605080011.
225 *In 2024, officials estimated that Benter*: Dan Ross, "Computer Assisted Wagering: Different Worlds, Different Fixes," Thoroughbred Daily News, October 1, 2024, https://www.thoroughbreddailynews.com/computer-assisted-wagering-different-worlds-different-fixes.
225 *In the United States, computer syndicates were*: Roeder, "I Used AI to Bet on Horse-Racing."
225 *rising to 40 percent in*: Ross, "Computer Assisted Wagering."
225 *The Australian Zeljko Ranogajec*: Brendan Cormick and Cameron Stewart, "Taxman Targets the King of Punters," *Weekend Australian*, December 24, 2011.
225 *"A substantial portion of our success"*: Chellel, "The Gambler Who Cracked the Horse-Racing Code."
226 *The halcyon days of 78,000 fans*: Laura Hillenbrand, *Seabiscuit: An American Legend* (Fourth Estate, 2001), Kindle, location 5037.
226 *"battered old sport"*: Joe Drape, "With Belmont in Saratoga, Horse Racing's History and Hope Are Linked," *New York Times*, June 10, 2024, https://www.nytimes.com/2024/06/07/business/belmont-stakes-saratoga-springs.html.
226 *"They're putting so much money"*: Roeder, "I Used AI to Bet on Horse-Racing."

PART 8: BILL NELSON

227 *In the spring of 2004, a tall*: Kit Chellel, "The Gambler Who Beat Roulette," Bloomberg Businessweek, April 6, 2023, https://www.bloomberg.com/features/2023-how-to-beat-roulette-gambler-figures-it-out.
227 *Reporters speculated, inaccurately*: Jeff Edwards, "Ritz Casino Hit by £1.3m Laser Scam," *Mirror*, March 22, 2004.
228 *The patented system was "statistically proven"*: "Product Brochure," TCS JOHNHUXLEY, February 19, 2007, https://web.archive.org/web/20070219045335/http://www.tcsjohnhuxley.com/products/LIVEGAMING/RouletteWheels/TraditionalWheels/en/pdfs/RouleteWheelsCIS0506v21300dpipdf.
229 *He'd be in a race against hedge funds*: Hooyeon Kim and Whanwoong Choi, "Ex-Quant Is Building a Chip to Save Traders Microseconds," Bloomberg, April 14, 2021.

229 *one of the fastest-growing economies*: Dorota Bartyzel and Adrian Krajewski, "Poland Booms as Consumer Demand Sends Economy to Peak Growth," Bloomberg, October 18, 2017.
229 *"Games are wonderful"*: Du Sautoy, *Around the World in 80 Games*, 410.

INTERLUDE: WHAT A FOOL BELIEVES

231 *"emptied punters' pockets"*: Atherton, *Gambling*, Kindle, location 2013.
232 *By 2015, FanDuel and DraftKings*: Chen, *Billion Dollar Fantasy*, xxii.
232 *"If you looked closely"*: "Everybody Hated Those DraftKings and FanDuel Commercials, Data Shows," Digiday, September 14, 2015, https://digiday.com/marketing/everybody-hated-draftkings-fanduel-commercials-data-shows.
232 *The two companies then went*: Eric Lipton and Kenneth P. Vogel, "Cigars, Booze, Money: How a Lobbying Blitz Made Sports Betting Ubiquitous," *New York Times*, November 20, 2022, https://www.nytimes.com/2022/11/20/business/sports-betting-lobbying-kansas.html.
232 *as of January 2025, sports betting*: "State of Play," American Gaming Association, Legal Landscape as of February 27, 2025, https://www.americangaming.org/research/state-gaming-map.
232 *Today, prediction markets allow*: "Markets," Kalshi, accessed on February 7, 2025. https://kalshi.com/.
232 *Americans are probably making more*: Silver, *On the Edge*, 10.
233 *"The more he responded"*: *RTM v. Bonne Terre Limited & Another*, High Court of Justice, King's Bench Division, 2025 EWHC 111(KB), Approved Judgment.
233 *When Dave Holmes, an online sports*: Katherine Sayre, "Sports Betting Companies Weed Out Winners. Gamblers Want to Know Why," *Wall Street Journal*, July 13, 2024.
233 *Nate Silver, the statistician and poker professional*: Silver, *On the Edge*, 200.
234 *"Bad as the mob is"*: Johnston, *Temples of Chance*, 297.

EPILOGUE

235 *A prominent player once*: Michael Kaplan, "The Blackjack Ball," *Cigar Aficionado*, July–August 2017, https://www.cigaraficionado.com/article/the-blackjack-ball-19426.
237 *Evolution, the biggest provider*: Chellel, "The Gambler Who Beat Roulette."
237 *In 2023, a betting syndicate won*: Eric Dexheimer, "Lottery Scheme Had Overseas Links," *Houston Chronicle*, October 6, 2024.
239 *The remains of clay dice have*: du Sautoy, *Around the World in 80 Games*, 38.
240 *Around 8 percent of suicides*: Gavin Finch, Harry Wilson, and Ann Choi, "Britain Opened the Door to Online Gambling. Now It's Living with the

Consequences," Bloomberg, December 1, 2022, https://www.bloomberg.com/graphics/2022-gambling-addiction-stories-how-uk-got-hooked-on-online-casino-betting.

241 *"It was like stepping back"*: A. D. Hopkins, "Steve Wynn," *Las Vegas Review-Journal*, February 7, 1999, https://www.reviewjournal.com/news/steve-wynn.

INDEX

Note: Page references in italics refer to photos.

PHOTO CREDITS

Pages 13, 33, 55, 93, 121, 157, 203, 227: Courtesy of William Nelson
Pages 19, 40, 79, 103, 129, 172, 195, 222: Courtesy of William Benter
Pages 23, 70, 164, 181, 215: Courtesy of Robert Reitzen
Pages 47, 109: Courtesy of Darrell Miers
Page 139: Courtesy of Norm Zada
Page 235: Courtesy of Kit Chellel

ABOUT THE AUTHOR

Kit Chellel is an investigative reporter at Bloomberg *Businessweek* and co-author of *Dead in the Water: A True Story of Hijacking, Murder, and a Global Maritime Conspiracy* alongside Matthew Campbell, published in the UK by Atlantic in 2022. The book was the winner of the True Crime Awards Book of the Year 2023 and shortlisted for the *FT* Business Book of the Year Award. It was also a Waterstones Best Books of 2022 pick and selected as a Book of the Year by *The Financial Times*, *The Times* and *The Economist*. Kit lives in West London with his three children.